COMBATING
THE ILLEGAL EMPLOYMENT
OF FOREIGN WORKERS

OECD

ORGANISATION FOR ECONOMIC CO-OPERATION AND DEVELOPMENT

ORGANISATION FOR ECONOMIC CO-OPERATION AND DEVELOPMENT

Pursuant to Article 1 of the Convention signed in Paris on 14th December 1960, and which came into force on 30th September 1961, the Organisation for Economic Co-operation and Development (OECD) shall promote policies designed:

- to achieve the highest sustainable economic growth and employment and a rising standard of living in Member countries, while maintaining financial stability, and thus to contribute to the development of the world economy;

- to contribute to sound economic expansion in Member as well as non-member countries in the process of economic development; and

- to contribute to the expansion of world trade on a multilateral, non-discriminatory basis in accordance with international obligations.

The original Member countries of the OECD are Austria, Belgium, Canada, Denmark, France, Germany, Greece, Iceland, Ireland, Italy, Luxembourg, the Netherlands, Norway, Portugal, Spain, Sweden, Switzerland, Turkey, the United Kingdom and the United States. The following countries became Members subsequently through accession at the dates indicated hereafter: Japan (28th April 1964), Finland (28th January 1969), Australia (7th June 1971), New Zealand (29th May 1973), Mexico (18th May 1994), the Czech Republic (21st December 1995), Hungary (7th May 1996), Poland (22nd November 1996) and Korea (12th December 1996). The Commission of the European Communities takes part in the work of the OECD (Article 13 of the OECD Convention).

Publié en français sous le titre :

COMBATTRE L'EMPLOI ILLÉGAL D'ÉTRANGERS

FOREWORD

This publication brings together a selection of the papers delivered at the seminar on "Preventing and combating the employment of foreigners in an irregular situation". This seminar, held in The Hague on 22 and 23 April 1999, was co-organised by the OECD and the Dutch authorities, with the support of the United States. It was an important step in the work that the OECD has been carrying out since 1995 on illegal immigration in OECD countries, particularly in relation to the labour market and the various programmes aiming at regularising foreigners in an irregular situation.

The main objectives of the seminar were to analyse the economic and political challenges posed by illegal immigration, to examine and compare the measures taken by OECD countries against the employment of foreigners in an irregular situation, and to evaluate their results. The seminar deliberately focused on the employment of foreigners in an irregular situation, even though the issue of illegal immigration also obviously includes border control and the fight against the networks of traffickers that facilitate illegal immigration.

The first part of the book analyses the impact of irregular immigration on the economy and the labour market. The second part presents attempts to analyse and evaluate the measures taken to combat the employment of illegal foreign workers. The book ends with a series of recommendations on the policies to be implemented in order to strengthen the coherence and efficiency of the sanctions relating to the illegal employment of foreigners. In addition to proposing improved co-ordination between the competent authorities, the authors underline the necessity of better informing the general public about the risks of detection and the penalties facing those caught employing illegal workers. Finally, strengthened co-operation between recipient and origin countries is advocated.

This volume is published on the responsibility of the Secretary-General of the OECD.

TABLE OF CONTENTS

Introduction – Preventing and Combating the Employment of Foreigners
in an Irregular Situation 7

Part 1
Impact of Irregular Migration on the Economy and the Labour Market

Chapter 1 – Irregular Migration: Economic and Political Issues
by Georges Tapinos 13

Chapter 2 – Immigrant Workers in an Irregular Situation: The Case of the Garment
Industry in Paris and its Suburbs
by Natasha Iskander 45

Chapter 3 – Some Lessons from Recent Regularisation Programmes
by the OECD Secretariat 53

Chapter 4 – The Regularisation of Temporary Migrant Agricultural Workers in Mexico
by Manuel Angel Castillo 71

Part II
Analysis and Evaluation of Measures Undertaken to Combat the Employment
of Illegal Foreign Workers

Chapter 5 – Review and Evaluation of the Measures Implemented
in OECD Member Countries
by Sophie Robin and Lucile Barros 81

Chapter 6 – Preventing and Combating the Employment of Foreigners
in an Irregular Situation in the United States
by John Fraser 101

Chapter 7 – Measures Taken to Combat the Employment of Undocumented
Foreign Workers in France
by Claude-Valentin Marie 107

Conclusion – Policy Recommendations 133

Annex – Review of the Relevant Legislation in Austria, Belgium, Germany, Japan,
the Netherlands and Switzerland 137

Measures Undertaken to Combat the Employment of Foreigners in an Irregular Situation
in Austria
by Viktor Riedel 139

Current Belgian Legislation on Sanctions against the Employment of Foreigners
in an Irregular Situation
by Jean-Claude Heirman 143

Combating the Irregular Employment of Foreigners in Germany: Sanctions against Employers
and Key Areas of Irregular employment
by Rainer Irlenkaueuser 151

Illegal Migration, Overstay and Illegal Working in Japan – Development of Policies
and their Evaluation
by Yasushi Iguchi 157

Current Dutch Legislation and Policy towards Preventing and Combating the Employment
of Foreigners in an Irregular Situation
by the Dutch Ministry of Social Affairs and Employment and the Dutch Ministry of Justice 166

Status Report on Measures to Prevent and Combat the Employment of Foreigners
in an Irregular Situation in Switzerland
by Kurt Rohner 177

© OECD 2000

INTRODUCTION

Preventing and Combating the
Employment of Foreigners in an Irregular Situation

On the initiative of the Dutch authorities and with the support of the United States, the OECD organised at The Hague on 22 and 23 April 1999 a seminar on "Preventing and combating the employment of foreigners in an irregular situation". This topic is a continuation of the work carried out at the OECD since 1995, and has facilitated the study of illegal immigration in several OECD Member countries, notably in relation to labour market and other programmes to regularise foreigners in an irregular situation. In preparing for this seminar, the OECD sent out a questionnaire to Member countries, the responses to which provided valuable information on the conditions surrounding foreigners' access to the labour market, on the sanctions imposed on the illegal employment of foreigners and their results.

The international dimension to this seminar was enriched by the participation of many delegates from Member countries, representatives from the General Secretariat of the European Commission, the International Labour Office (ILO), the International Office for Migration (IOM) and the Vienna-based International Centre for Migration Policy Development (ICMPD) as well as representatives of the social partners, notably from the Trade Union Advisory Committee to the OECD (TUAC) and the Business and Industry Advisory Committee to the OECD (BIAC).

The seminar at The Hague had, as its principal objectives, analysing the economic and political challenges posed by illegal immigration, examining and comparing the measures implemented in OECD countries to prevent and combat the employment of foreigners in an irregular situation and evaluating the results of these actions. A further aim of the seminar was to provide information on co-operative policies (bilateral or multilateral) and to invite the participants to formulate proposals which would extend this co-operation. The objectives of the seminar were deliberately oriented around the employment of foreigners in an irregular situation even though the issue of illegal immigration is also, of course, one of border control and the fight against the networks of traffickers which facilitate illegal immigration and/or the counterfeiting of documents.

This publication contains the majority of the papers presented at the seminar and an annex containing detailed notes prepared by senior civil servants which provide a comprehensive overview of the legislation in force in many OECD Member countries regarding the employment of foreigners in an irregular situation. The first part of the book is devoted to analysing the impact of irregular migration on the economy and the labour market. The second part presents attempts to analyse and evaluate the measures undertaken to combat the employment of illegal foreign workers.

1. THE IMPACT OF IRREGULAR MIGRATION ON THE ECONOMY AND THE LABOUR MARKET

Analysing the economic and political issues surrounding irregular migration, *Georges Tapinos* presents the different situations of irregularity and insists on the fact that illegal immigration has a time dimension which has important implications regarding the measurement and the characteristics of illegal immigrants. The author takes the view that insofar as the effects of illegal immigration, by producing labour costs that are lower than those of legal immigration, are linked to a reduction in labour costs and the rate of the equilibrium wage, it has, other things being equal, a more pronounced positive macro-economic effect. As for the labour market impact of illegal immigration, it would appear, according to the author, that economic analyses of the labour market have not identified and incorporated within the models the specific features of illegal immigration. This being the case, the difference in the economic impact of illegal and legal immigration appear therein to be merely a matter of degree rather than of nature.

Turning to an analysis of the attempts to curb illegal immigration and the sanctions imposed on employers, Tapinos highlights the differences in the approaches of Europe and the United States. In Europe, combating the employment of foreigners in an irregular situation forms part of a wider strategy directed against undocumented employment in general whereas in the United States it is not first and foremost a legal instrument aimed at regulating the labour market.

Three papers then illustrate the issues raised by the presence of foreigners in an irregular situation in the labour market and examine the question of regularisation programmes.

Natasha Iskander, taking the example of immigrant workers in an irregular situation employed in the garment industry in Paris and its suburbs, attempts to demonstrate how the strategies used by firms to develop the flexibility of their productive systems and to succeed in competing under new economic conditions have changed the nature of undeclared work. Undocumented immigrants in the labour market can now be divided into two categories: those who are sufficiently skilled to remain competitive despite the new constraints and the unskilled who are employed in the most onerous conditions and whose prospects of upward social mobility are becoming increasingly remote.

The paper drafted by the Secretariat presents some of the lessons to be drawn from the regularisation programmes undertaken recently in certain OECD countries. The first section analyses the reasons behind these countries' decisions to effect these operations. The second section shows first of all that the individuals regularised tend to be young workers employed in sectors with a high concentration of foreign labour. They bring greater flexibility to the productive system. The regularisation experiences examined in this paper also highlight the key labour market role of certain categories of illegal immigrants. As a consequence, the measures taken to combat the hiring of illegal immigrants must address the problem of undeclared work in general and not just the employment of illegal immigrants.

Manuel Angel Castillo deals with a specific flow, that of seasonal migrant workers who move mainly from the border region of Guatemala to Soconusco in Mexico, an agricultural area which produces mostly coffee and sugar cane. The growing proportion of foreign labour in the agricultural sector did not attract the attention of the Mexican authorities until the end of the 1980s. The beginning of an important flow of undocumented transit migrants, who passed through the frontier in order to reach northern Mexico and to attempt to illegally enter the United States, also played a significant role.

According to the author, evaluating the scale of these movements is still very difficult, as is defining their principal characteristics. It would appear however that the temporary migrant population is overwhelmingly dominated by adult males, adolescents and young adults and that this population is essentially rural. For some years now, an awareness campaign regarding the situation of undocumented workers has been undertaken, and the mechanisms for effecting regularisations have been put in place. For example, the issuance of individual work permits has replaced the collective authorisations granted previously.

2. ANALYSIS AND EVALUATION OF MEASURES UNDERTAKEN TO COMBAT THE EMPLOYMENT OF ILLEGAL FOREIGN WORKERS

In this second part of the publication, *Sophie Robin* and *Lucile Barros* analyse the preventive measures and sanctions relating to the employment of foreigners in an irregular situation in place in a number of OECD Member countries. *John Fraser* and *Claude-Valentin Marie* present in turn evaluations of the measures undertaken to combat the employment of illegal foreign workers in the United States and in France respectively.

Robin and Barros present an overview and an evaluation of the policies implemented in OECD Member countries concerning preventing and sanctioning the employment of foreigners in an irregular situation. Their analysis is based on the replies received to a questionnaire addressed to the Member countries of the OECD. In the first section, the authors examine the types of sanctions set out in the legislation both against workers who do not possess a work permit and their employers, as well as the penalties which can be imposed against those who abet illegal employment, focussing in particular on the administrative structures set in place to curb illegal employment and emphasising the greater effectiveness of joint actions. The authors then draw attention to the fact that whilst preventive measures could be expected to be quite effective they are, in fact, accorded only a relatively modest role.

In the second section, the authors reveal the limitations of the measures implemented to curb the employment of undocumented foreigners and analyse their development. They point to the difficulties which enforcement services encounter in field operations, their lack of information for conducting effective controls and their lack of data with which to assess the outcome of inspection and reporting procedures. Finally, they point to the fact that international co-operation in this area not very extensive, and that which exists is most often bilateral.

Fraser looks at the prevention and the combating of the employment of foreigners in an irregular situation in the United States. According to the author, the United States authorities recognise clearly that employment is the primary impetus for illegal immigration. In addition to border control, this country applies two basic strategies to prevent and combat illegal employment on its territory: generosity regarding the granting of legal immigrant status for employment purposes combined with law enforcement at the workplace level. However, the author notes that despite the considerable volume and massive increase in investment in its comprehensive law enforcement efforts, as well as the continuing development and adjustments to the law enforcement strategy and tools employed, illegal immigration and employment continues to increase.

In his paper on the measures taken to combat the employment of undocumented foreign workers in France, their place in the campaign against illegal employment and their results, Marie presents first of all an outline of the legal framework for the employment of foreigners before proceeding to a detailed analysis of the measures implemented to combat their illegal employment. He examines the penalties which can be imposed against principals and intermediaries as well as against employees without a work permit. He also presents the information gathered from reports recording violations observed at the national and departmental level. He notes that nearly 60% of all violations are discovered in service industries. He goes on to analyse the clandestine labour market and the insecurity experienced by the workforce concerned, and notes that more and more French nationals are being hired illegally. Finally, the author points out that clandestine employment is far and away the most common reason for conviction on charges of illegal employment and that heavier fines are imposed for employing undocumented foreigners than for clandestine employment itself.

PART 1
IMPACT OF IRREGULAR MIGRATION ON THE ECONOMY AND THE LABOUR MARKET

CHAPTER 1

Irregular Migration: Economic and Political Issues
by
Georges Tapinos
(Professor, Institut d'Etudes politiques de Paris)

1. INTRODUCTION

Considered over a long period of time (since the 1970s), and against a backdrop of otherwise moderate growth in international migration (Tapinos and Delaunay, 2000), the increase in the variety of forms of clandestine residence and the growing length of stay of clandestine immigrants have had the effect of reducing the debate on immigration policy to one on the issue of clandestine immigration. The curbing of illegal inflows and of foreigners' irregularity with regard to residence and employment has become one of the priorities of migration policy. This policy orientation is now common to all the countries of Europe, particularly the new countries of immigration in the south (*i.e.* Italy, Spain, Greece and Portugal), as well as to North America, although the United States and Canada are still open to regular immigration.

To examine the economic and political challenges deriving from clandestine migration is to investigate whether clandestine migration possesses specific features as compared to regular migration. It is from such a perspective that this paper considers the problems of measurement, the economic dimension and control policies.

2. ILLEGAL MIGRATION

Illegal migration: a multi-faceted concept

The extent of States' sovereignty defines the scope of clandestine migration flows. The clandestine nature of such migration is defined by reference to the rules of law (and their shortcomings), the restrictions on entering and leaving a country, and the regulations governing access to the labour market. By definition, clandestine immigration eludes registration and statistical coverage. The first difficulty confronting one is that of how to define and measure clandestine immigration.

Convention No.143 adopted by the 1975 ILO Conference defines clandestine or illegal migration movements as those where migrants find themselves "during their journey, on arrival or during their period of residence and employment [in] conditions contravening relevant international multilateral or bilateral instruments or agreements, or national laws or regulations" (Moulier Boutang *et al.*, 1986). This definition places the stress on the diverse aspects of irregularity: entry, residence in the host country and the undertaking of an occupation.

In a world without restrictions on entering or leaving a country illegal immigration would be a concept without reference. Unless there simultaneously exists both restrictions and a degree of tolerance illegal immigration cannot take place. It is a manifestation of an imbalance between the effectively unlimited supply of candidates for emigration and the limitations placed by recipient countries on the acceptance of new entrants.

In countries like the United States and Canada which remain essentially open to immigration, illegal immigration is an alternative entry procedure for those who do not meet the required criteria, for those who would have to wait longer than they would wish in order to obtain an immigrant's visa, as well as for those for whom unauthorised immigration is less expensive. Where opportunities for entering and staying in a country are limited, as in Europe at the present time, illegal entry is, excepting being the subject of a family reunion application or applying for asylum, the only option available to candidates for migration. In the cases of both types of country, once there exists a statutory maximum length of stay, whether this depends on the type of visa (*e.g.* for tourists, students and temporary workers) or whether indeed there is any obligation to have a visa at all, overstaying[1] places the person concerned outside the law.

This fundamental distinction is easier to draw in the United States where there exists at entry a statutory dividing line between immigrants and non-immigrants, and where the statistical system estimates the number of non-immigrants by counting those who do not amend their status after entry, whose departure from the country is not registered, and who are assumed to be still in the country after the expiry date of their visa.

In European countries, where no such distinction is made on entry, overstaying usually occurs when an immigrant is turned down after applying for the obtention or renewal of a residence permit. This situation, the reflection of rules governing legal residence, can result not only from wilfulness on the part of migrants but also from the ambiguity or incoherence of the rules themselves. For example, in countries like Italy and Spain where there have been frequent regularisation programmes and where a permit obtained at the time of a regularisation exercise is normally limited to a period of one year, with the possibility (non-automatic) for it to be renewed, repeated regularisations of the same people have been observed. By contrast, in the United States, those who benefited from the amnesty law of 1986 [the Immigration Reform and Control Act (IRCA)]

---

1. The relative proportion of these two components in the number of illegal migrants varies from country to country. In the United States, it has been estimated that illegal entries (entries without inspection) and overstayers each account for 50% of total illegal immigration (Warren, 1994). A more recent estimate by the INS puts the figures at 60% and 40% respectively.

obtained permits enabling them to remain in the country until they met conditions for the obtention of a permanent residence permit (Green Card).

Illegal immigration also has a time dimension as it can be defined by length of stay. From the immigrant's point of view, illegality may represent either a temporary phase in the migration cycle (as was the case in France during the 1960s where there existed the possibility for illegal immigrants to be regularised) or a permanent state (in the absence of regularisation or when regularisation is exceptional and non-renewable – which is what American regularisation in 1986 and certain of the regularisation programmes recently undertaken in European countries are assumed to be). This distinction also holds from the point of view of the recipient country, which may be either a country of first entry or one where the immigrant intends to settle permanently. In this regard, the situation develops over time. When Spain and Italy, emigration countries *par excellence*, began to accept immigrants at a time when traditional European immigration countries were closing their borders to immigration, the authorities in these countries liked to think they were countries of first entry. By the late 1980s and early 1990s, it had become clear that these countries had in turn become settlement countries with a significant number of clandestine immigrants.

The examination of clandestinity cannot be reduced to the clandestine migrant himself. The analysis of the phenomenon and the formulation of policies to combat it should look at the whole length of the chain of clandestinity, which brings into play a series of agents: the migrant, the intermediary who facilitates his passage or placement, the company for whom the migrant works and, according to the case, the principal contractor. One is therefore confronted by a wide array of complex situations and circuits which range from the arrangement of the meeting between the clandestine immigrant and the employer through to far-reaching and powerful organisations which control a veritable trade in labour. In America, workers from Mexico or Central America endeavour to cross the border with the help of a smuggler, who might also arrange their obtention of employment. Elsewhere, nationals of sub-Saharan Africa enter Algeria by aeroplane, continue their journey by land through to the Spanish enclave of Melilla in Morocco in the hope of being transported to Spain at the time of a regularisation programme.

The organisations involved in smuggling operations can be of considerable scale. In the United States, the INS dismantled in 1998 an organisation which had arranged the passage to the United States of approximately 10 000 people; in November of the same year two million fake identification papers were seized in Los Angeles (US Department of Justice, 1999). The clandestine chain sometimes goes further back than the migrant himself. For example, the Moroccan youths who are known to have entered Europe were not, as one might have supposed, unoccupied youths who had taken the initiative to emigrate clandestinely, rather they had been sent by their parents who had elected to take advantage of their children's minority which, in Europe, protects them against expulsion. This extreme heterogeneity should rule out judgements on this phenomenon made on purely humanitarian or, conversely, purely criminal bases.

These distinctions have considerable implications for the measurement and characterisation of illegal migrants, the economic impact of illegal migration, administrative effectiveness and the aspect of control policy.

Measurement methods

Estimating the number of people in an irregular situation is inherently problematic. Account must be taken not only of the legal system of immigration, the system of statistical observation and mechanisms involved in undocumented living, but also, given that such estimates rely to varying degrees on survey evidence, of the perception that the clandestine migrants have of the acceptance of their clandestinity by the local population and of the nature of the risks that they are taking.

In that it concerns the measurement of an unobservable event, the measurement of irregular migration runs into well-known problems. The difficulties are particularly severe in the case of clandestine migration for whilst measurement in this field can only be indirect, the absence of regularities in the phenomena that might be linked to this form of migration limits the usefulness of indirect methods. Indeed, the classic demographic distinction between direct and indirect methods is hard to sustain. Strictly speaking, one rarely has direct observations at one's disposal. At best, observations are incomplete; in every case complementary information is required – which is itself often estimated – for the phenomenon to be satisfactorily understood.

Figures for apprehensions in border regions, for example, have to be adjusted to take account of the number of times that individual migrants attempt to cross. Figures derived from regularisation programmes need to be amended to take account of those excluded for failing to meet the criteria (particularly those relating to the date of arrival, the obligation to remain in the country continuously, and the presentation of a work permit). Similarly, surveys that focus directly on the clandestine population ("snowball" sampling or the Delphi technique) which presume to identify from the outset people who are known to be in an irregular situation contain substantial biases. Measurements made in the frontier zones of sending countries before migrants cross the frontier (the COLEF survey) constitute an exception.

It is important first of all to know what one is measuring. Is it numbers (stocks) or movements (flows)? Is it workers or the whole of the population? To measure clandestine *entries*, is to attempt to assess the volume of the *flows* of people entering the country without the required legal administrative documentation, whether they cross the frontier with false papers or at a point that is not controlled. By contrast, irregularity in respect of those who *reside* concerns *stocks* which comprise both the net cumulative flows of people who have entered without authorisation and are not regularised, and those who have entered clandestinely but have lost their right of residence and are still in the country. It should also be considered essential to attempt to measure the number of foreigners in irregular employment, in so far as the employment status of those in an irregular situation will also, logically, be irregular.

Defining the groups in these ways allows one to distinguish the possible estimates, those of: *clandestine entrants* (inflow of illegal migrants over a given period), *clandestine residence* (the total foreign population residing in the country illegally at a given moment) and *clandestine workers* (the number of clandestine workers in employment at a given moment).

Figure 1 summarises the different entry, residence and employment situations in which foreign migrants can find themselves. It is possible to identify six categories of clandestinity:

- Migrants who have entered the country legally with a legal residence permit, but who are working illegally either because the job is not declared or because their residence permit does not allow them to work.

- Migrants who have entered the country legally, who are living in the country illegally (either because their work permits are invalid or have expired, or because they do not have residence permits), and who are working illegally. It is assumed that a migrant without a residence permit cannot work legally under the legislation in force.
- The same category as above, but covering inactive migrants.
- Migrants who have entered the country clandestinely, who have no residence permit, and who are working illegally.
- The same category as above, but covering inactive migrants.
- Migrants who have entered the country clandestinely, who have a residence permit (*e.g.* following regularisation, or by variation in their status through marriage) and are working illegally.

The problem is how to go from administrative statistics, which are marked by characteristics specific to each country, to a method of measuring the phenomenon.[2] Most methods rely on data from the recipient country, and they are based on two kinds of logic with the estimate of the stock of clandestine immigrants made either by comparing statistics on entry and modifications to status with data relating to stocks, or by using comprehensive registers of demographic events such as births and deaths.

Methods of estimating the clandestine population were first developed and applied in the United States. Direct calculation, through comparing entry statistics and modifications to status from INS (Immigration and Naturalization Service) data, permitted the inference of the number of visa overstayers. To this component of the stock of clandestine immigrants should be added clandestine entrants (*entries without inspection*) estimated by means of an indirect procedure (Warren, 1994).

"Residual" estimating is based on census data. From the total *foreign-born* population counted at the time of the census, 1990 say, and the theoretical legal *foreign-born* population estimated for the same point in time from INS figures, an estimate of the population of clandestine immigrants picked-up by the census can be obtained by subtracting one from the other. To be of analytical interest, the censuses would have had to have counted a high proportion of the illegal migrants (Clark *et al.*, 1995). Mention should also be made of estimates of clandestine entries arrived at by adjusting the number of arrests on the basis of the likelihood of being apprehended at the United States-Mexico border (Espenshade, 1995).

---

2. One can not always distinguish these different categories in the administrative statistics. Indeed, these record either legal movements or infractions which, when they are penalised, measure clandestinity at the very moment that it has ceased to exist. Moreover, administrative statistics, cross-sectional by nature, record the events or migrants affected by the events without, in general, it being possible to attach the events to a reference population. Further, there is distinction to be drawn as to the reliability of the information: between administrative records which can include a fiscal dimension or an element of sanction which might incite inexact declarations, and data which respond to a desire for socio-economic knowledge such as censuses and some surveys; they do not necessarily have the same utility when one seeks to determine the number of clandestine immigrants. When clandestine immigration is tolerated, it is quite possible that a census will record a non-negligible proportion of the clandestine immigrants. Conversely, when it is not tolerated, it is less likely that a census will record a non-negligible proportion.

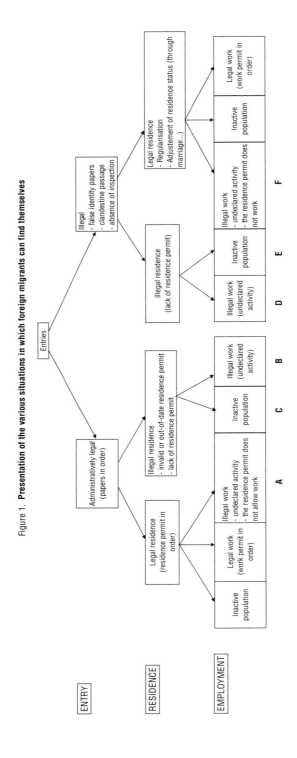

Figure 1. **Presentation of the various situations in which foreign migrants can find themselves**

In Europe, measurement of clandestine migration has been attempted only relatively recently. The wide range of methods contemplated and used is a reflection of the similarly wide range of statistical observation systems employed but is above all testament to the exploratory nature of these first attempts. Tables 1 and 2 summarise the results of comparative research carried out by Eurostat in some ten European countries; its objectives were to compile a register of methods used in the various countries and to suggest viable procedures in the light of the kind of data available (Delaunay and Tapinos, 1998). In practice, given that any measure of clandestinity necessitates a piece of information, the measurement is based initially on direct observation of the individual in a an irregular situation or considered likely to be so, either at the moment of his crossing the border (for example data on apprehensions and forced departures), during his residence (for example, from regularisations and refusals of asylum). Such information constitutes the basis for only an imperfect measure. This is why recourse to indirect estimation methods is necessary.

Estimates based on the population of sending countries are really an application of classical expected-population and gender ratio methods integrating additional information derived from data from immigration countries. The "expected population" method involves a comparison between expected and observed stocks broken down by age and gender in two successive censuses. Starting from the population distribution on that date (t), and allowing for deaths and births registered or estimated during the period (t, t+k), the difference between the population actually observed and that extrapolated in (t+k) gives an estimate of the sending country's net migration during the inter-census period. Evaluating clandestine migration involves comparing this net

Table 1. **Typology of the methods used to estimate clandestinity**

Direct measures	Administrative statistics	Statistics on refusals	Visas / entries
			Political asylum
			Residence and work permits
		Infractions	Entry / border
			Stay
			Work or job
		Regularisations	Mass
			Exceptional
	Surveys	without sample	Delphi "method"
		with sample	"Snowball" technique
			At the time of the regularisation
			On employment
			On mobility / border flows
			Biographical
Indirect estimates	Comparison of sources		Expected populations
			Pairing of files
	Inferences from secondary events		Sex-ratio
			Common law crimes
			Births and deaths
			Statistics on school attendance
			Social / health benefits
	Work statistics		National data

Source: Delaunay and Tapinos, 1998.

Table 2. **Tested or conceived methods of estimates**

Category	Method	No.	Europe	United Kingdom	Belgium	France	Greece	Netherlands	Italy	Portugal	Czech Rep.	Switzerland
Entry/ Exit	Visa refusals	1										
	Entry refusals	1										
	Passenger cards						■					
	Apprehensions at border	4									■	▨
	Biographical inquiries	14										
	Surveys on flows	13						■			■	
Residence	Breaches of residence regulations	5										▨
	Refusals residence permits	3										
	Refusals of political asylum	2										
	Regularisations	8				■	▨		■	▨		
	Common law crimes	18						■				
	Comparison of sources	16			■	■			■			▨
	Deaths and births	19						▨	■	▨		
	Expected populations	15	■									
	Sex-ratio	17	■									
	School, social assistance	21							■			▨
	Delphi Method	10						■	■		■	▨
	Surveys by stage	11										
Work	National data	22							■			
	Employment infraction	6										
	Surveys on irregular employment	12										

Methods being applied ■
Collaborators' proposals ▨

migration estimate with variations in stocks (or in net migration) registered world-wide for nationals of these countries which necessitates knowledge of the stocks in recipient countries of the nationals of the country concerned. Such a method is appropriate only under the hypothesis that the nationals of the country concerned migrate to a very small number of countries.

The second method focuses on the high proportion of men among clandestine migrants; this is observed by default in gender ratios (women appear to be in a majority) of populations counted in sending countries. An estimate of those missing is then possible if one knows the ratios of men among those remaining and among all nationals registered both in their own countries and abroad. These indirect methods are not reliable. A small weakness in one of the links of the estimating chain (*e.g.* in census coverage, or in measuring the death rate) can easily lead to a substantial variation in the measure of clandestinity. Furthermore, they only provide an overall estimate of the number nationals who are living abroad; their distribution by recipient country would remain unknown.

In so far as clandestine immigrants work in the hidden economy, it will be possible to consider an estimate of clandestine immigration as a by-product of a measurement of the hidden economy,[3] defined as those activities which evade payment of tax and social security contributions. This approach has two limitations: firstly, with a few exceptions, clandestine migrant workers account for only a small proportion of those clandestinely employed; secondly, the methods used to measure the hidden economy reflect concerns linked to taxation and national statistics (*e.g.* the amount of, and growth in, GDP), and are not directly concerned with the legal status of migrant workers. Moreover, in the hidden economy the dividing line between clandestine employment and registered employment tends to be very difficult to draw.

The most elaborate attempts to estimate the number of clandestine foreigners by measuring the hidden economy have been made in Italy. They have relied on observed divergences in the national accounts between declared added value and estimates of added value based on average productivity throughout a given sector and anomalies observed in changes in participation rates.

Three concluding remarks on these measurement methods.

- It is not possible to place on the same plane, on the one hand, the innumerable *guestimates* (guess estimates) that tend rather to reflect the feeling of anxiety (or the need to give reassurance) that their authors feel with regard to clandestine immigration and, on the other hand, the difficult and imperfect attempts, conducted in conformity with the procedures of scientific research, to arrive at a statistical measurement. Most certainly, there is no guarantee that the measurements arrived at on the latter basis will more closely correspond to reality than those based on the former approach. However, that their method of calculation, the field covered, the hypotheses used and statistical biases

---

3. It is a gross over-simplification, but we can identify three overlapping types of procedure. Firstly, there are surveys that have the advantage of including characteristics of economic sectors and the workers concerned, but do not identify variations over time. Then, there are numerical methods that focus on anomalies between observed and assumed developments; the variables customarily used are participation rates, the disparity between national revenue and expenditures, the proportions of expenditure using cash and large-denomination notes, and household electricity consumption. These methods need a blank sheet in which it is reasonable to assume that the hidden economy is, to all intents and purposes, non-existent. It is then possible to identify growth in the hidden economy over time. A more ambitious econometric procedure uses a theoretical model of the informal economy that involves the introduction of a series of variables defining determiners (e.g. fiscal pressure or regulations covering employment) and indicators of the hidden economy (e.g. participation rates). Because of the wide variety of procedures used and specific features of the statistical factors requested and the field covered, it is difficult to make comparisons. As a percentage of GDP, estimates range between 4% to 20%, with particularly high levels for certain sectors such as building, hotels and catering and domestic services.

are all explicit does present a considerable advantage. Such an approach, in offering the possibility of subjecting to comparison the results obtained through a variety of statistical methods, is the sole means of coming close to an accurate estimate.

- The issue is not so much the number of clandestine immigrants but rather the characteristics and the mechanisms of the reproduction of clandestinity: these give real meaning to the estimate of the stock obtained. The stock of clandestine immigrants results from the difference between their inflow and outflow and depends therefore on the average length of time spent in the state of clandestinity. It is of some importance to know the relative extents to which a change in the stock of clandestine immigrants is due to a change in inflows and a change in the average duration of clandestine stay.[4]

- Irregular migration is by definition a breach of immigration law, and we have long pretended that it was an exceptional phenomenon. This allowed us to believe that we were dealing with a problem to which we had to find a solution. This confusion between normative and positive had the effect of concealing the need to put in place a statistical apparatus that would provide for both measurement and the carrying out of longitudinal surveys with a view to understanding the mechanisms of migration and the characteristics of clandestine migrants. Clandestine immigration is not an exceptional, non-renewable event. It is an inevitable phenomenon, one that is likely to grow as globalisation, economic transition and inter-ethnic conflict continue.

3. THE ECONOMIC IMPACT

Is there an economic dimension that is specific to illegal migration as compared to legal migration? To what extent are the economic implications of illegal labour immigration linked to the foreign workers' legal status?

In the standard model of the labour market, the incidence of immigration, legal or illegal, depends on the nature of the migration process and the degree to which immigrants and nationals complement or substitute for one another. In this way, one may contrast the situation according to which immigration derives from an economy-wide or sectoral labour shortage and may therefore be seen as endogenous, with that where immigration is exogenous and likely to engender competition with the pre-existing domestic labour supply. Under this latter hypothesis, which standard labour market theory assumes to be the case, the equilibrium wage falls; the quantitative impact on the employment of nationals depends on the (downward) elasticity in the supply of nationals' labour compared with the (upward) elasticity of employers' total labour demand.

---

4. Despite the multiplicity of conceivable procedures, for most of the countries concerned we do not have a single estimate worthy of the name. For the European countries, one is obliged to content oneself with very partial measurements, typically estimates inferred from the number of asylum or regularisation applications refused. In the United States, however, the civil service furnishes one of the most reliable estimates of the stock of clandestine immigrants. The number in October 1996 was put at 5 million, there having taken place between 1992 and 1996 an annual growth of 275 000 (US Statistical Abstract 1996 and US General Accounting Office,1999).

A significant displacement effect is only observed where a lower equilibrium wage rate leads to a substantial withdrawal by nationals from the labour market without a significant increase in labour demand.

The empirical scope of such a prediction is dependent on the extent to which we can determine the elasticity of the various segments of the workforce's labour supply (*e.g.* with regard to age, gender, marital status and skills) and the nature of changes in labour supply (*e.g.* variations in participation rates, hours worked, etc.). Another school of thought sees labour market segmentation as a key factor underlying the resort to immigrant workers. Layard *et al.* (1991) suggest, given the differing characteristics of jobs in the primary and secondary sectors, that a fall in wage rates in the primary sector causes labour demand to rise, whereas a fall in wage rates in the secondary sector causes labour supply to fall. This could be expected to have a positive impact on the employment of foreigners in the latter sector.

Could the anticipated effects be extended to irregular immigration? The highlighting of an effect that is specific to irregular immigration or irregular employment would necessitate an examination of the behaviour of labour supply and demand and the institutional variables that influence it (in particular the existence of an informal sector) and the specific impact of illegal immigration at a macro-economic level with regard to resource allocation, distribution and taxation.

The behaviour of labour supply and demand

For the migrant, there can be advantages in clandestine employment, but illegality is rarely the result of choice.[5] When a regularisation exercise is in progress, the eagerness of most people who meet the criteria to file an application shows that illegal workers have a marked preference for legal status.[6] However, the argument that clandestine workers (who are assumed to be more interested in financial gain than in working conditions) are prepared to accept longer working hours needs qualification. In an attempt to isolate the sole impact of incentives and constraints on working hours, Dunn (1990) sought to assess the extent to which pay rates match the marginal rate of substitution between income and leisure. To that end, he compared the results obtained from three samples distinguished by the existence and amount of bonuses linked to long working hours and the fixed costs linked to obtaining employment. It appeared that in agriculture, the economic sector that comes closest to the hypothesis of economic theory (*i.e.* the absence of overtime bonuses, low fixed job-obtention costs, plentiful information on wages, and competition between employers), there was no difference between the working hours of legal and illegal workers. From this, the author concluded that preferences in respect of working hours are independent of a worker's legal status.

---

5. This can vary for nationals and established regular migrants. Although there is certainly more of an incentive for nationals to work in the informal economy than for undocumented foreigners, the advantages for the former outweigh the risk; this is not so for illegal workers. Contini (1982) cites the example of Fiat whose staff between the mid-1960s and the early 1970s left for employment with smaller enterprises where there was more work and higher capitalisation and profits. Regular migrants, too, have accepted restrictions that limited their mobility.

6. However, it should be pointed out that there are cases where undocumented migrant workers have lost their jobs following regularisation; they are less likely to repeat the experience another time.

The advantages of illegal migration tend to be on the employers' side. In that the migrant's illegal status vis-à-vis his residence or employment places him in a situation of marked dependence rendering him more willing to accept a very low wage, often below the legal minimum, the employer might expect to benefit. The threat of being caught weighing on the migrant is for the employer a source of protection against being penalised himself. And conversely, legal residence status combined with semi-clandestine employment status can represent for the employer an advantage in so far as they allow a part of the work undertaken by the migrant to go undeclared or for the migrant to be considered as an independent worker. The monograph recently published by Iskander (1999) on the garment fabrication sector in Paris and the Parisian suburbs shows that employers' preference for one or the other of these situations depends on whether the firm's strategy is oriented more towards producing a quality product or to the minimisation of wages. There exists for the employer, leaving aside the cost of sanctions against unauthorised employment (this issue is examined below), three reasons for preferring clandestine foreign workers: differences in pay, differences in social charges, and flexibility in the production process.

For the employer to benefit from lower labour costs, undocumented migrants have to accept wages below the current market rate. Taking into account differentials in pay, standards of living and job opportunities in the sending and host countries, both legal and illegal migrants normally have a lower reserve wage. Do clandestine migrants have a lower reserve wage than documented migrants?

On the one hand, those embarking on clandestine emigration have to evaluate the expected costs of their illegality; these mainly comprise the cost of entering the country (e.g. the likelihood of being arrested in the course of each attempted entry, the average number of attempts made before a successful entry,) and similarly the expected cost of being penalised for taking up clandestine employment. On the other hand, the threat of being caught coupled with the desire, perhaps obligation, to pay back rapidly the monies spent on entering the country limit the incentive of prolonging job-search efforts. Clandestine immigrants are therefore inclined to accept a lower rate of pay than nationals and regular immigrants of the same skill category.

As far as social charges and non-wage costs are concerned, *ceteris paribus*, the advantage for employers in hiring undocumented workers increases in line with the proportion of labour costs that would otherwise be accounted for by mandatory deductions and conformity with health and safety regulations. In this context, we might talk of a *"welfare magnet"*, but in a quite different sense from how it is normally understood, that is to say, more favourable for the employer than the employee. Moreover, given the precariousness of his situation and weak negotiating power, clandestine status also renders him more susceptible to discriminatory practices.

Undocumented migrant workers and the hidden economy

The structure of the labour market and the hidden economy constitute for both the employer and the worker the critical element in their decision making processes. It is by no means true to say that the hidden economy and clandestine foreign employment cover one and the same domain, but equally they are not unrelated given that the hidden economy is the only way for foreigners in an illegal situation and with no work permits to enter the labour market. Clandestine work by foreigners is the point at which two domains converge: on one side, irregular migration (which is located within the dynamic of international migration) and, on the other, the hidden economy (which is linked to changes in the labour market, but cannot be simply reduced to the work of foreigners in an irregular situation) (Moulier-Boutang, 1991). For clandestine foreign workers, these two domains are superimposed upon one another. Work carried out by foreigners in an irregular situation is therefore located in the overall dynamic of the labour market, independent of the dynamics of international migration. The emergence of a hidden economy is part of a complex process of labour market hierarchisation and the bypassing regulations directed at responding to competition through achieving greater flexibility in production and pay. It is also accompanied by formal "desalarisation" and frequent movement from employee status to non-employee status (from salaried employment to self-employment, for example in the building industry), and the activation of community (*i.e.* family, ethnic and political) links in employment relations. These strategies for managing work are particularly important in highly seasonal jobs that demand a rapid response to variations in demand and changing tastes.[7]

These "atypical" jobs are performed by different categories of the labour force: young school-leavers and students, women looking for a second job, home helps, and foreigners in a precarious situation (whether regular or otherwise in terms of residence status) are the most commonly employed on such a basis.[8] Irregularly employed foreigners constitute one of the elements of the hidden economy; they are not the cause of its existence. However, the existence of a hidden economy that is broadly tolerated by society as a whole makes the recruitment of unauthorised migrants more likely, particularly as networks of migrants make it easier to hire undocumented workers in this sector.[9] However, though the recourse to clandestine foreign labour can regarded as an element of a flexibility strategy, were precariousness to be extended to other segments of the labour force the relative advantage of hiring clandestine foreign labour would diminish (Iskander, 1999).

Clandestine employment is also observed among sole traders (such as door-to-door salesmen and people who sell goods in underground railway stations). In such cases, clandestinity can be both a necessity and a choice for immigrants.[10] It would appear that these activities are more the consequence of an exogenous inflow than a response to a demand for labour in the host country. That said, it cannot be denied, in that the "African" products sold by Senegalese street-sellers in Italy are in fact produced locally within the informal sector.

There is an interrelationship between declared and undeclared employment, that reflects both the prohibition/tolerance dialectic of control policy and the complementarily/substitutability

---

7. The decision to sub-contract part of production reinforces, and often conditions, the opportunity to reduce wages and avoid mandatory deductions (*i.e.* taxes and social security).

8. Sub-contracting, a practice that responds to a logic of efficiency, also allows bogus companies to expand by employing unauthorised labour. For example, a French legal judgement refers to a sub-contractor who employed eight people, five of whom had no residence permits or work permits, and one of whom had no work permit. Work was supervised by a charge-hand from the main company, the workers were lodged in huts hired by the same company, and all the equipment and materials used for production were also the property of the main company. Sub-contracting enabled the main company to avoid paying taxes and social charges (Pupier, 1992).

9. Unauthorised migrants often have a better understanding of conditions in the informal labour market than nationals and immigrants who have been in the country for a long time, particularly in the services sector. This gives them a comparative advantage.

10. For example, some Sri Lankans who had no real intention of settling, applied for asylum in order to take advantage of the slow pace at which the application process is conducted, and used the time to build up their savings before returning home (Costes, 1991).

debate on the labour market. Whether it involves legal activities that breach tax and employment legislation or illegal activities (*e.g.* the sale of prohibited goods), the informal sector develops from the formal sector in the same way as immigration is a consequence of the existence of a system of legal immigration. The informal sector results from institutional rigidities in the formal sector (*e.g.* tax regulations and working time rules) and could not thrive unless tolerated by society.

Impact on the labour market: empirical results

To what extent does the employment of clandestine immigrants affect the employment and wages of nationals and legal immigrants? What differences in wages are observed between nationals, legal migrants and illegal migrants? For otherwise identical individuals, are these differences the outcome of market adjustments or an expression of discriminatory practices?

Ten years of scholarly debate on the subject in the United States from the end of the 1970s through to the end of the 1980s have highlighted the problems one encounters when one attempts to isolate the specific effect of migrants' legal status and the difficulties one meets when attempting to reconcile apparently contradictory results. One requires, in fact, data which allow one to take into account self selection effects (age, sex, marital status, education, time spent in the United States, social capital, etc.), the self selection of those who return and also unobservable events (for example, attitude towards risk). The kind of data that we have at our disposal rarely allow us to exploit the sophisticated statistical techniques that might eliminate these biases. The research undertaken by Massey (1987) on four Mexican communities observed in the United States and in Mexico is exemplary in this regard. It shows that the resulting status of inequality does not of itself lead to a lower wage but does exert an indirect influence in the sense that it is associated with interrupted periods of residence and to shorter total periods of stay. Experience in the United States is consequently limited and the workers tend to be confined to badly paid jobs, factors which have the effect of diminishing wages, be the persons legal or illegal. One of the earliest studies in the United States on the relative impact of illegal and legal immigrants on the wages of nationals shows that illegal migrants have a smaller negative impact (Bean *et al.*, 1988). The explanation for this outcome may lie in the fact that most legal immigrants enter the country irrespective of labour market conditions in the United States, whereas illegal migrants respond more to an endogenous demand for labour in that country. Other studies concluded that the results obtained should be subject to some qualification. On the whole, the results are not clear-cut, and the impact, if there is one, is moderate. In Europe, in the absence of appropriate data, the results have been more contrasted.[11]

---

11. We have indeed very little research material of the statistical quality necessary to make an assessment. One of the monographs worthy of note, that by Venturini (1997) measured the elasticity of regular employment compared with unauthorised, irregular employment and threw doubt on the hypothesis that there is competition from irregular foreign labour. Using ISTAT data on the hidden economy during the period 1980-1994, she showed in 14 branches in 5 sectors (agriculture, industry, construction, tradable services and non-tradable services) that there are variations between sectors, in particular that the depressive effect is more pronounced in agriculture, but that the overall impact is small. However, in another context, other studies show that the pay of undocumented workers is lower than that of nationals (allowing for different levels of productivity), and that they perform lowly regarded jobs with few differences in pay determined by qualifications, gender or age (Lianos *et al.*, 1996; Markova and Sarris, 1997).

In addition to the methodological problems already mentioned, these divergences may be explained by the heterogeneity of the forms of illegal migration, differing contexts, as well as by the differing dynamics underlying the process of unauthorised migration. In France during the 1960s, for example, when regularisation programmes were frequent, enterprises had a two-tier strategy whereby they directly recruited irregular workers who were already in the country whilst at the same time, as an insurance mechanism for times when they might find themselves unable to recruit such labour, they also went through legal procedures to hire migrant workers.

For migrants, too, it was a short-cut compared with the legal recruitment system; it enabled them to cut down their waiting time and, in some cases, even the cost of migration (Tapinos, 1973). Illegal immigrants would accept the first job they were offered, and usually at the lowest rates of pay. As soon as they were regularised, they had little difficulty, at a time of substantial industrial growth and labour shortages, in finding jobs that were sometimes better paid than those of the legal immigrants who continued to accept minimum wage rates.

The impact of a migrant's legal status can also be measured indirectly by looking at how migrants' wages have changed following their regularisation. Figures are generally lacking, and where they exist they come from cross-country surveys that contain biases and are therefore difficult to interpret. An exception to this has been the exploitation of two American surveys, the Legalised Population Survey (LPS) and the Current Population Survey (CPS) which incorporate a longitudinal follow-up (Tienda and Singer, 1995). This analysis seeks to break down salary variation since regularisation according to characteristics at entry that are specific to illegal workers (*e.g.* younger, more likely to come from non-English-speaking countries, lower standard of education, a shorter period of residence in the United States), and to factors that may have influenced increases in their wage in the United States (*e.g.* education, command of English, professional experience, changes in the labour market, entry cohort, the first sector of activity, economic indicators in the geographical area of activity, and changes in the economic situation in the United States). Results point to a substantial rise in the wage of workers following regularisation, correlated with the year of entry and the duration of residence, with major variations according to country of origin.

The macro-economic impact, distribution and taxation

What, then, is the total macro-economic impact specifically attributable to the employment of illegal foreign labour on distribution and taxation. According to standard economic theory, immigration reduces the equilibrium wage, increases total employment (*i.e.* nationals and immigrant workers) and alters the distribution of income between labour and capital. The greater the fall in wages rates due to immigration, the higher the surplus and return on capital investment. Do variations in the amount of surplus and its distribution depend on the legal status of the migrant workers? Insofar as the effects of illegal immigration are linked to a reduction in labour costs and the equilibrium wage rate, illegal immigration, by offering the possibility of labour costs lower than would be the case under legal migration, has *ceteris paribus* a more pronounced positive effect on GDP than legal migration.

However, it is also important to take account of the characteristics of migrants, their skills, the sectors and branches in which they are employed, the conditions of supply and demand for nationals, and the time horizon in question. For example, Djajic presents an open economy model with full employment in two sectors: unskilled workers, both nationals and unauthorised migrants, are employed in branches whose product is an input for branches where only nationals are employed. The effects on wages and flexibility in a sector brought about by the employment of undocumented workers increase the total product and *per capita* product for the workforce as a whole. In the long term, the employment of illegal foreign workers may promote the acquisition of skills and the upward mobility of the domestic labour force, and thereby raise incomes for society as a whole (Djajic, 1997). However, results are linked to migrants' skill levels and to their exclusive concentration in a branch or sector, rather than to their illegal status. A structure of this type provides an equally good description of both legal and illegal migration in Europe during the 1960s and early 1970s (Lutz, 1963; Tapinos, 1973).

By contrast, given the current situation in Europe, particularly in southern Europe where the labour supply and unemployment are both high, substantial non-wage labour costs in the formal sector and the shortage of capital can lead to a displacement of capital and workers towards the low-cost informal sector. This is an undesirable consequence in the long term (Dell'Aringa and Neri, 1989). It is a hypothesis that needs checking; the detailed sectoral analyses required for this have yet to be carried out (Venturini, 1997).

The most sensitive area concerns the effects of undocumented migration on the most disadvantaged workers in society. Insofar as immigration increases the total product, specific groups affected by immigration could receive compensation. The minimum wage and other forms of guaranteed income seek to meet this redistributive objective for the most disadvantaged. However, the existence of such measures can itself encourage illegal immigration. The argument is not that undocumented migrants are attracted by the *"welfare magnet"*, but rather that by raising the reserve wage of nationals, welfare-state policies increase the return for employers on the use of illegal immigrant workers and, to a lesser extent, on the use of legal immigrant workers.

It is precisely considerations of this type that are adduced in support of restrictive policies. However, restrictions on legal and illegal immigration that aim to protect the least skilled groups on the labour market have to be compared in an open economy with effects on the same groups that would result from an equivalent increase in labour-intensive imports. Potential migrants unable to leave their countries would specialise in the production and export of labour-intensive products; the employment and earnings of unskilled workers in what would otherwise have been immigration countries would thereby be affected.

The fear of a crowding-out effect on nationals and legal migrants is reinforced when illegal immigration occurs during situations of rising unemployment. According to a neo-classical approach, an increase in unemployment would be analysed as a further voluntary withdrawal by nationals and legal immigrants from the labour market, their reserve wages being higher than the now lower equilibrium wage brought about by the employment of illegal foreign workers. What exactly voluntary unemployment and reserve wage mean in such a model is, to say the least, somewhat ambiguous, particularly in an open economy with the possibility of temporary labour migration.

Let us imagine a large inflow of undocumented foreigners ready to accept jobs at a wage 50% below the market rate – a movement that could lead to a massive withdrawal of nationals from the labour market. To consider these nationals as voluntarily unemployed because their reserve wage is too high would be to render the notion of a reserve wage meaningless. The reserve wage is established in relation to certain expectations that workers have with regard to their standard of living – taking into account time and place, to use the academic definition of the right price. Migrants are prepared to accept wages which, given the constraint of an irreducible level consumption in the country where the jobs are, provide a standard of living desired for family members who stayed behind through remittances that increase in value with improvements in the terms of trade. The reserve wages of residents of immigration countries and of potential migrants are associated with different reference spaces and life styles. Differentials may explain why people resort to unauthorised immigration, but they also pose the problem of an inter-personal comparison of utilities.

The question of labour market competition needs to be examined together with concerns for the fiscal impact of illegal immigration. This brings us back to an examination of the extent to which deductions and benefits are linked to territoriality, nationality and regularity in respect of residence.

In terms of taxation, whatever calculation technique is used to itemise the expenditures and resources put into immigration as a whole (it is a calculation that cannot be simply reduced to a cross-sectional analysis, and has aroused a debate notable for its extremely divergent positions), the fiscal impact of unauthorised foreign workers and their families is generally positive as far as the national budget is concerned. Illegal migrants pay indirect taxes in the same way as all other consumers and although they avoid paying income tax their revenues are generally such that the loss to the public exchequer cannot be significant and is unlikely to exceed what they obtain in return, given that their use of community services tends to be even lower than their incomes. The only real "cost" linked to irregularity is for services whose use is not determined by the legality of residence status; these mainly concern the education of children of illegal immigrants.

As far as social protection is concerned, contributions and entitlements are linked to regularity in respect of residence and work. On the hypothesis that regular migrants realise a net gain from the social protection system, a relative increase in the proportion of illegal immigrants in the immigrant population who do not contribute – but do not draw benefits either – actually reduces the cost of the system. On the hypothesis that the contributions of regular migrants are greater than the benefits they receive, which is usually the case, a similar relative increase in the proportion of illegal immigrants represents a loss to the system, but not a specific cost. Whichever of these hypotheses is retained, the claim that the money that illegal migrants take out of the social protection system is a motivating factor behind their decision to migrate should be treated with caution. There is, however, an argument in favour of reallocating resources between the various administrative tiers in order to pay for higher charges at the local level.

The research by McCarthy and Vernez (1997) that reports on the results of surveys conducted by the Rand Corporation in California can be cited as an example. According to United States law, illegal immigrants are not eligible for certain assistance programmes, although they do qualify for education and for food programmes. Children qualify for assistance in the same way as all children born in the United States. In fact, the drawing of social benefits depends more on migrants' socio-economic status than on their legal status. However, it is noteworthy that: a) hospitalisation is higher among children born in the United States of illegal immigrants; b) many illegal immigrants qualify for access to certain social programmes (*e.g.* AFDC, food stamps and Medicaid) insofar as their children born in the United States are eligible or one of the parents has the status of legal immigrant; and, c) illegal immigrants tend not to apply for reduced tax liability.

The final element to be considered in this calculation is the cost of control, which can indeed be very high. Entry control seeks to counter a wide range of illegal activities including drug trafficking and terrorism. Not all the costs incurred in entry control can be attributed to illegal migration. Moreover, the specific cost of applying laws (*e.g.* frontier controls, the imposition of penalties on employers, and the investigation and sending back of foreigners lacking the proper documents) are an integral part of general immigration policy and as such is the price to be paid for operating a legal migration regime – unless, that is, we were to imagine a totally open-frontier system. In other words, for illegal immigration to represent a fiscal burden, it would have to be assumed that the cost of control (properly adjusted) exceeded the positive net balance of fiscal revenues less social expenditures attributable to it. That is a highly unlikely outcome given the extent of illegal immigration's positive impact on GDP.

In conclusion, in order for the phenomenon of clandestine immigration to be comprehended it is essential that its economic dimension be taken into account. It would appear however that economic analyses of the labour market have not identified and incorporated within its models the specific features of clandestine immigration. This explains why the majority of the studies of illegal immigration, in particular to the Unites States, analyse the employment of illegal immigrants as if it were coterminous with that of unskilled legal immigrants. The difference in the economic incidence of illegal and legal immigration appears then as a matter of degree rather than of nature

4. COMBATING CLANDESTINE IMMIGRATION

Before turning to an examination of the administrative effectiveness of controls, the questions of the legitimacy of restrictions on movement and settlement and their economic efficiency, from both the world and national point of view, should be examined.

With regard to economic efficiency, as defined by some criterion of world or national welfare, there are arguments in favour of both an open frontier and a control policy. Using very restrictive hypotheses, particularly an otherwise fixed national supply of labour, it is possible to demonstrate that total world welfare would increase were all frontiers opened up (Hamilton and Whalley, 1984). At a national level, one may more realistically say that, for the recipient country, immigration has distributive and *"free rider"* effects in that it allows new entrants to benefit from the past accumulation of capital and technological progress, the cost of which has been borne by previous generations. However, looking over the long term, there are too many non-measurable parameters. That is why immigration policies are usually founded on short-term economic arguments, or on arguments of political philosophy that have nothing to do with the issue of economic impact.

In this regard, two observations can be made. First, in a democratic society, whilst the regulation of inflows and the definition and implementation of rules for accepting new members of the community are seen as forming part of the legitimate attributes of a nation-state, the issue of sending immigrants back against their will is much more problematic. There is an asymmetry here which, for the individual, recalls the asymmetry between the right to leave one's country and the absence of an equivalent right to enter another. Liberal societies have also made a commitment not to close their frontiers to refugees and asylum seekers. What, then, in these conditions, are the options for the state?

The combating of clandestine immigration is effected by measures that attempt to control inflows and length of stay, and curb the clandestine employment of foreign labour. These two elements are closely linked: curbing the clandestine employment of foreign labour aims to limit clandestine inflows and residence; the main justification for the control of flows is to protect the domestic workforce from unfair competition thought to come from the clandestine employment of foreign labour. To these two administrative activities, we must add free trade and co-operation policies that seek to reduce the propensity to emigrate.

Frontier control and controlling the length of stay

To measure the effectiveness of administrative measures requires that the policy's objective has been clearly defined. If the objective is to reduce illegal immigration and settlement in the country, are entry restrictions efficient? Do they represent the best option? To answer these questions, we need to take account not only of the direct effects on inflows, but also of the effects on net migration. However, entry control is only one of the possible ways of limiting inflows and settlement in the country. It follows, therefore, in relation to the established objective, that we need to compare the cost-effectiveness of frontier controls with other indirect methods, for example the imposition of penalties on the employers of clandestine foreign workers or policies of co-operation with origin countries.

The policy of *controlling inflows* responds to general principles of immigration policy regarding the number and characteristics of legal migrants. In settlement countries, in particular the United States, this involves defining immigration criteria and measures for combating clandestine immigration; in the European Union, it takes the form of severely restricting labour immigration from non-member countries. Whether they limit access to the country through a policy of visas or prevent the clandestine crossing of frontiers, these policies of controlling migration flows have revealed themselves to be both effective and limited. Although they have reduced the number of entries of the categories concerned, they have also led to their substitution, to some degree, by those categories whose entry continues to be possible and/or less controlled, and who have subsequently transformed themselves into clandestine residents. Clearly, policies for controlling inflows cannot on their own hope to regulate immigration. The international opening of economies, the volume of cross-border movements, the maintenance (indeed the heightening) of economic imbalances between rich and poor countries, and the existence of networks sustained by the presence of established foreign communities ensure that control is not simply a matter of visas and frontier police.

In the context of globalisation, entry control presents a real problem for developed countries. First, outside a closed system (such as that of the Soviet Bloc or the Berlin Wall), and in a democratic environment, a selective, partial system of control is difficult to implement. Moreover, it is generally the case that countries that attract migrants are often those that also attract entrants of all kinds, mainly tourists and family visitors. The problem is how to distinguish clearly at the point of entry between potential migrants and other flows. No administrative measure [*e.g.* visa policies that distinguish between different categories of inflow, the insistence on special conditions for tourists such as the obligation to have a return ticket and/or a certain amount of money, and the recently withdrawn French system of an "accommodation certificate" (*certificat d'hébergement*)] has proved itself sufficient to meet the problem[12].

---

12. However, as statistics on flows into European countries show, it would be wrong to under-estimate the impact of the visa policy.

In this context, the United States' migration policy, which focuses mainly on entry (*i.e.* the visa system)[13] and the surveillance of land frontiers, provides a particularly good illustration. How effective is the threat of being apprehended by the Immigration and Naturalization Service (INS)? Research by Espenshade (1995) does not offer a firm response.[14] There is a 30% chance of being apprehended each time an attempt is made to enter the United States, but of course migrants can simply keep trying until they succeed. There is a 1-2% chance of being apprehended on American soil. It is clear that, when migrants reach the American border, they will cross it eventually, and once they are inside the country, there is very little likelihood of their being arrested. It appears, then, that there is no link between the perceived risk of being arrested at the border and the total number of illegal immigrants in the United States. However, Espenshade concludes that implementation of INS policies "does have some dissuasive effect". Over recent years, although the strengthening of INS controls has increased the risk of apprehension it has also been accompanied by an enlargement in the number of crossing points.

Assessing the administrative effectiveness of control policy by its impact on flow reduction can be deceptive as soon as there exists ambiguity in the policy's objective. In North America and Europe, the stepping up of controls does not rule out a degree of acceptance of irregular entries. In the United States, at least until 1994, the declared control policy at the Mexican border was exercised somewhat selectively.[15] In Europe, after frontiers were closed the admission of asylum seekers was for a time and without calling the principle of closure into question an indirect and more efficient means of selecting entries.

Control over entry in no way guarantees control over the length of stay. The strengthening of external controls, however effective they may be as far as inflows are concerned, does have an impact on the rate of migration return, on length of stay and, therefore, on the stock of illegal immigrants in these countries. In the United States, where the risk of being apprehended at the frontier has increased over recent years, migrants have tried to compensate for the additional cost by crossing the border less often and spending more time in the United States. In Europe, the closing down of frontiers has had the effect of slowing down the rate at which labour migrants return home (with marked differences by nationality), consolidating the family reunion process, and extending the length of stay.

---

13. Under American law, obtaining a visa from an American consulate abroad does not remove the right of immigration officers to refuse entry at the point of entry.

14. In 1993, the INS spent USD 362 million on implementing the policy; to this sum, we must add the USD 12.2 million spent on equipment used in achieving the same objective. That year, 1 282 000 apprehensions were carried out by border patrols; another 45 000 were made inside the United States. In 1998, the INS spent around USD 900 million for the Budget Authority for Border Patrol (Tightened Controls and Changing Flows: Evaluation the INS Border Enforcement Strategy by R. Suro in Research Perspectives on Migration, Vol. 2, n°1, 1999).

15. This has been well documented by the Zapata Canyon Project (Bustamante, 1990). Illustrations of this include the fact that most migrants do not choose to cross the frontier where the geographical conditions are least dangerous, but where there is a large labour market on the American side (*e.g.* the Tijuana-San Diego border), and a large number of "illegal commuters".

Democratic and liberal states face a range of political, legal and administrative difficulties. Sending back long-standing foreign residents, particularly if they are in employment is, irrespective of their legal status, open to question. Among developed countries, no recipient country has introduced plans for a mass-scale repatriation. Public opinion is in favour of restrictive measures at entry, but is much more reluctant to accept coercive repatriation measures. There are also legal and technical difficulties that hinder the implementation of forced departure measures. The law requires compliance with strict conditions for repatriation or expulsion: these take the form of individual legal or administrative decisions, notifying the foreigner of the decision personally, and the possibility of verifying the individual's identity and citizenship. There is no shortage of examples of people against whom decisions have been taken, but which have proved impossible to carry out: these include individuals who have had their identity papers taken away from them and cannot be expelled or escorted to the border, and cases where, despite strong evidence of a person's nationality, it has been necessary, in the absence of formal proof, to obtain acknowledgement of citizenship from the consulate in the country of origin, the latter's co-operation in such matters being linked to considerations outside the field of migration. Readmission agreements are specifically aimed at dealing with this type of problem.

The asylum applications system is a typical illustration of the limitations affecting the control of inflows and length of stay. The asylum system seeks to guarantee legal protection for asylum seekers in situations where they are few in number and where there exists an indisputable means of assessing personal risk in the country of origin. In the late 1980s and early 1990s, the use of the asylum procedure by candidates for migration, when all other means were out of the question or more difficult, has been reflected in a substantial growth in the number of asylum seekers in western Europe, particularly Germany – to the point of severely hampering the functioning of the system. This crisis has led to reform of national legislation.

Let us take the case of someone entering a country and applying for asylum. He files an application but, because of the large number of requests outstanding, the processing can sometimes take longer than two years. In most cases, the request is rejected in the first instance and the application goes through to appeal, a procedure designed to ensure so far as possible that no legitimate request for refugee status is turned down. The appeal procedure is suspensive; the person can therefore stay in the country for the duration of the procedure. During this time, the country has to decide between the following alternatives: either the asylum seeker obtains a work permit, which means that if the appeal is rejected (which is what usually happens), the asylum seeker is to all intents and purposes settled and the implementation of the judicial decision (which should involve sending him to a foreign country) turns out to be technically and humanely out of the question; or the country does not grant the asylum seeker a work permit, and this involves giving him financial assistance and enabling him to qualify for social security benefits while he awaits the final decision. In the latter case, the charge increases over time and becomes increasingly difficult to justify, especially so given that some asylum seekers manage to find jobs in the hidden economy.[16]

---

16. It is interesting to note that countries choosing the former option (*e.g.* France) have subsequently gone for the latter, and countries choosing the latter (*e.g.* Germany) have subsequently adopted the former.

Countries faced with this dilemma have initially chosen to speed up the process by increasing the budgets of the government departments responsible for refugees. This has been effective. However, it ultimately proved necessary to make the asylum scheme more restrictive: in Germany, this resulted in an amendment to Article 16 of the Basic Law; in Europe more generally, it took the form of implementing the Dublin Convention whereby candidates may make only one application in the European Union. These measures have led to a significant reduction in the number of asylum seekers. Yet greater financial resources and stronger controls do not affect the principle of the asylum system. There is therefore reason to believe that the asylum route will continue to be one of the key components of migration flows. The asylum procedure, which is specific with regard to entry, illustrates the general difficulty of controlling the length of stay.

It appears therefore that there is an inter-relationship between entry control and the regulation of migration return. A country which makes entry more difficult reduces thereby the incentive to leave for those already present. However, when confronted with the difficulty of exerting control over length of stay, countries react by raising barriers to entry, often going further than the degree of closure that was initially planned and seen by the country as desirable. Immigration control can only be carried out at entry, but the economic, social and political problems of immigration are more the result of the settlement of migrants.

As soon as unauthorised migration is, in the absence of reliable data, assumed to reach proportions deemed "large", governments face a dilemma: either they apply the existing legislation and thereby create a group of marginalised individuals, or they decide on an amnesty which has to be presented and perceived as an exceptional and "one-off" operation. In the latter instance efforts are made in the hope of ensuring that the amnesty does not attract new inflows,[17] and in particular that it does not stimulate expectations of another amnesty.

The European experience, particularly since 1973-74, and the American experience (IRCA, 1986) show that no regularisation exercise has ever put an end to the presence of clandestine immigrants, in the sense that none have affected the decisive factors and mechanisms underlying illegal migration. This does not mean that regularisation programmes should be ruled out, rather that it is important to realise that amnesties (partly) efface the past, but have no effect on the future. However, the American example shows that, even in the absence of any prospect of a new amnesty, illegal migration has once again increased; this makes it quite clear that there does not need to be the prospect of a new amnesty for the stock of clandestine immigrants to increase. Recent experience in Europe shows that it is not an option to decide whether to have an amnesty or not; rather, the choice is between repeated amnesties and discreet amnesties carried out on a case-by-case basis.

Employment controls and penalties against employers

The imposition of penalties against employers who use clandestine labour, that is to say the second form of control, aims to influence the determining factors of unauthorised migration but, like regularisation, it is a means after the fact of dealing with the problem.

---

17. This assumes that provision is made for deadlines, the type of proof that the applicant is indeed residing in the country, and possibly further proof that he has a job.

In the light of the most recent European and American experiences, sanctions against employers would appear to be of very limited effectiveness. There are a number of reasons for this. First, there are intrinsic difficulties in implementing such a system; some are legal or technical, while others are linked to the socio-cultural environment. In most cases, employers are not asked (or, more accurately, they cannot be asked) to check the validity of documents produced by migrant workers. As a result, even if the employer is under a duty to check on a worker's status, he can only be punished for not ensuring that the documents were valid. More importantly, the system of sanctions can only be effective if it is perceived by society, particularly at local level, as a legitimate element of labour market intervention.

In reality, there is usually quite a gap between being found breaking the law and being found guilty in a court of law. It is hardly surprising, therefore, that the legal process comes to a halt somewhere between the two as a result of local considerations and political pressures that highlight the difficulties that enterprises would face if they had to pay for labour at the current market rate and the risks that a cessation of activities would have on the employment of nationals.

Sanctions against employers also have an economic dimension. The effectiveness of the system of sanctions depends on the extent to which a sanction reduces the demand for unauthorised workers by adding a risk premium to their wage. This effectiveness also depends on the extent to which sanctions encourage the replacement of clandestine immigrants by nationals or legal immigrants thereby reducing clandestine entries. There is a price that entrepreneurs are prepared to pay to be able to hire unauthorised workers; the problem may be formulated within the theory of optimal taxation (Hill and Pearce, 1990). Entrepreneurs will risk employing unauthorised foreigners for as long as the expected cost of being penalised (a function of the expected size of the penalty and the likelihood of being caught) is lower than the difference between the labour costs of illegal and legal migrants.

The unknown element for the employer is the likelihood of being checked up on. It can however be calculated, or at least its determinants can be assessed on the basis of such factors as the amount of money invested by the competent government department (the INS, for example), the degree of geographical and sectoral concentration of illegal workers, and the size and location of the company. This economic analysis needs qualification in the case of European countries. The vision of the market economy ignores the shame that can go with being found guilty of employing illegal workers. Clandestine workers can be hired by small enterprises in the formal and informal sectors, but not by large firms. These latter possess, however, the political influence to recruit the migrants they need through other, more widely accepted, means. It follows that the perceived concentration of illegal workers in certain jobs, and in firms marked by certain characteristics, can be deceptive.

There remains the question of the discriminatory effect that employer sanctions have on legal migrant workers. An honest employer who does not seek to hire illegal migrants might refuse to hire workers who display characteristics that point to a high probability of their being clandestine (e.g. a low level of skills, or a poor command of the language). Paradoxically, law-abiding employers who have no intention of discriminating are more likely to operate on this basis thereby actually discriminating against legal workers. However, this legitimate concern must not be used as an excuse for relaxing a system of sanctions that aims to prevent unfair competition among unskilled workers (North, 1994). In any case, that administrative effectiveness is limited does not justify the conclusion that there should be no controls at all. After all, that the police will never succeed in completely stamping out criminality would not justify disbanding them.

The significance and scope of these measures also depend on the context in which they operate and on the importance attached to the socio-economic and legal dimensions of the offence. In European countries such as France, the combating of the employment of foreigners in an irregular situation forms part of the wider campaign against clandestine employment. It aims above all to secure compliance with employment legislation with a view to preventing the unfair competition that would result from hiring clandestine labour. The penalties are directed at employers, not at workers. To this end, drawing upon the lessons learned from applying the law, in particular the variety of legal devices used with the aim of evading employment and taxation regulations, attempts have been made to strengthen and reposition control provisions (*i.e.* prevention), the justification for which goes beyond administrative and economic efficiency. The question of the efficiency of sanctions, notably with regard to how much they reduce clandestine immigration and what impact they have at the macro-economic level, has been accorded rather less attention.

The perspective in the United States is different. The imposition of penalties on employers seeks to reduce clandestine entry and residence; it is not first and foremost a legal instrument of regulating the labour market. Here, as a result of experience acquired since 1986, less effort has been made to alter labour market regulation in response to the inventiveness of clandestine workers and their employers. Instead, questions have been asked about the relative efficiency of implementing laws against employers as compared with measures aimed directly at curbing clandestine inflows at frontiers. Taken to their logical conclusion, were it to be shown that by comparison with legal immigration, illegal immigration is of greater benefit to the economy, such considerations of economic efficiency would lead to the conclusion that implementing laws against employers has a negative economic impact.

This means that sanctions are efficient only if they reflect society's view of the legitimacy and necessity of combating clandestine employment and form part of a more general policy directed to this end. Real control is social control, as the Swiss example testifies. It necessitates at the local level a consensus on the need to combat the phenomenon and implement sanctions against employers. The new strategic orientation adopted by the INS, which proposes to associate local communities and the implementing agencies in its actions in order to "identify and define the problems linked to illegal immigration" is in line with such an view (US Department of Justice, 1999).

Policies designed to reduce the propensity to emigrate

In a world where demographic and economic imbalances produce a supply of emigrants out of all proportion to the reception capacities and demand in developed countries, it has become necessary to re-situate migration in the context of development, and to promote a strategy of trade liberalisation, incentives for private investment, aid and co-operation, from which one might eventually hope to see a reduction in inequalities between nations and less incentive to emigrate. The realism of this approach, and the confidence we can have in it, depend on the answers to two lines of inquiry. What effect can the liberalisation of national economies and trade liberalisation be expected to have on growth in revenues and employment? What effect can stronger economic growth in origin countries be expected to have on the incentive to emigrate?

The impact of external opening on the growth of economies is highly debatable. The analysis mainly (and often solely) focuses on the impact on exports and imports and on growth in the economy; it is more discreet about the effects on employment and income distribution.[18]

The relationship between economic growth and emigration is even more uncertain. Economic theory and empirical observation suggest two possible approaches. If the explanation for migration is mainly to be found in income differentials (this is the only scenario produced by the theory of international trade that assumes full use of factors of production) and employment (the neo-classical theory of allocation of factors), and if the opening up to trade and movements of capital is likely to encourage growth in the revenues and well-being of all trading partners and stronger growth among the less developed countries, it is possible to predict that the surplus workforce will be absorbed and that there will be convergence in wages.

A reduction in the incentive to emigrate follows from this; free trade and development aid are then an alternative to population movements. On the other hand, if it is true that the origin of migration lies in the breakdown of the demographic-economic equilibrium, which results notably from the take-off of the development process, then an increase in internal mobility, which is inherent to this process, normally extends outside the confines of the country. According to this hypothesis, development and international migration go hand in hand (Tapinos, 1973; Massey, 1988). This hypothesis finds confirmation in empirical studies of the American and European cases. The two viewpoints may be reconciled through the introduction of a time dimension. In the medium term, the kind of development fostered by trade liberalisation strengthens the incentive to emigrate; in the long term, improved standards of living make emigration less advantageous for potential candidates.

The decrease in clandestine migration is envisaged in this way as the consequence of a fall in the general propensity to emigrate. However, the selective character of migration needs to be taken into account. If those who are disposed to migrate clandestinely are different from other potential migrants, whether these characteristics be observable or otherwise, then the question of the specific impact of development and trade liberalisation will remain open. A partial indication in this context was provided by Hanson and Spilimbergo (1996), who showed that illegal migration as measured by apprehensions is a function of wage differentials between Mexico and the United States, but that it is more responsive to variations in real wages in Mexico than to variations in real wages in America. Generalisation on the basis of this observation would not, of course, be warranted.

5. CONCLUSION

What lessons can we draw from this examination of the economic and political issues of international migration in the light of experiences in North America and Europe? What is the

---

18. Given the wide range of experiences, it is particularly interesting to identify the factors likely to influence the direction of variations and to measure their effects. In a review of the literature, Edwards (1993) selects five elements: liberalisation measures, in particular the distinction between, on the one hand, the removal of quota and tariff barriers and, on the other, devaluation that can become necessary as a result of the opening; the time-tabling and speed of the opening; the stage of development that the country has reached; the international environment; and labour market distortions.

scope for public intervention in the context of accelerating globalisation alongside the persistence of demographic and economic disequilibria between the rich and poor countries and the instability resulting from intra- and inter-national conflicts?

The phenomenon of clandestine migration is not confined to any one migration regime in particular. Neither a regime open to regular migration such as that in North America nor one of closed borders such as that prevailing in Europe guarantees the containment of clandestine entries and the prevention of unauthorised residence by foreigners in an irregular situation. The diversity of the potential forms of clandestinity, the multiplicity of the objectives in the fight against clandestine immigration, the conflicts of interest between different groups in recipient countries and the ambivalence of public opinion necessitate the implementation of a range of measures. The effectiveness of these measures rests on the assumption that migration is a process with inflows and outflows. It is the obstacles to entry which have the effect of ultimately inducing an increase in the number of illegal immigrants greater than would be the case under a more liberal system of entering and leaving.

The problem of the control of migration flows should not be viewed as being uniquely bilateral. The emergence of new geographic areas for migration imposes on governments forms of co-operation ranging from the exchange of experiences to co-ordination in the methods they employ to regulate migration flows.[19] Yet in a world increasingly open to the circulation of goods and capital, where the reduction in transport costs leads to considerable cross-border movements linked to tourism, the acquisition of tertiary education and professional training and business travel, it is anachronistic to conceive of immigration control exclusively in terms of sovereignty.

An initial distinction needs to be made between *movement*, the expression of the human right to come and go, and *settlement* which is conditional on the legitimate prerogative of societies to decide the extent to and the conditions under which they are ready to accept new members. For all that, the difficulty of managing the risk that incomers will remain beyond the duration of their visa cannot legitimise the imposition of restrictions on the circulation of persons, for this would be detrimental to the majority of them who desire merely and with honest intent to undertake a brief stay.

It should be noted also that migrants belong neither to their country of origin nor to their country of destination. It is an illusion to imagine that irregular migration can be eliminated solely by state intervention and improved co-operation between the origin and destination countries. Clandestine migration, as well as being a breach of the law is also a manifestation of individual liberty. Between the inspector who carries out his duty and the migrant in search of his destiny, the issues are not of the same nature. This is the root of the problem.

---

19. Hence the lifting of internal controls within the European Union and the drafting of common regulations for external border control (the Schengen inter-governmental agreement and the Dublin Convention on asylum seekers). For all this, none of the countries concerned has ruled out the possibility of applying special conditions to certain categories of would-be entrants.

BIBLIOGRAPHY

BAGANHA, M.I. (1998), "Immigrant involvement in the informal economy: the Portuguese case", *Journal of Ethnic and Migration Studies,* Vol. 24, No. 2, April, pp. 367-385.

BEAN, F.D., LOWELL, B.L. and TAYLOR, L.J. (1988), "Undocumented Mexican immigrants and the earnings of other workers in the United States", *Demography*, Vol. 25, No. 1, February, pp. 35-52.

BENEDETTI, L. (1991), "Le travail clandestin entre le travail choisi et le travail possible", in Montagne-Villette, S. (ed.) *Espace et travail clandestin*, Masson, Paris, pp. 65-70.

BERANEK, W. (1982), "The illegal alien work force, demand for unskilled labour and the minimum wage", *Journal of Labour Research*, Vol. III, No. 1.

BHAGWATI, J.N. (1981), "Alternative theories of illegal trade: economic consequences and statistical detection", *Weltwirtschaftliches Archiv.*, 117, pp. 409-427.

BOND, E.W. and CHEN, T.J. (1987), "The welfare effects of illegal immigration", *Journal of International Economic,* Vol. 14, pp. 315-328.

BORJAS, G., FREEMAN, R.B. and KATZ, L.F. (1986), "Searching for the effect of immigration on the labor market" in *American Economic Review*, May, pp. 246-251.

BRATSBERG, B. (1995), "Legal vs. illegal U.S. immigration and source country characteristics", *Journal of International Economics*, pp. 715-726.

BUCCI, G.A. and TENORIO, R. (1996), "On financing the internal enforcement of illegal immigration policies", *Journal of Population Economics*, Vol. 9, pp. 65-81.

BUSTAMANTE, J. (1990), "Undocumented migration from Mexico to the United States: preliminary findings of the Zapata canyon Project" in *Undocumented Migration to the United States. IRCA and the Experience of the 1980s,* , Rand Corporation, Santa Monica, California, The Urban Institute, Washington, D.C.

CHISWICK, B.R. (1986), "Illegal aliens: a preliminary report on employee-employer survey", *American Economic Review*, Vol. 76, No. 2, May, pp. 253-257.

CHISWICK, B.R. (1986), *Illegal Aliens: Their Employment and Employers,* WE Upjohn Institute for Employment Research.

CHISWICK, B.R. (1988), "Illegal immigration and immigration control", *Journal of Economic Perspectives*, Vol. 2, pp. 101-115.

CLARK, R.L., PASSEL, J.S., ZIMMERMANN, W.N. and FIX, M. with MANN, T.L. and BERKOWITZ, R.E. (1995), *Fiscal Impacts of Undocumented Aliens: Selected Estimates for Seven States,* The Urban Institute, January, Washington D.C.

COBB-CLARK, D. A., SHIELLS, C. R. and LOWELL, B. L. (1995), "Immigration reform: the effects of employer sanctions and legalization on wages", *Journal of Labor Economics*, Vol. 13, No. 3, July, pp. 472-498.

COMMISSION FOR THE STUDY OF INTERNATIONAL MIGRATION AND COOPERATIVE ECONOMIC DEVELOPMENT (1990), *Unauthorized Migration: An Economic Development Response,* Report, July.

CONTINI, B. (1982), "The second economy of Italy" in Tanzi V. (ed.), *The Underground Economy in the United States and Abroad,* DC Heath and Co., Boston, pp. 199-208.

COSTES, L. (1991), "Immigrés et travail clandestin dans le métro" in Montagne-Villette, S. (ed), *Espaces et travail clandestins*, Masson, Paris.

CORNELIUS, W.A., MARTIN, P.L. and HOLLIFIELD, J.F (1994), *Controlling Immigration: A Global Perspective*, Stanford University Press, Stanford, California.

DELAUNAY, D. and TAPINOS, G. (1998), *La mesure de la migration clandestine en Europe. Vol.: Rapport de synthèse,* Eurostat Working Paper (Population et conditions sociales).

DELL'ARINGA, C. and NERI, F. (1989), "Illegal migrants and the informal economy in Italy" in I. Gordon and A.P Thirwall, (eds), *European Factor Mobility (Trends and Consequences),* Macmillan, pp. 133-147.

DJAJIC, S. (1997), Illegal immigration and resource allocation", *International Economic Review*, Vol. 38, No. 1, February, pp. 97-117.

DJAJIC, S. (1997), "Dynamics of immigration control", Centre for Economic Policy Research Workshop, 14-15 February, Athens.

DONATO, K.M., DURAND, J. and MASSEY, D.S. (1992), "Stemming the tide? Assessing the deterrent effects of Immigration Reform and Control Act", *Demography*, Vol. 29, No. 2, May, pp. 139-157.

DUNN, L. F. (1990), "An empirical study of labour market equilibrium under working hours constraints", *Review of Economics and Statistics*, Vol. 72, No. 2, May, pp. 250-258.

EDWARDS, R. (1993), Rights at Work: Employment relations in the post-union era. A Twentieth Century Fund book, Brookings Institute, Washington DC.

ESPENSHADE, T.J. (1995), "Using INS border apprehension data to measure the flow of undocumented migrants crossing the U.S.-Mexico Frontier", *International Migration Review*, Vol. 29, pp. 545-565.

ETHIER, W.J. (1986), "Illegal immigration", *The American Economic Review,* Vol. 76, No. 2, May, pp. 258-262.

GARSON, J.P. and THOREAU, C. (1997), "Lessons from regularisation programmes and measures taken to combat employment of foreigners in irregular situations", Centre for Economic Policy Research Workshop, 14-15 February, Athens.

GONZALES, J.G. (1994), "Illegal immigration in the presence of labor unions", *International Economic Journal*, Vol. 8, pp. 57-70.

GROSSMAN, J.B. (1984), "Illegal immigrants and domestic employment", *Industrial and Labour Relations Review*, Vol. 37, No. 2, January, pp. 240-251.

HAMILTON, B. and WHALLEY, J. (1984), "Efficiency and distributional implications of global restrictions on labour mobility", *Journal of Development Economics*, Vol. 14, pp. 61-75.

HANSON, G. H. and SPILIMBERGO, A. (1996), "Illegal immigration, border enforcement, and relative wages: evidence from apprehensions at the U.S.-Mexico Border", National Bureau of Economic Research, Working Paper n° 5592, May.

HAUT CONSEIL À L'INTÉGRATION (1992), *L'emploi illégal des étrangers* (rapport particulier).

HILL, J.K. and PEARCE, J.E. (1990), "The incidence of sanctions against employers of illegal aliens", *Journal of Political Economy*, Vol. 98, No. 1, pp. 28-44.

ISKANDER, N. (1999), "Immigrant workers in an irregular situation: the case of the garment industry in Paris and its suburbs", The Hague Seminar, OECD, 22-23 April.

KARAMESSINI, M. (1996), "Labour flexibility and segmentation of the Greek labour market in the eighties: sectoral analysis and typology", European Association of Labour Economists, 8ème conférence annuelle, Crete, 12-22 September.

LAYARD, R., NICKELL, S. and JACKMAN, R. (1991), *Unemployment, Macro-economic Performance and the Labour Market*, Oxford University Press.

LEVINE, P. (1995), "The welfare economics of legal and illegal migration", Centre for Ecomomic Policy Workshop, 14-16 September, Halkidiki.

LIANOS, T. P., SARRIS, A. and KATSELI, L.T. (1996), "Illegal migration and local labour markets. The case of Northern Greece", *International Migration*, Vol. XXXIV, No. 3, pp. 449-484.

LUTZ, V. (1963), "Foreign workers and domestic wage levels, with an illustration from the Swiss case", *Banca Nazionale del Lavoro Quarterly Review*, March, pp. 3-68.

MARIE, C.V. (1994), *La verbalisation du travail illégal, les chiffres de l'année 1994*, Mission de liaison interministérielle pour la lutte contre le travail clandestin, l'emploi non déclaré et les trafics de main d'oeuvre, Paris.

MARIE, C.V. (1997), "La loi du 11 mars 1997 sur le travail illégal: les donneurs d'ordre en ligne de mire", *Regards sur l'actualité*, No. 235, November, pp. 31-53.

MARKOVA, E. and SARRIS, A. H. (1997), *The Performance of Bulgarian Illegal Immigrants in the Greek Labour Market,* Department of Economics, Athens University, February.

MASSEY, D. S. (1987), "Do undocumented migrants earn lower wages than legal immigrants? New evidence from Mexico", *International Migration Review*, Vol. XXI, No. 2, pp. 236-274.

MASSEY, D.S.(1998), "Economic development and international migration" in *Population and Development Review*, September, pp. 383-413.

McCARTHY, K. F. and VERNEZ, G. (1997), *Immigration in a Changing Economy – California's Experience,* Rand Corporation, Santa Monica, California.

MIGRATIONS-SOCIÉTÉ (1995), "Marché de l'emploi et clandestinité", Vol. 7, No. 39, May-June, pp. 30-91 (series of articles).

MOULIER-BOUTANG, Y. (1991), "Dynamique des migrations internationales et économie souterraine: comparaison internationale et perspectives européennes", in *Espaces et travail clandestin,* Montagné-Vilette (S.), Paris, Masson, pp. 113-121.

MOULIER-BOUTANG, Y., GARSON, J.P. and SILBERMAN, R. (1986), *Economie politique des migrations clandestines de main d'oeuvre*, Publisud, Paris.

NORTH, D. (1994), "Enforcing the minimum wage and employer sanctions", *Annals AAPSS*, Vol. 534, pp. 58-68.

NORTH, D. and HOUSTON, M. (1976), *The Characteristics and Role of Illegal Aliens in the U.S. Labor Market: an Exploratory Study*, Report, U.S. Department of Labour, Washington D.C.

OECD (1990), "Comparative analysis of regularisation experience in France, Italy, Spain and the United States" in *SOPEMI* , Paris, pp. 65-101.

PALLIDA, S. (1990), "L'immigration entre l'économie ethnique et l'économie souterraine", in Abou Sada, G., Courault, B. and Seboulou, Z. (eds), *L'immigration au tournant*, CIEMII, L'Harmattan, Paris.

PHILIBERT, J.P. and SAUVAIGO, S. (1996), *Rapport sur l'immigration clandestine et le séjour irrégulier d'étrangers en France*, Commission d'enquête; Rapport n°2699 de l'Assemblée nationale, Tome 1: Rapport, Tome 2: Audition, Paris.

PORTES, A., CASTELLS, M. and BENTON, L. A. (eds.) (1989), *The Informal Economy — Studies in Advanced and Less Developed Countries*, The Johns Hopkins University Press, Baltimore and London.

PUPIER, A. (1992), "La fausse sous-traitance dans le bâtiment et les travaux publics", *Sociétés contemporaines*, No. 10, pp. 153-170.

REYNOLDS, C.W. and McCLEERY, R.K. (1988), "The political economy of immigration law: impact of Simpson Rodino on the United States and Mexico", *Journal of Economic Perspectives*, Vol. 2, No. 3, pp. 117-131.

RICCA, S. (1984), "Administering migrant workers in an irregular situation in Greece, Italy and Spain", Working Paper No. 11E, ILO, Geneva.

ROBIN, S. and MARIE, C. V. (1995), "A comparative analysis of legislation in several European countries aimed at the illegal employment of foreigners", OECD Working Party on Migration, Paris.

ROTHMAN, E.S. and ESPENSHADE, T.J. (1992), "Fiscal impact of immigration to the United States", *Population Index*, Vol. 58, No. 3, pp. 381-415.

SLIMANE, L. (1995), *L'immigration clandestine de la main-d'oeuvre dans la région bruxelloise*, Bruylant, Brussels.

SURO, R. (1999), "Tightened Controls and Changing Flows: Evaluation the INS Border Enforcement Strategy", in *Research Perspectives on Migration*, Vol. 2, n°1.

TANZI, V. (ed.), (1982), *The Underground Economy in the United States and Abroad*, Lexington Books, Lexington, Massachusetts.

TAPINOS, G. (1973), *L'économie des migrations internationales*, Fondation nationale des Sciences politiques/Armand Colin, Paris.

TAPINOS, G. (1992), "La pression migratoire: sentiment d'inquiétude ou concept analytique ?", in Tapinos, G. and Keely, C.B. *La migration international: deux approches,* Programme mondial pour l'emploi, Working Paper, ILO, Geneva, May, pp. 1-14.

TAPINOS, G. (en collaboration avec de RUGY, A.) (1993), "The macroeconomic impact of immigration. Review of the literature published since the mid-1970" in *Trends in International Migration*, OECD, Paris.

TAPINOS, G. and DELAUNAY, D. (2000), "Can one really talk of the globalisation of migration flows?" in *Globalisation, Migration and Development*, OECD, Paris.

TAPINOS, G., LACROIX, P. and RUGY, A. de (1996), *Les méthodes d'évaluation de l'immigration clandestine dans certains pays étrangers*, Fondation nationale des Sciences politiques, December, Paris.

TIENDA, M. and SINGER, A. (1995), "Wage mobility of undocumented workers in the United States", *International Migration Review*, Vol. XXIX, No. 1, Spring, pp. 112-138.

TODARO, M.P. and MARUSZCO, L. (1987), "Illegal migration and U.S. immigration reform", *Population and Development Review*, Vol. 13, No. 1, March.

UNITED NATIONS (1998), *World Population Monitoring, 1997: International Migration and Development*, United Nations, New York (Economic and Social Affairs).

UNITED STATES DEPARTMENT OF JUSTICE (1999), *Backgrounder*, Immigration and Naturalization Service, Interior Enforcement Strategy, March.

UNITED STATES GENERAL ACCOUNTING OFFICE (1997), *Illegal Immigration Southwest Border Strategy Inconclusive: More Evaluation Needed*, December.

UNITED STATES GENERAL ACCOUNTING OFFICE (1999), *Illegal Aliens-Significant Obstacles to Reducing Unauthorized Alien Employment Exist*, GAO, April.

UNITED STATES STATISTICAL ABSTRACT (1996)

VAN HAMERSFOORT, H. (1996), " Migration: the limits of governmental control", *New Community*, Vol. 22, No. 2, April, pp. 243-257.

VENTURINI, A. (1997), "Do immigrants working illegaly reduce the natives's legal employment? Evidence from Italy", paper presented for the Centre for Economic Policy Research Seminar on Illegal Migrants, Athens.

WARREN, R. (1994), "Estimates of the unauthorized immigrant population residing in the United States by country of origin and state of residence", October, P.A.A. Meeting, April 1995.

YOSHIDA, C. (1996), "The global welfare of illegal immigration –no discernment case", *Indian Journal of Economics,* Vol. LXXVI, No. 303, April, pp. 537-550.

CHAPTER 2

Immigrant Workers in an Irregular Situation: The Case of the Garment Industry in Paris and its Suburbs

by

Natasha Iskander

(Department of Urban Studies and Planning,
Massachusetts Institute of Technology)

1. INTRODUCTION

Immigrants in the French workforce face a labour market whose structure has changed meaningfully over the past twenty years. New market pressures and production realities have modified their status as workers and have amended the structure of the employment opportunities available to them. Moreover, these changes have altered the role of work permits as a mediating factor determining their access to jobs, wages, and training.

This paper shows how the strategies that firms have used to build into their production systems the flexibility needed to compete under new economic conditions have change the nature of informality. Their modification of production processes and employment patterns have blurred the line between formal and informal labour almost to the point of being indistinguishable. Firms have complemented their increasing reliance on part-time and temporary labour with hybrid forms of informality that are more sophisticated and elusive than the precursors, with at least one facet of employment arrangements gilded with the appearance formality. Examples include full-time work declared as part-time, "free-lancers" who work consistently for a single employer, temporary contracts which mask layoffs during periods of low demand, and convoluted subcontracting relationships that make it difficult to pinpoint a worker's employer. Through these newer brands of undeclared work, firms have been able to informalize and make more contingent the segment of their workforce that they would have previously considered their essential labour. These "core employees" are the workers that theories of labour market dualism would have comfortably located in the primary sector of the labour market. Yet, the new work forms have enabled firms to obtain the standards of performance and skill levels expected from that segment of the labour market without providing the associated job security, employment guarantees and compensation. The impact of this trend has been particularly devastating for undocumented immigrant workers.

As these hybridised forms of informality become more widespread, undocumented immigrant workers lose their competitive edge of offering firms "no-strings-attached" employment. While undocumented immigrants traditionally provided firms with a cheap buffer against economic flux – they could be hired quickly and easily to meet temporary increases in market demand, and then released without consequence when demand contracted – firms are increasingly adopting flexibility strategies that integrate better in their production operations. As a result, being an undocumented immigrant is no longer an advantage. In fact, it has even become something of a liability because it means that they cannot work under semi-formal employment arrangements with one or more facets that are declared and above board.

As a consequence of these changes, a disturbing economic divide has emerged among undocumented immigrants. On one side of this yawning chasm are undocumented immigrants endowed with enough skills to remain competitive in the labour market. On the other side are undocumented immigrants who are unskilled and who have, in a sense, been left behind. They work for substantially lower wages and under more arduous and difficult conditions. Moreover, because they work at a geographical or qualitative distance from their skilled peers in the production process, their opportunities for acquiring new skills through observation, casual exchange, and informal "learning-by-doing" are limited. As a result, these undocumented workers are forming a permanent underclass whose possibilities for upward mobility are increasingly remote.

The garment industry in Paris illustrates these trends well. Clothing production is highly sensitive to shifts in market demand and international competition in this sector has been fierce – in this industry, making production processes as flexible as possible has been a matter of survival. Additionally, the garment industry in France, as in many other industrialised nations, has relied and continues to rely heavily on immigrant labour, documented or not.

2. THE FRENCH GARMENT INDUSTRY

The French garment industry has been hard hit by international competition; it has ceded its international market share to new garment producing and exporting giants, such as China and Chinese Tapei. The proportion of worldwide garment exports produced in France slipped from 6% in 1980 to 3.7% in 1994. Figures from the French Ministry of Economy, Finance, and Industry indicate that since 1990, this sector has lost a fifth of its enterprises and a fourth of its workers. Government data also show that the structure of the industry has changed, with the number of large firms (with 500 employees or more) shrinking by almost a third since 1990 and the proportion of subcontractors growing from a fifth to a third of all firms in the last decade. Production tasks have also undergone a kind of rationalisation along firm lines, so much so that firms increasingly specialise in only one stage of the production process. They focus, for example, exclusively on design, fabric cutting, assembly or distribution. In 1986, 38% of firms completed more than one phase of the production process, but this proportion dropped to 28% by 1996. Links between the different stages of production, thanks to temporary and relatively fragile inter-firm relationships, are becoming an industry norm. Subcontracting networks have become more complex, with links between firms resembling more an intricate web than a neat cascade.

Entrepreneurs and workers in Paris – the heart of the French garment industry - reported that the sting of international pressures had been particularly sharp in recent years. Owners of sewing and assembly firms in particular explained that competition had intensified significantly, and that subcontractors had ratcheted up their standards while at the same time lowering their payments for orders. They reported that they were receiving anywhere from 10% to 30% less per garment assembled than a few years earlier. They added that subcontractors had also tightened the turnaround time they allowed for orders, requiring higher quality items to be produced in less time. They also specified that a small error in assembly or a missed deadline for deliver, had consequences that were increasingly severe: such a mistake could seriously jeopardise, if not permanently sever, ties between a subcontractor and subcontractee. Firm owners thus indicated that there was little, if any, slack in the system, and that the requirements for remaining competitive had become much more stringent.

Two different production strategies seem to have emerged as a result of these economic pressures. The first relies on a so-called "high-road" approach, using high skilled labour to produce higher quality items under tighter time constraints, and the second is a "low-road" method that maintains competitiveness by cutting costs, primarily wages, without any upgrade in quality. Of course, high-road and low-road production strategies are not new to Paris's garment industry; they have long featured in the repertoire of tactics that firms use to sharpen their competitive edge. These strategies, however, have become increasingly discrete. Firms' commitment to one "road" or the other is reflected in adjustments made to numerous aspects of their production processes, ranging from their hiring practices to the target markets. Furthermore, a geographical separation has accompanied this disaggregation of approaches, such that firms that rely on "high-road" production tend to be concentrated in the heart of the city, whereas firms that use more straightforward, "no-road" cost-cutting strategies tend to locate production in the capital's suburbs.

This separation of approaches has significantly affected the status of undocumented immigrants in the labour market supplying the garment industry, and has changed the importance of legal work permits for workers seeking to gain access to employment and training. Explaining why requires a more detailed analysis of these two types of production strategies and the manner in which they draw on immigrant labour.

3.   THE CASE OF THE GARMENT WORKSHOPS IN THE SENTIER DISTRICT OF PARIS

Garment workshops opting for the high-road production approach tend to be clustered in the centre of Paris, the Sentier district. This neighbourhood hosts firms that focus on different stages of the production process. Those specialising in pattern design or distribution are located caddy-corner to firms performing the cutting or sewing and assembly portions of garment production. This constellation presents distinct advantages for garment firms in this area: subcontractors can deploy orders to smaller firms quickly and can easily reconfigure their links with these enterprises to meet the specific production requirements of a given batch of garments. Clothing items can be cycled through firms responsible for the various stages of production with relative speed and with negligible transportation costs, and firms can exchange information about product design, especially design flaws, with facility. The close relationships between firms, engendered by this geographical proximity, allow for a quick turnaround on products and make this multi-firm production process flexible and lithe.

Flexible production system demanding high standards

Firms in the Sentier district complement the agility and adaptability offered by clustering with a judicious use of undeclared labour. Enterprises at every stage of the production process incorporate informal practices into their operations; in fact, analysts have argued that firms could not be profitable without such "off-the-books" gains. The geographical concentration of these firms, however, makes them visible, and means that their employment practices are subject to greater government scrutiny than they would otherwise be. As a result, firms have turned to more convoluted and slippery forms of informality to mask their illegal use of labour. A series of highly publicised crackdowns on the employment of undocumented labour in the garment industry in the last few years has made camouflaging illegal uses of labour an even greater priority than before. Full-time workers are routinely declared as part-time, others are hired under temporary contracts (that often last less than a week) every time an order comes in, some are "borrowed" from other firms, and still others are classified as "freelance".

While no data quantifying this shift is available, infractions of employment law in the garment industry as a whole – which is in any case concentrated in Paris – reflect this trend. The French Inter-ministerial delegation for the control of illegal labour (DILTI) reports that in 1992, 40% of all citations in the garment industry were for the employment of undocumented workers, and 60% were for informal practices in more hybrid arrangements, that is, work set-ups that tend to display attributes of both formal and informal employment. By 1997 that distribution had shifted, such that only 20% of citations were for the use of undocumented immigrant labour, and 80% were for the use of undeclared labour in its various forms.

Because these hybrid partially undeclared jobs depend on a façade of formality to conceal informal employment practices, they are only available to workers with legal work permits whose presence in a firm can, on some level, be declared. Undocumented immigrants are therefore precluded from holding these positions, thereby substantially narrowing their access to the labour market for high-end firms in the garment industry. Such workers increasingly face a labour market where holding a legal work permit is a prerequisite for working *informally*.

Despite the contingent nature of these contracts, the skill level of workers employed in these workshops is relatively high. Some employees are hired with skills in one or more aspects of garment production already developed and perfected. Many others, however, acquire and/or diversify their skills on the job, through the informal training of "learning-by-doing". Employers facilitate this process through frequent quality controls of the merchandise as it is being produced. Interviewees reported that they regularly cycle through workstations, verifying the garments (or portions of garments) assembled by their employees. Many specified that they check production often enough to ensure that no more than a handful of garments pass unseen through any one stage of the production process or through the hands of any one worker between inspections. Because this style of quality control is so intensive and interactive, it acts as a form of training. Workers learn through the feedback that their employers give them, and are able to correct and improve their technique, addressing their weaknesses with precision. Additionally, because workers labour in very close physical proximity (sewing machines are often crammed into tight rows), they learn from their colleagues, through casual exchanges where tips on sewing techniques accompany congenial small talk.

Because firms in this cluster place such a high premium on quality, the wages paid to their employees are fairly competitive. Interviewees reported than in a good month – a month during which they consistently worked very long hours – they could easily earn two or three times the minimum wage. (However, it is important to note that because the availability of work in this industry is so sensitive to market demand, months are not uniformly or even regularly "good"). Employers explained that because producing quality merchandise reliably is crucial to receiving orders, they feel compelled to pay salaries high enough to attract skilled workers. They also clarified that they were generally willing to negotiate with workers over whether compensation for labour should be by the piece, the hour, or some combination of both. Furthermore, because most firms closely match their workforce to production requirements and scramble to hire workers only after they have received a work order, firms have to offer wages substantially enough to draw skilled workers on very short notice, with, in many cases, less than a day of lead time to assemble the necessary labour.

4. LOW-ROAD PRODUCTION METHODS

While firms in the Sentier district have by and large adopted high-road production practices, they are surrounded by a ring of production sites in Paris's poorer neighbourhoods and in its suburbs where low-road production methods are the norm. As they are not "firms" *per se*, the more inclusive term of "sites" is used here. They are in fact extensions of firms: satellite production spaces for the completion of the sewing and assembly phase of garment production. General contractors or firm owners whose enterprises focus on either cutting or sewing and assembly drop off sets of cut fabric for assembly, and then return to collect the finished order a specified number of days later.

Many of these sites fit the traditional profile for homework production set-ups, with one or more family members producing garments for a contractor directly out of a family home. Others are more formal arrangements, with workers gathering in a separate location. However, all of these arrangements are concealed from easy public view: they are tucked away in basements or living rooms of suburban houses, squeezed into extra bedrooms or kitchens of crowded city slum apartments, or hidden in tool shacks at the edges of overgrown vegetable gardens.

Perhaps the most important reason why these production spots are covert is their complete reliance on undeclared labour. Their employment arrangements are uniformly and wholly undeclared. As is generally the case in underground workshops, the wages that employees receive are sub-par. Workers are paid by the piece and, during a "good" month, earn about half the minimum wage, substantially lower than earnings in the Sentier cluster. Work conditions are often far below standard requirements. Ventilation and lighting are generally inadequate, machinery tends to be in poor condition, and with exits blocked with boxes and with heaps of textile scraps, fire hazards a real concern.

These production arrangements undoubtedly offer firm owners and contractors a low-cost venue for at least the sewing phase of garment manufacture. Employers, however, are less than enthusiastic about this cheap mode of production. The remote location of these production sites significantly complicate quality control. Instead of being able to check the clothes being assembled, firm owners are constrained to inspecting the garments when they collect them, after the whole order has been completed. As a result, assembly errors often run through the entire set of garments produced. Furthermore, stitching mistakes also have fairly significant consequences: employers, who are themselves accountable to another firm or contractor, are obliged to send clothes back to workers for re-stitching, incurring a delay of at least several days. In this industry where quick and reliable turnaround is critical, deferral on delivery can mean lasting damage to a firm's relationship with its subcontractor. Even when incorrect stitches are removed, the mistake permanently spoils the garment because the original stitches leave a visible mark in the fabric, thereby reducing the sale value of the item. This sort of error in production not only costs a firm revenue on its order; it can cost it its reputation in the market.

The skill level of workers in these production satellites intensifies the problem of quality control for employers. By and large, assembly workers in these underground workshops have mediocre sewing skills: their stitching is often imprecise, the finish on the items tends to be slapdash, and their adherence to merchandise design is frequently approximate. The likelihood that such unsupervised production will yield flawed or lower quality goods is relatively high. But the merchandise produced at these locations does not compete directly with those from Sentier, with its high-road production style. These informal workspaces target low-end markets in both Western and Eastern Europe, where their proximity keeps transportation costs down and gives them a very slight, but very important, edge on dynamic foreign competitors (specifically garment producers located in places such as China, Hong Kong, China, and Turkey). Their more established counterparts in Sentier, on the other hand, cater to more high-end markets throughout Europe, where customers purchase clothes to keep up with fashion trends but nevertheless demand certain standards of quality.

Unequal opportunities

The dramatic division of skills between high-road and low-road production styles is not simply a matter of supply and demand, with higher compensation and better working conditions attracting skilled workers. Instead, the different types of undeclared work in the two production regimes have exacerbated the skill distribution between them – they have ensured that those employed under low-road conditions remain unskilled.

As new hybridised semi-formal work arrangements become more and more typical of the "high-road" production method, undocumented immigrant workers who do not have legal work permits, and who, therefore, cannot be employed under work set-ups where one or more facet of the job is formal undeclared, find themselves largely excluded from the labour pools that supply the more established, upscale, and visible garment firms of the Sentier. These workers find themselves relegated to firms that take the "low-road" to competitiveness, where informality is of the more traditional, straightforward ilk. The only undocumented workers to escape this rough rule of thumb are those that are highly skilled at what they do. Their abilities make them attractive to employers despite the hazards of hiring a worker who can only labour under completely informal arrangements.

The risk that firm owners run by having an undocumented immigrant worker on business premises is by no means insignificant. They face possible prosecution and fines. This practice also makes other hybrid illegal hiring activities more vulnerable to government scrutiny. If a labour inspector reviewing a workshop discovers that one of the immigrant workers is unable to provide work papers, the work arrangements of other employees are likely to undergo more careful examination. Furthermore, although firms have a number of means at their disposal to evade penalties for illegal employment practices, these strategies have other indirect costs that are perhaps more damaging to the firm over the long term. A common method of avoiding fines, for example, is declaring bankruptcy and closing down, only to reopen the business a short while later, registering it under the ownership of a family member (a brother, a child, a cousin), and perhaps also changing the name. Resorting to this method, however, means sacrificing a firm's relationships – at least temporarily – with subcontractors and suppliers, jeopardising its reputation for reliability and its name recognition.

For undocumented immigrant workers who have not already developed skills marketable enough to offset the risk involved in hiring them, employment prospects are grim. The "low-road" production sites to which they are largely confined offer very limited possibilities for on-the-job training or informal learning-by-doing. Furthermore, because unskilled workers cannot access the workshops in the Sentier where that training is available, the likelihood that they will ever acquire the skills to cross-over into the labour pool for firms that use "high-road" production approaches is very slim. This situation has generated a widening skill and economic divide among undocumented immigrant workers: on one side of the split are *skilled* undocumented immigrants who work alongside immigrants with work papers for wages that are often decent; on the other are *unskilled* undocumented immigrants, working in isolation for miserable wages, with no prospects for advancement. This gulf will remain unbridgeable so long as the legal right to work is denied these immigrants.

5. CONCLUSION

This paper uses the garment industry in Paris and its suburbs to illustrate how the status of undocumented immigrants in the labour market has changed. As firms face intensifying pressures for flexibility and as new hybrid forms of informality become widespread, undocumented immigrants' access to informal employment has become more complex. Legal work permits and skill levels play an increasingly significant role in determining the types of jobs that undocumented immigrants are able to secure. A widening economic rift divides workers in this industry, with workers on the losing side of the chasm working under unacceptably exploitative conditions.

But this disturbing divide is not unique to the garment industry. It seems to be emerging in a variety of sectors that display features similar to those highlighted in this case study. They are industries where flexible production strategies are increasingly indispensable, where the quantity of work available fluctuates considerably according to demand, and where workers pass through numerous employers, working for each for relatively short periods of time. For undocumented immigrants and industries where this divide is a defining trait, opportunities to escape this hermetic economic entrapment are few and far between.

Demonstrations by undocumented immigrants throughout France in the past three years are, in a very real sense, a challenge to the hegemony of the legal boundaries that exclude them. By resorting to dramatic action, such as church occupations and extended hunger strikes, protesting immigrants are demanding legal status in France. They have invoked the right to family life and work stability, free from discrimination.

CHAPTER 3

Some Lessons from Recent Regularisation Programmes[1]
by
The OECD Secretariat

1. INTRODUCTION

Illegal migration, though measured poorly, accounts for a large proportion of aggregate international migration flows. All major centres of migration are affected; in new immigration countries, illegal migrants often form the largest component of the foreign or immigrant labour force. This was so only a few years ago in Italy and Spain, and more recently in Portugal. It is currently the case in Greece, and in the newly emerging migration areas of Central Europe and Asia.

The causes of illegal migration are legion, as are the different types of illegal situations. Apart from unlawful entries into host countries, most other instances now involve migrants who overstay their host country visas or fail to have their visas, residence permits and/or work permits renewed. Other examples include seasonal workers who do not return home when their contracts expire and asylum seekers who are not granted political refugee status. The spectre of illegal migration is spreading[2] and a large proportion of illegal migrants occupy undeclared jobs.

In a number of OECD countries, illegal migration is at the centre of political debate – first, because of the magnitude of these population flows and, second, because the phenomenon has persisted despite the clearly expressed determination of many countries to combat illegal immigration and trafficking in labour. Illegal immigration also continues to exist in countries that take in large numbers of immigrants under active immigration policies and programmes to recruit permanent settlers. This is especially true in the United States.

---

1. Two room documents were prepared to support this report: (Palidda, 1999) and (Izquierdo Escribano, 1999).
2. The authors have identified 17 types of illegal situations (Moulier-Boutant *et al.*, 1986).

Amnesties, which can be long-established and recurrent processes (as in France) or the result of a decision taken after lengthy preparations and extensive debate (as in the United States in 1986 or Greece in 1998), have been used repeatedly in recent years in Spain, Italy and Portugal. For the moment, most other OECD countries grappling with illegal migration do not wish to resort to legalisation programmes, although some have experimented with such procedures in the past.[3] They are nonetheless paying close attention to recent amnesties in the six countries mentioned above, as well as to measures taken in conjunction therewith.

As a rule, the volume of illegal migration depends first and foremost on a government's capacity to set migration legislation and, in accordance therewith, to regulate conditions for the entry and residence of foreigners and for the granting and renewal of residence and work permits. Strict application of such laws delineates the borderline between legality and illegality. A home country's prevailing economic, social and political conditions have a decisive impact on decisions to emigrate and in some cases prompt migrants to defy a host country's restrictive laws and try their luck, often at the cost of their lives. They act either individually or through the organised or informal channels set up by smugglers, labour traffickers and purveyors of forged documents. And insofar as some illegal migrants hold jobs in their host countries, pull factors remain strong, even in countries where unemployment rates for both citizens and foreigners have endured. In response to labour shortages in certain localities and certain industries, employers do not hesitate to employ illegal immigrants, thus helping to maintain the flow of illegal migration.

As it is impossible to cover the wide spectrum of illegal migration, this paper will focus specifically on illegal immigrant workers. But it is important to stress that employment of illegal immigrants is tied in with the broader question of undeclared work. Such illicit employment has perverse effects on social protection schemes and represents a form of unfair competition vis-à-vis those employers and workers who comply with applicable labour market legislation. As a rule, all factors conducive to undeclared work aggravate the illegality of illicit forms of activity and employment. Such practices exist in practically all OECD countries. They are more widespread in some countries than in others, and illegal immigrant workers are just one part of the equation.

Illegal foreign workers are immigrants or other foreigners who work without possessing all of the official documents required of workers by the host country's administrative authorities. This definition cannot encompass all undeclared work by foreigners (let alone that of host country citizens), because it excludes, *inter alia*, legally resident foreigners, whether employed or unemployed, engaged in work that is partially or totally undeclared. The definition nevertheless corresponds to the category of illegal migrants targeted by recent amnesties in OECD countries. This study will first address the issue of why and in what context certain OECD countries undertook exceptional legalisation programmes in recent years, and will then analyse the information gathered, focusing on the profile of illegal foreign workers and the sectors of activity involved.

---

3. Canada declared an amnesty in 1993, Austria in 1974, the Netherlands in 1975, Belgium in 1975 and 1980, the United Kingdom in 1977, and Australia in 1973, 1976 and 1982. For a detailed analysis of such legalisation programmes in a number of OECD countries, see OECD, 1990, Chapter 3.

2. WHY AND IN WHAT CONTEXT DID CERTAIN OECD COUNTRIES UNDERTAKE LEGALISATION PROGRAMMES?

A large number of OECD countries do not wish to grant amnesties, citing above all the risk of attracting new migrants, who might seek to take advantage of the programme at once or remain illegally in anticipation of a future amnesty. Another argument against amnesties is that they alone are not enough to legalise the status of the entire population of illegal immigrants because not all of those immigrants are eligible. Finally, to declare an amnesty is to acknowledge implicitly that the systems set up to control and regulate migratory flows are in some way ineffectual. Recent amnesties in OECD countries also had political repercussions. Opponents of legalisation have at times voiced immoderate arguments, alluding to the alleged laxity of authorities and the risks of "invasion" or "surge of hoards of migrants" from less developed countries.

Today, however, the accumulated experience of amnesties in OECD countries is sufficient to broach the issue with far greater serenity and to attempt to explain, first, the reasons that prompt certain countries to take such measures and, in some cases, to repeat their experience with these purportedly "exceptional" campaigns.

The legal framework and context in which legalisation programmes are carried out

Governments carry out legalisation programmes when applying laws or decrees, which in some cases are preceded by vast democratic debates. Lawmakers generally view them as exceptional, even though in the past 15 years amnesties were ordered on three or four different occasions in Spain and Italy.

In countries that have not instituted amnesty programs, it is nonetheless possible for certain migrants, under certain conditions, to obtain legal resident status. But such procedures are discretionary. In the particular case of recurrent regularisation,[4] the procedure is not strictly discretionary. It does however differ from an amnesty by its recurrent nature, the limited number of persons involved and the extent to which decisions are taken at the local level – most often in response to labour market needs or to address situations with complex humanitarian aspects. In the past decade, for example, a number of OECD countries granted legal status to asylum seekers whose applications had been denied. In some cases, such people had stayed on long after being notified of the refusal, while in others they had had to wait years for a ruling. Because of other decisions – of a more political nature – a status other than of "refugee" has been granted to illegal migrants from countries afflicted by serious political or economic difficulties. In these specific instances, government decisions were not perceived as genuine amnesties.

Recent amnesties in the United States, France, Italy, Spain, Portugal and Greece (Table 1) all gave rise to legal procedures and the introduction of considerable technical and human resources, distinguishing them from discretionary regularisation. But the amnesties all took place in different economic and political contexts. For example, the 1981-1982 campaign in France was adopted

---

4. This refers to regularisation procedures carried out annually as a function of labour market requirements. Such procedures were always used in France until 1974, and in some years the number of workers to be regularised exceeded that of workers brought in through legitimate channels. Today, this system of "creeping" regularisation is the exception, and it applies to a much smaller number of workers.

Table 1. **Main regularisation programmes of immigrants in an irregular situation in selected OECD countries, by nationality**

Thousands

France (1981-1982)[1]

Nationality	
Tunisia	17.3
Morocco	16.7
African countries	15.0
Portugal	12.7
Algeria	11.7
Turkey	8.6
Other	39.1
Total	**121.1**

France (1997-1998)

Nationality	
Algeria	12.5
Morocco	9.2
China	7.6
Dem. Rep. of Congo	6.3
Tunisia	4.1
Other	38.1
Total	**77.8**

Greece[2] (1997-98)

Nationality	
Albania	26.8
Egypt	3.1
Bulgaria	3.0
Pakistan	3.0
Romania	2.2
Poland	1.6
Other	11.3
Total	**51.0**

Italy (1987-88)

Nationality	
Morocco	21.7
Tunisia	10.7
Senegal	10.7
Former Yougoslavia	10.0
Philippines	8.4
China	7.1
Other	50.1
Total	**118.7**

Italy (1990)

Nationality	
Morocco	49.9
Tunisia	25.5
Senegal	17.0
Former Yougoslavia	11.3
Philippines	8.7
China	8.3
Other	97.1
Total	**217.7**

Italy (1996)[3]

Nationality	
Morocco	23.0
Albania	20.2
Philippines	18.6
China	8.9
Peru	8.8
Romania	5.9
Other	62.4
Total	**147.9**

United States (1986)[5]

Nationality	
Mexico	2 008.6
El Salvador	152.3
Caribbean	110.5
Guatemala	64.0
Colombia	30.3
Philippines	25.7
Other	293.5
Total	**2 684.9**

United States (1997-1998)[6]

Nationality	
El Salvador/Guatemala	300.0
Haiti	50.0
Nicaragua	40.0
Eastern Europe	10.0
Cuba	5.0
Total	**405.0**

Portugal (1992-1993)

Nationality	
Angola	12.5
Guinea-Bissau	6.9
Cape Verde	6.8
Brazil	5.3
Sao Tome and Principe	1.4
Senegal	1.4
Other	4.8
Total	**39.2**

Portugal (1996)

Nationality	
Angola	6.8
Cape Verde	5.0
Guinea-Bissau	4.0
Sao Tome and Principe	2.0
Brazil	0.3
Other	3.7
Total	**21.8**

Spain (1985-1986)[4]

Nationality	
Morocco	7.9
Portugal	3.8
Senegal	3.6
Argentina	2.9
United Kingdom	2.6
Philippines	1.9
Other	21.1
Total	**43.8**

Spain (1991)

Nationality	
Morocco	49.2
Peru	7.5
China	5.7
Argentina	5.5
Poland	4.2
Dominican Rep.	3.3
Other	34.7
Total	**110.1**

Spain (1996)

Nationality	
Morocco	7.0
Peru	1.9
China	1.4
Argentina	1.3
Colombia	1.1
Philippines	0.8
Other	7.8
Total	**21.3**

1. Excluding seasonal workers (6 681 persons) and around 1 200 small traders not broken down by nationality.
2. A total of 374 000 people had been granted a white card (first stage of the regularisation). The 51 000 people mentioned in the table is a sample out of the total of the requests in process.
3. A total of 258 761 applications were received but the provisional results, broken down by nationality, cover only permits granted for reasons of work. If spouses and minor children were included, 227 300 permits were granted. In 1998, another programme was held. A total of 350 000 applications were received. Details by nationality are not available. Morocco, Albania, Philippines, Tunisia, and the former Yugoslavia are among the main nationalities.
4. Number of applications received.
5. Data refer to all persons granted a permanent residence permit (excluding their dependents) during the period 1989-1996 following the 1986 Immigration and Reform Control Act. Data are broken down by country of birth.
6. Foreigners who benefited from the Nicaraguan Adjustment and Central American Relief Act (November 1997) and from the Haitian Refugee Immigration Fairness Act (October 1998).

Sources: France: Office des migrations internationales; Greece: National Employment Observatory; Italy, Portugal and Spain: Ministry of the Interior; United States: INS.

even though new labour immigration had been officially suspended since July 1974. At the time, the French economy was also characterised by low growth and high unemployment. In the United States, conversely, the 1986 amnesty took place in the context of regular, permanent immigration and a favourable economic situation in terms of growth and employment alike.

Italy, Spain and, more recently, Portugal have conducted regularisation programmes. In all three countries, the labour supply had been inadequate in certain industries, and there were scarcely any immigration laws on the books – which is highly reminiscent of how things used to be in some of Western Europe's traditional immigration countries. The geopolitical environment also explains the origins of the nationalities concerned and the magnitude of illegal flows, particularly in the case of Italy.

Greece's current legalisation programme has had economic and political repercussions that go far beyond the question of whether such a procedure is advisable. Indeed, the number of illegal migrants is so great that it is difficult for Greece, due to lack of adequate statistical tools, to quantify the foreign population more precisely except through a legalisation programme. The Greek authorities' 1998 decision to launch such a procedure came following a debate that lasted more than two years. The main problem Greek authorities face today is to decide what status to confer on beneficiaries of the programme (some 375 000 applications have been registered to date, most of which concern employed persons). That the Greek labour force has been estimated at just over four million means that nearly 10% of it consists of people who are in Greece illegally.

A number of recent surveys in Greece show that a substantial number of Greek citizens were also involved in informal or partially declared employment in several sectors of the economy. To grant permanent status to amnesty beneficiaries without at the same time radically overhauling labour relations would profoundly alter labour market flexibility and would no doubt trigger an immediate increase in unemployment for Greeks and foreigners alike. The main question in Greece, therefore, is whether or not to limit, for the time being, the number of beneficiaries entitled to residence permits which are valid for longer than one year and automatically renewable.

Information obtained through amnesties

Amnesties generally provide authorities with information on the number of illegal migrants who fulfil the required conditions, on the networks that had enabled them to live illegally, on the industries in which they tended to be employed, and on the workings of the labour market. Data on the number of beneficiaries do not of course provide a precise account of the number of illegal immigrants, although they do suggest the magnitude of the phenomenon. Figures from recent studies in a number of OECD countries are nevertheless much lower than the unrealistic estimates that circulate in public opinion.

But apart from this general information, follow-up on legalisation programmes shows that amnesties uncover situations that governments had not expected. It is sometimes necessary to extend deadlines and/or ease conditions for eligibility. Authorities charged with implementing amnesties discover that people find themselves in illegal situations as a result of administrative dysfunction or gaps in the law, especially with regard to family members, minor children and special cases of unjustified non-renewal of residence or work permits. Amnesties also reveal categories of illegal immigrants that had been involuntarily excluded or underestimated in the list of prospective amnesties (itinerant vendors, self-employed persons, retirees, and so forth). For example, the main purpose of the legalisation procedure adopted in France in June 1997 was to rectify certain situations of illegality, primarily affecting migrants' family members. As a result of successive amendments to legislation governing the entry and residence of foreigners, or due to certain gaps in the law, many remained illegal.

Public security objectives

Legalisation programmes also help fulfil public security objectives. Governments that tolerate the persistence and recurrence of serious levels of illegal immigration in which most illegal immigrants have jobs encourage firms to exploit immigrants deprived of rights, endanger their health and expose them to illicit or criminal activities. While public opinion on the whole is not favourably disposed to amnesties, such programmes do tend to limit the frequency of discrimination and racism, which is even more painful when inflicted on immigrants deprived of all rights.

In the current debate between partisans of amnesty procedures and staunch opponents, rarely is the accent placed on information gathered during such procedures or on the lessons learned by officials undertaking them. Yet information on the profiles of beneficiaries and their status in society and host-country labour markets has made it possible to customise actions to inform and, if necessary, sanction employers who recruit illegal immigrants. The debate between proponents and opponents of amnesties should be conducted from this perspective. But do governments truly heed the lessons of earlier amnesties and do they adopt suitable policies that reduce the need for such programmes?

3. LEGALISATION PROGRAMMES AND THE LABOUR MARKET: LESSONS FROM RECENT AMNESTIES

Amnesty programmes, as formulated in a number of OECD countries, have never attempted to cover the entire range of illegal migration. Even after successive amendments, eligibility conditions make such amnesties selective (such as entry prior to a specific cut-off date, employment or possession of a labour contract and proof of direct family ties with citizens or legal aliens). It is nevertheless easier to interpret the illegal immigrant population's profile if the conditions for legalisation are liberal and the procedure is carried out flexibly and in good will, which can sometimes lead to successive modifications.

By definition, the contours of the illegal immigrant population are fairly vague, especially since more and more foreign tourists decide to remain in host countries after their visas expire. It is therefore impossible to know with any precision the number of immigrants in an irregular situation and the share of those who are employed. And because recent economic restructuring in many OECD countries has caused substantial job loss and shifts in employment, the results of legalisation programmes can provide only a rough idea of how the labour market works. Regardless, these amnesties yield a wealth of information about migrant profiles and the nature of illegal employment.

Amnesty beneficiaries tend to be young workers employed in sectors with a high concentration of foreign labour

Illegal immigrants are generally fairly young. According to figures from amnesties in France (1981-82), Italy and Spain, three-quarters of those involved were under 40. In the United States

(Table 2), migrants taking advantage of the 1986 amnesty law were significantly younger than the population as a whole, as measured by the 1990 census.

Those granted legal status were found in industries where legal immigrants were also working (or had been working until recently). The continued tendency of certain sectors to hire foreign labour may be an indication of employer preference for immigrant workers, legal or illegal. It may also reflect the fact that illegal immigrants are an integral part of the migratory process as a whole. As such, they fully benefit from the experience of their elders (home, ethnic community and networks of mutual assistance and support) in entering, living and finding jobs in the host country.

Table 2. **Comparison of the age structure of regularised immigrants in 1987 and the total population in 1990, United States**

Percentages

Age group	Regularised immigrants at the time they applied to the regularisation programme[1]	Age structure of the total population in 1990 [2]
18-19	4	4
20-24	14	10
25-29	23	11
30-34	22	12
35-39	14	11
40 and over	23	52
Total	**100**	**100**

1. Data were extracted from a 1989 survey of persons who benefited from the general regularisation programme. Most of the immigrants applied in 1987 or 1988. Breakdown of the population aged 16 years and over.
2. Breakdown of the total population aged 18 to 64 (1990 Census).
Source: U.S. Department of Labor, 1996.

Industries in Italy, Spain and Portugal with high concentrations of illegal immigrants correspond, with few exceptions, to those that mainly employ other foreigners with legal status (agriculture, small industry, tourism, hotel and catering, and household and business services). The same pattern was revealed in France during the exceptional amnesty of 1981-82, as well as for former illegal workers who were granted a permit in another manner (Tables 3, 4 5 and 6).

Amnesty beneficiaries bring greater flexibility to the productive system

Agriculture, manufacturing, construction and public works, and certain categories of services employ the bulk of illegal immigrant workers. Because of the seasonal nature of agricultural activities and the high labour turnover, agricultural employers are always seeking workers willing to endure harsh, intensive work that in many cases, in addition to excellent physical stamina, requires technical expertise. Under such circumstances, illegal immigrants fulfil a labour demand that citizens or legal immigrants cannot or do not care to meet. The use of illegal immigrants also

Table 3. **Regularisation of permanent workers according to the activity of their employer, 1995-1997, France**

	1995		1996		1997	
	Number	%	Number	%	Number	%
Real estate, renting and business activities	523	14.3	532	19.4	645	22.5
Trade	430	11.7	345	12.6	369	12.9
Community, social and personal services	296	8.1	266	9.7	287	10.0
Domestic services	422	11.5	255	9.3	285	9.9
Hotels and restaurants	229	6.3	198	7.2	229	8.0
Construction	413	11.3	184	6.7	196	6.8
Health and social work	162	4.4	175	6.4	170	5.9
Education	440	12.0	250	9.1	159	5.5
Transport and communications	105	2.9	88	3.2	81	2.8
Mining and quarrying (except fuel)	152	4.1	83	3.0	43	1.5
Agriculture and fishing	35	1.0	22	0.8	40	1.4
Textile manufacture, clothing	76	2.1	49	1.8	37	1.3
Other	903	24.7	301	11.0	330	11.5
Total	**3 663**	**100.0**	**2 748**	**100.0**	**2 871**	**100.0**

Source: Annuaire des migrations, Office des Migrations internationales, 1995, 1996 et 1997.

Table 4. **Immigrants who benefited from the 1986 regularisation programme according to the activity of their employer, prior to U.S. entry, at application and in 1992,[1] United States**
(percentages)

	Last job outside the United States	At application[1]	1992
Eating and drinking establishments	4	13	10
Construction	8	10	10
Private household services	5	8	6
Clothing production	3	5	4
Agriculture	24	3	2
Landscaping, horticulture	..	3	2
Hotel and motel	1	3	4
Furniture	1	2	1
Hospital and nursing home	2	2	3
Automobile repair	2	2	2
Grocery, retail	3	2	2
Other	47	47	54
Total	**100**	**100**	**100**
Number of applications for regularisation General Programme (thousands)	-	1 760	-
Number of applications for regularisation Seasonal Agricultural Workers (SAW) Programme (tho	-	1 272	-

1. Most of the applications were received in 1987 and 1988.
Sources: 1989 and 1992 surveys of persons who benefited from the general regularisation programme;
U.S. Department of Justice, 1991.

reflects the systematic attempts by firms to minimise labour costs (wages and social insurance contributions) and maximise labour flexibility (with highly intensive work for limited periods in time), especially in Europe and the United States. Governments clearly encounter greater difficulties in combating the employment of illegal immigrants in agriculture than in other sectors of the economy. Still, seasonal work is very well suited to the cyclical needs of many agricultural activities (here the experience of France, Canada and, more recently, Germany deserves closer attention).

But it is clear that some agricultural employers are reluctant to accept the idea of granting legal status guaranteeing elementary rights to immigrant workers. This is especially so in the United States.

The manufacturing industry accounts for a relatively large number of amnestied immigrants, and for nearly half of those in Italy and France. In France, the textiles/garment and construction/public works sectors employ the most illegal immigrants. One might have expected to find fewer illegal immigrants given the decline in business in both sectors. But, in reality, companies have sought to cushion the impact of the downturn by systematically resorting to subcontracting and, in some cases, to cascading subcontracting. Given the financial constraints and very short deadlines employers face, subcontracting prompts them to employ illegal immigrants, among others.

Table 5. **Regularisation programme for workers in an irregular situation, Italy, 1996**
Residence permits delivered for work reasons according to the activity of the job and the kind of contract
Thousands

	Fixed-term	Indeterminate	Total
Agriculture	11.1	9.2	20.4
Industry	11.2	20.3	31.5
Public sector	2.5	8.3	10.8
Domestic	5.3	53.9	59.2
Other	6.7	19.3	26.0
Total	**36.8**	**111.0**	**147.9**

Sources: Census and Ministry of Labour.

Table 6. **Regularisation programmes in Spain**
Work permits delivered by activity

1985-86			1991			1996		
Activity	Number	%	Activity	Number	%	Activity	Number	%
Services	4 923	33.6	Domestic services	23 289	21.2	Domestic services	2 814	21.6
Trade	3 517	24.0	Construction	16 784	15.2	Hotels	2 231	17.2
Agriculture	2 381	16.3	Agriculture	15 719	14.3	Construction	2 187	16.8
Hotels	1 461	10.0	Hotels	13 437	12.2	Agriculture	1 839	14.1
Construction	944	6.4	Retail	8 685	7.9	Retail	1 311	10.1
Education	594	4.1	Business activities	8 997	8.2	Other services	1 945	15.0
Iron and steel industry	544	3.7	Other	23 202	21.0	Industry	679	5.2
Chemicals	274	1.9				Not classified	70	
Total	**14 638**	**100**	**Total**	**110 113**	**100**	**Total**	**13 076**	**100**

Source: Ministerio del Trabajo y de la Seguridad Social (31 November 1987)

Source: Ministerio de Asuntos Sociales (31 December 1993)

Source: Ministerio del Trabajo y Asuntos Sociales.

Source: Izquierdo Escribano, 1999.

The development of subcontracting is part of a process whereby labour management is totally or partially externalised by encouraging salaried workers to acquire self-employed status. In most cases, the self-employed continue to work exclusively for the subcontracting firm, which in some cases actually provides them with essential tools and machinery. This form of concealed dependent employment allows the contracting firm to cut its social insurance contributions and escape the constraints of labour legislation, while leaving the subcontracting firm free to recruit legal or illegal workers – the important thing being to accomplish the subcontracted task.

In this context, it is frequently small and medium-sized enterprises that enhance the flexibility of the production system and adjust to economic shifts. In some cases, the adjustments in question are organised and lead to the formation of networks of companies specialising in international labour lending at unbeatable prices; and, under the guise of service contracts, it becomes possible to evade national laws restricting the employment of new immigrant workers (Robin, 1996).

In the service sector, in contrast to what has happened in industry or agriculture, the presence of illegal immigrants has been accompanied by a rise in employment. But this growth is part of a transformation in the nature of the services on offer and of an adjustment of these activities to consumer demands. These transformations take a variety of forms: extension of seasonal activities (tourism) and non-standard working hours (retail trade and restaurants), occupations shunned by host country citizens (cleaning and, in some cases, teaching), growth in services to businesses (equipment maintenance and security) and households (childminding and other domestic services), and the development of outsourcing in leading-edge activities such as information technology and engineering.

Illegal immigrants are found in all these service activities, especially in the case of France and the United States. Firms providing these services are in the market for workers who, along with certain qualifications, possess the required flexibility to compensate for drawbacks stemming from the nature of the work involved. In Italy, as in Spain, recent amnesties have spotlighted the predominant role of household employees in the service sector. In the case of Italy, those primarily involved are women from the Philippines, Sri Lanka, Mauritius and Cape Verde, and in the case of Spain, from the Philippines and mainly the Dominican Republic (Oso, forthcoming).

Amnesty beneficiaries come from the same areas as legal immigrants, reflecting two parallel trends: the persistence of traditional areas and the emergence of new nationalities of immigrants

Table 1, which presents regularisation programmes for immigrants in six OECD countries, according to natgionality, shows that the majority of amnesty beneficiaries come from a limited number of countries. Migrants to France generally come from Africa and migrants to the United States from Mexico and Central America. In Italy and Spain, immigrants from North Africa make up the largest group, followed by those from the Philippines, in the case of Italy, and from Central and South America, in the case of Spain. In Portugal, most beneficiaries come from the former Portuguese colonies of Africa. One initial observation is clear: geographical proximity and traditional immigration patterns explain the large share of certain nationalities in the five countries studied. New nationalities are however emerging: Senegalese, Chinese, Albanians and Romanians in Italy; Chinese and Poles in Spain; and Haitians, Zairians and Chinese in France.

Recent legalisation programmes in Spain and Italy show that beneficiaries can slip back into illegality

In 1996, Italy and Spain conducted their third legalisation campaigns for illegal immigrants. While the final results of the two amnesties are not yet available, it is interesting to note that the main beneficiaries of the 1996 programmes were immigrants who obtained legal status in earlier amnesties. What then happens to immigrants after they are legalised? Important factors are the status offered them and, in particular, the conditions to renew their residence and/or work permits, along with their type of employment (or unemployment) after legalisation. It is also important to determine who replaces legalised immigrants at the time of amnesty once they leave their jobs – the same labour needs obviously remain.

In the case of the United States, most amnested people obtained resident visas and after four years were able to gain permanent immigrant status. This entitled them not only to live permanently in the United States and pursue the occupation of their choice, but also – under certain conditions – to bring in family members. The freedom that resident visas confer on amnestied workers enables them to look for jobs in industries other than those in which they were working at the time of amnesty.

The geographical and occupational mobility of amnestied immigrants therefore depends on labour market conditions and any qualifications they may have, including those acquired in their home countries. Such mobility is obvious in the case of the United States (Table 4) and was even anticipated by the authorities, who, just after amnesty, introduced programmes to recruit immigrant workers, especially in the farming sector, to replace amnesty beneficiaries who left the sector. "New" illegal immigrants therefore replaced the old. In the case of France, a survey carried out one year after the 1981-82 legalisation programme shows that a large number of immigrants changed employers or occupations. In some cases, the authorities had not anticipated such behaviour (immigration of new workers had been officially suspended since 1974), and amnestied immigrants were replaced by "new" illegal ones.

Longitudinal studies on what becomes of workers whose status has been legalised show that such people behave as suppliers on the labour market, and that the jobs they hold, while not yet legal, do not necessarily correspond to the full range of their professional experience and qualifications. If new job prospects come their way, they will try to improve their situation and their occupational standing (in the host country or upon return to their country of origin). Unlike certain employers who do not hesitate to systematically hire illegal immigrant labour, immigrants tend rather to consider their illegal status as temporary, and as a necessary step on the road to legality, in the hopes of future occupational and/or geographical mobility. Illegality is perceived and envisaged by the migrant as merely a passing phase, whereas it is difficult for certain employers to give up having a workforce composed of illegal immigrants.

In Spain, out of a total of 110 000 foreigners benefiting from the 1991 amnesty, only 82 000 held valid permits in 1994. Unfortunately, the information available does not indicate what happened to the 30 000 other beneficiaries (Table 7) who "disappeared" from the labour market. It does, however, show that most beneficiaries of the 1996 programme were immigrants who had also benefited from earlier amnesties. One might ask whether administrative procedures that grant short-term work permits to amnestied immigrants do not contribute, in the event those permits are not renewed, to an increase in the number of illegal immigrants, in particular when manpower needs persist in certain sectors of the economy.

Table 7. **Foreigners who benefited from the 1991 regularisation programme
and whose residence permits were renewed in 1994, Spain**

	Number of foreigners who benefited from the regularisation programme	Permits renewed
	1991	1994
Total	**110 113**	**81 906**
Sex		
Men	78 808	58 770
Women	31 305	23 136
Breakdown by country of origin		
Morocco	49 155	38 972
Argentina	7 474	4 768
Peru	5 708	4 939
Dominican Rep.	5 548	4 718
China	4 153	3 281
Poland	3 339	2 593
Other	34 736	22 635
Breakdown by economic sector		
Services to private households	23 289	16 254
Construction	16 784	13 303
Agriculture	15 719	9 977
Hotels	13 437	11 124
Trade	8 685	5 389
Business activities	8 997	6 950
Other	23 202	18 909

Source: Dirección General de Migraciones, Ministerio de Asuntos Sociales.

Two OECD studies on illegal immigration in Italy (Palidda, 1996*a* and 1999) show it to be an increasingly endogenous phenomenon, due to a combination of two factors: (a) the non-renewal of residence permits and employment contracts of immigrants who had benefited from the three previous amnesties since 1986, and (b) the growth of the underground economy and the benefits it generates for those who have an interest in migratory flows, providing those flows remain illegal. As a result, between 1991 and 1994, over 300 000 foreigners were unable, or did not attempt, to renew their residence permits, with some even becoming illegal again.

In this context, is it not a paradox to require immigrants to have stable jobs in order to have their status legalised or their residence and work permits renewed? In point of fact, host country citizens increasingly have insecure jobs, and the scope of the underground economy has been expanding continuously – and with it the systematic use of undeclared labour (foreign or not). A 1995 survey by the Italian Ministry of Labour of more than 29 000 businesses with nearly 740 000 employees (including 18 000 non-EU foreigners) shows that the irregularities noted (undeclared employment and/or absence of valid residence permits) appeared mainly in agriculture, trade, tourism, and the hotel and service industry. And, as in other countries (the United States,

France and Spain), companies have a higher percentage of irregularities in some regions than in others (Table 8).

The example of Italy clearly shows how important it is to reconsider the issue of illegal immigration, tying it in more closely with economic and social changes in host countries. The systematic use of undeclared workers can in part explain the persistence of illegal immigration. Unless governments effectively combat the spread of the underground economy, most immigrants who try to renew their residence permits or obtain a job in the mainstream labour market will risk illegality (and at times illicit or criminal activities).

Table 8. **Non-EU workers in an irregular situation,[1] by region and by economic activity, 1995, Italy**
(percentage of the total of the non-EU workers surveyed)

	North	Centre	South	Total
Agriculture	37.2	53.2	52.3	45.9
Industry	99.6	53.0	57.5	23.3
Crafts	99.8	65.9	68.8	39.3
Trade	45.0	50.8	57.6	46.9
Tourism	43.4	55.6	94.1	55.7
Entertainment	39.6	17.5	64.5	25.3
Transport	14.4	32.9	-	17.0
Hotels	42.6	39.8	70.7	43.9
Cleaning services	31.1	34.3	69.2	33.0
Private household services	50.0	44.6	74.6	55.5
Total (all activities)	**31.1**	**43.3**	**59.4**	**37.1**
Of which:				
Irregularity linked to residence permits	8.4	15.8	32.8	12.9

1. Irregularities are linked to the absence of a valid residence permit or to the employment of undeclared workers.
Source: Survey by the Ministry of Labour of 29 097 enterprises, employing 738 437 salaried workers (of whom 17 913 are non-EU foreigners).

4. CONCLUSION

Illegal immigration is a core component of migratory flows. The fact that it persists in periods of economic decline or slowdown, and in countries that maintain active pro-immigration policies shows that it is illusory to think the phenomenon can be eradicated. It is possible, however, to reduce its magnitude. The fight against illegal immigration and, to a more limited extent, against the employment of illegal immigrants, is crucial in efforts to restore production and labour systems that are compatible with fair competition and respect for fundamental workers' rights.

In periods of economic growth, the number of illegal immigrants is probably higher than it is when the economy is slowing down. But at least economic growth increases the chances of such people to find regular work and obtain residence and work permits through legitimate channels.

In the second case, however, they may have to remain illegal for a long time, with no or little rights, be overexploited and even eventually revert to delinquency and criminality.

Recurrent and exceptional amnesties, and discretionary or disguised legalisation, enable some illegal immigrants to escape illegality, acquire a status more conducive to the enjoyment of human rights, and envisage better economic and social integration, either in their host countries or when returning to their countries of origin.

The results of the regularisation exercises recently carried out in some OECD countries demonstrate clearly the key role that certain categories of illegal immigrants play in the labour market. This observation implies that at the same time as efforts are being made to control migration flows more should be learned about the constraints bearing on the labour market, notably the increased need for flexibility within the wider context of the productive system's adaptation to the changes taking place. It is without doubt here where the principal limitations of measures to combat the employment of foreigners in an irregular situation are to be located. These limitations derive from the fact that the policy measures can not be undertaken uniquely against the employment of foreigners in an irregular situation but rather must be directed on clandestine labour in general.

BIBLIOGRAPHY

BACH, R.L. and MEISSNER, D. (1990), *Employment and Immigration Reform: Employers Sanctions: Four Years Later*, Immigration Policy Project, Carnegie Endowment for International Peace, Washington, D.C.

BRIZARD, A. and MARIE, C.V. (1993), "Travail illégal et suites judiciaires", *Etudes et Statistiques Justice 1*.

BUSTAMANTE, J. (1990), "Undocumented migration from Mexico to the United States: preliminary findings of the Zapata Canyon Project", in Bean. F., Edmonston, B. and Passel J.S. (eds.), *Undocumented Migration to the United States: IRCA and the Experience of the 1980s*, Urban Institute Press, Washington, D.C.

CHISWICK, B.R. (1988), *Illegal Aliens: The Employment and Employers*, W.E. Upjohn Institute for Employment and Research, Kalamazoo, Michigan.

de LARY, H. (1994), "Les fondements juridiques et les modalités du contrôle des migrations dans la Communauté européenne", *Migration et développement : un nouveau partenariat pour la coopération*, OCDE, Paris.

DELAUNAY, D. and TAPINOS, G. (1998), "La mesure de la migration clandestine en Europe", Eurostat Working Papers, Vol. 1.

DIMARZIO, N. and PAPADEMETRIOU, D. (1988), "US Immigration Reform: Challenges and Choices for the Future", Migration and Refugee Services, US Catholic Conference, Washington, D.C

DJAJIC, S. (1997), "Illegal immigration and resources allocation", *International Economic Review*. Vol. 38, No. 1.

ETHIER, W.J. (1986), "Illegal immigration: the host-country problem", *American Economic Review*, Vol. 76, pp. 56-71.

FASSIN, D., MORICE, A. and QUIMINAL, C. (dirs.), (1997), *Les lois de l'inhospitalité, les politiques de l'immigration à l'épreuve des sans-papiers*, La Découverte/Essais, Paris.

FRASER, J.R. (1994), "Illegal immigration in the United States and the limits of sanctions against employers", *Migration and Development: New Partnerships for Co-operation*, OECD, Paris.

GARSON, J.P. (1985), "Migrations clandestines, régularisations et marché du travail en France : contraintes nationales et internationales", Working Paper, ILO, Geneva.

GARSON, J.P. (1987), "L'emploi d'étrangers en situation irrégulière et le travail clandestin dans le B.T.P.", *La lutte contre les trafics de main-d'oeuvre en 1985-86*, Report to the Ministre des Affaires sociales et de l'Emploi, La Documentation française, Paris.

IZQUIERDO ESCRIBANO, A. (1997), "Caractéristiques et résultats de la troisième opération de régularisation des immigrés en situation irrégulière en Espagne", paper presented at the Meeting of the Working Party on Migration, June, OECD, Paris.

IZQUIERDO ESCRIBANO, A. (1999), "L'immigration irrégulière en Espagne à la lumière des régularisations et de l'expérience des contingents annuels des travailleurs étrangers", paper presented at The Hague Seminar, 22-23 April.

KLABATSEAS, G.G. (1998), "Développements récents du programme de régularisation en Grèce", paper presented at the Meeting of the Working Party on Migration, September, OECD, Paris.

LEITAO, J.M. (1997), "La régularisation de 1996 au Portugal", paper presented at the Meeting of the Working Party on Migration, June, OECD, Paris.

MARIE, C.V. (1984), "De la clandestinité à l'insertion professionnelle régulière : le devenir des étrangers régularisés", *Travail et Emploi*, No. 22.

McMAHON, V. (1994), "Immigrant integration and the labour market in Australia". *Migration and Development: New Partnerships for Co-operation*. OECD, Paris.

MEISSNER, D. and PAPADEMETRIOU, D. (1988), *The Legalization Countdown: a Third Quarter Assessment*, The Carnegie Endowment for International Peace, Washington, D.C.

MINISTRY OF SOCIAL AFFAIRS AND EMPLOYMENT AND MINISTRY OF JUSTICE (1994), "Illegal employment in the Netherlands: extent and effects", The Hague.

MOULIER-BOUTANG, Y. and GARSON, J.P. (1984), "Major obstacles to the control of irregular migrations: prerequisites to policy", *International Migration Review*, No. 67, Vol. 18, pp. 579-592.

MOULIER-BOUTANG, Y., GARSON, J.P. and SILBERMAN, R. (1986), *Economie politique des migrations clandestines de main-d'oeuvre. Comparaisons internationales et exemple français*, Publisud, Paris.

NORTH, D.S. (1993), "Why democratic governments cannot cope with illegal immigration?" *The Changing Course of International Migration*, OECD, Paris.

OECD (1990), 1989 SOPEMI Report. OECD, Paris.

OSO, L. (forthcoming), "Women, the pioneers of migration chains: the case of Spain", International Migration and Labour Market Policies, Occasional Papers, OECD, Paris.

PALIDDA, S. (1996a), "L'immigration irrégulière en Italie", paper presented at the Meeting of the Working Party on Migration, June, OECD, Paris.

PALIDDA, S. (dir.), (1996b), "La construction sociale de la déviance et de la criminalité parmi les immigrés en Europe", Brussels, European Community.

PALIDDA, S. (1999), "Les migrations clandestines en Italie", paper presented at The Hague Seminar, 22-23 April.

PASSEL, J.S. (1996), "Recent efforts to control illegal immigration to the United States", paper submitted to the Working Party on Migration, June, OECD, Paris.

POZO, S. (ed.), (1986), *Essays on Legal and Illegal Immigration*, W.E. Upjohn Institute for Employment Research, Kalamazoo, Michigan.

ROBIN, S. (1996), "Prestations de services et circulation des travailleurs dans les pays de l'Union européenne", Occasional Paper No. 2, OCDE/GD(96)63, OECD, Paris.

ROBIN, S. and MARIE, C. V. (1995), "L'accès au marché du travail et la lutte contre l'emploi illégal des étrangers", paper presented at the Meeting of the Working Party on Migration, June, OECD, Paris.

RUDDICK, E. (1994), "The selection and management of immigration to Canada", *Migration and Development: New Partnerships for Co-operation*, OECD, Paris.

TAPINOS, G. P. (1985), *Eléments de démographie*, Presses de la Fondation nationale des Sciences politiques, Armand Colin, Paris.

U.S DEPARTMENT OF JUSTICE (1991), Statistical Yearbook of the Immigration and Naturalization Service, Washington, D.C.

U.S. DEPARTMENT OF LABOR (1989), *The Effects of Immigration on the US Economy and Labor Market*, Washington, D.C.

U.S. DEPARTMENT OF LABOR (1996), *Characteristics and Labor Market Behavior of the Legalized Population, Five Years Following Legalization,* Washington, D.C.

VAILLANT, E. (1997), "La régularisation au Portugal : le point de vue des immigrés", paper presented at the Meeting of the Working Party on Migration, June, OECD, Paris.

CHAPTER 4

The Regularisation of Temporary Migrant Agricultural Workers in Mexico

by

Manuel Angel Castillo

(Professor, Researcher, Center of Demographic and Urban Development Studies,
El Colegio de Mexico)

1. NATURE OF THE MIGRANT FLOW

Mexico's southern border forms a frontier with Guatemala and Belize. As on other frontiers, towns, villages or merely small crossing points witness great flows of goods and people. But more intense areas of migration do exist and some are used mainly for labour reasons.

Several types of migration flows take place over this border. Most analysts, however, agree that the major flows consist of temporary migrant workers, border residents, local temporary visitors and transmigrants – both authorised and unauthorised. Of particular importance is the case of the Guatemalan refugees, acknowledged or not by local authorities, who settled in this region in the last decade. But the determining factors of migration vary in each case, though they are not necessarily exclusive. Flows also frequently overlap (Castillo, forthcoming).

This paper focuses on the flow of seasonal migrant workers who move mainly from Guatemala's border region to the area in Mexico known as the Soconusco – an agricultural area whose most important produce is coffee, a crop destined mainly for exportation. Because of its quality, coffee from Chiapas, the southernmost border state, is highly valued on the demanding US and European markets. Though on a minor scale, the region also produces sugar cane, which like coffee production requires a seasonal workforce, but in considerably lower numbers.

Coffee production units recruit mostly during harvest and employ very few workers during the rest of the agricultural cycle. Workers on coffee plantations therefore need other sources of income in order to survive. They usually own or have access to a small plot of land for basic production to satisfy essential needs, whether for total family consumption or partial sale in small local markets. A similar situation exists on sugar cane plantations, which also require larger numbers of workers during harvest. Other agricultural activities, banana and other fruit production, and cattle raising, have different workforce needs; their impact on labour migration is considerably less than that of coffee production.

Subsistence production on family-owned plots and temporary paid-migrant labour are complementary activities that give rise to a cycle of social reproduction, which has proven its ability to sustain generations of peasants. Activities in domestic units take place outside periods of labour demand by export plantations. Wages obtained from seasonal work are an important source of cash income, increasingly necessary in market economies. Peasants require manufactured products, instead of handicrafts no longer available in domestic units, which can only be purchased with hard cash.

2.   THE HISTORICAL CONTEXT

Coffee production in Chiapas began at the end of the century. Mostly German, American, British, and Mexican entrepreneurs settled in the region to produce the grain (Martínez Velasco, 1994; García de León, 1981). At that time, producers started to bring Guatemalan workers into the region, where they became part of and contributed to the region's population (Fábregas *et al.*, 1985). During the first half of the century, however, most of the seasonal workforce required by coffee plantations was made up of peasants coming from the northern part of the state of Los Altos.

There has never been a full investigation of the conditions and reasons for the progressive disappearance of native (national, though not regional) workers from the coffee working population. There is of course the common idea that in border regions foreign workers now replacing natives are subject to worse labour conditions and higher levels of exploitation. Different historical factors have also modified the living and working conditions of former migrants in their places of origin.

It seems clear, however, that important changes occurred in the Los Altos region, which altered the readiness of peasants to travel each year to work on coffee plantations in the Soconusco in Chiapas. Colonisation programmes, grants of productive land, migration to growing urban areas, and frequent displacements to emerging and closer economic poles (such as, tourist complexes, oil producing areas and hydroelectric projects) offered new opportunities to Chiapas' peasants, which enabled them to leave behind temporary migration as a survival strategy.

From the 1950s onward, the inflow of Guatemalan migrants for work in the coffee harvest began to increase. The undocumented and unregistered nature of historical migration means that it is impossible to record and review its performance precisely. Observers agree that by the end of the 1970s, Guatemalan migrants outnumbered nationals.

A significant aspect of this traditional migration is how Mexico viewed the border region. For a long time, southern Mexico was an underprivileged area, overlooked by government programmes and not well thought of in public opinion. Levels of social isolation and abandonment by official programmes, as denounced at the start of the Chiapas conflict in 1994, are evident in the deeply rooted inequalities and marginalization of its population.

The lack of federal institutions was a handicap in attempts to control or regulate border social phenomena such as migration flows. Population mobility across the border was relatively low and perhaps, as reports and chronicles indicate, the major stream was that of seasonal workers during the coffee harvest. But the local population largely assessed these movements as "natural" and inherent to regional life. Guatemalan peasants were not really considered foreigners, but recognised regional workers, essential for production and general economic needs in Chiapas, and more specifically in the Soconusco.

Social sensitivity at a national level towards the presence of foreigners did not emerge with the arrival of refugees in the early 1980s. Concern and more hostile attitudes have come out more recently in the face of the increasing presence of transmigrants, and especially of undocumented migrants. They are not only Guatemalan nationals, but citizens of other Central American countries and even from other regions of the world, who attempt to cross the border, traverse Mexican territory and ultimately reach and cross the Mexican-US border.

3. IRREGULAR EMPLOYMENT AND THE ISSUE OF VOLUME

Such border relationships have given rise to elaborate freedom of movement in the region. But the presence of foreigners – mostly Guatemalans – seems to be closely related to traditional cross-border links, which facilitated their admittance and acceptance in a variety of regional activities, and their intertwining with Mexican families and regional and local social networks.

The recruitment of Guatemalan peasants as temporary workers on coffee plantations was favoured by this generally positive – or at least neutral – view of Guatemalan citizens, not only by Chiapas' employers but also by regional society in general. But this familiarity with foreigners also meant that official regulations were practically non-existent. Migrant workers crossed the border without any control from Mexican authorities. Employers benefited from this situation as the demands of productive activities were easily fulfilled by an expanding and unregulated cross-border labour market.

The increasing proportion of foreign workers in agricultural activities did not attract the attention of Mexican authorities until the mid-1980s. By the middle of the decade, the border region was receiving a notable inflow of Guatemalan refugees who settled in Mexican territory after fleeing armed conflict in their country. Both the public and private sectors in Mexico suddenly attached greater importance to the geo-economic and geopolitical profile of the southern border.

Another contributing factor was the increasingly significant immigrant flow of undocumented transmigrants attempting to cross Mexico and illegally enter the US. The question of population mobility in the southern border area became an emerging issue on the national and foreign affairs agenda.

Many questions arose regarding the nature, background, and current profile of migrant labour flows. It was evident that very little was known about this regional social process, which in part could be explained by the little attention it received until then.

A whole series of figures for migration flows were produced, mostly with little or no evidence. Analyses of volumes offered by different actors and institutions were heavily influenced by ongoing debates about regional and national conflicts. A review of the different estimates for migration seems to indicate that they are notoriously lacking in rigour (Castillo, forthcoming). The numbers ranged from 18 000 to 150 000, but the majority did not explain the basis of their estimates, and only those offering very low figures indeed contained some references to extremely limited official records.

One serious effort to obtain a well-founded estimate, developed by Professor Mosquera Aguilar (1990), nevertheless deserves recognition. He made an estimate based on a series of assumptions including, among other factors, the extension of cultivated surface, productivity levels, the average length of stay, and the proportion of foreign workers in the workforce, and proposed a total of 75 000 temporary immigrant workers. One of the limits of such an estimate is the difficulty including other influential factors, such as, differentials in productivity, the proportion of family members (women and children), and the multiple counting of labourers working in more than one unit.

Progress in calculating the number of migrants is possible only by improving the documentation process, which would boost confidence in official statistics. It does, however, seem reasonable at present to assume that the total flow of temporary migrants is not greater than 100 000, including family members (women and children).

4.   SOCIO-DEMOGRAPHIC CHARACTERISTICS OF MIGRANT WORKERS

The limited knowledge of agricultural workers' immigration trends obviously extends to the description of its main features, other than volume. The first known systematic attempt to define the socio-demographic characteristics of temporary migrants was a survey conducted in 1986 by *El Colegio de Mexico* with the sponsorship of the *Consejo Nacional de Ciencia y Tecnología* (CONACYT) of Mexico. The main aspects of the inflows and characteristics of migrants were analysed and discussed in several articles (Castillo and Casillas, 1988; Castillo, 1990 and 1992).

Other attempts followed. None, however, were general enough to portray a complete picture of the migratory process. Their lack of statistical coverage, mainly due to technical obstacles, prevented them from creating a random representation of migrant workers' universe. Any assessment, therefore, refers only to those groups considered in specific samples taken in each case. That certain features recur, however, constitutes a sufficient basis upon which to generalise with only minor probabilities of error.

The first salient feature of migrant populations is male dominance. Recent partial official records, however, suggest some changes in sex composition. In the survey in question, for instance, only two women interviewed claimed to be individually employed workers. In 1997, unpublished data gathered as part of a joint research project conducted by *El Colegio de la Frontera Sur, El Colegio de Mexico* and *El Instituto Nacional de Migracion* (INM) and based on partial official records showed that of a sample of seasonal workers 9.5% were females. In another sample of the flow between November 1997 and December 1998, the INM recorded a rise in the number of females to 11.8% of the total (INM, 1999). Partial results such as these nevertheless suggest a trend, observed in other migration flows, that women are taking a greater part in migration flows, even in temporary and agricultural labour displacements in which conditions are very unattractive.

All sources and monitoring confirm the overwhelming presence of adolescents and young adults in the temporary migrant population. Most migrants are between 15 and 39 years of age. Recent data show a breakdown of 24.97% aged 15-19, 32.75% aged 20-29 and 16.31% aged 30-39 which, when combined, account for almost three-quarters of the total (INM, 1999). The high participation levels of economically active persons between 15 and 39 matches the profile of workers in arduous productive activities, especially coffee harvesting.

The Guatemalan migrant population is mostly rural and agricultural, characterised by high levels of illiteracy. In tandem with the cyclical nature of seasonal migration, the majority have access to very small plots of land (individually or family owned, leased or borrowed) mainly dedicated to subsistence production. Most travel alone or in groups of male relatives or community members. In many cases, however, the male head of family is formally employed while other family members partake in labour activities suitable to their age and capabilities. Women and children usually participate in complementary activities to contribute to family income.

5. FROM A NON-POLICY SITUATION TO AN EXPLICIT REGULATION OF MIGRANT WORKERS

Large-scale unauthorised border crossings and seasonal employment in Chiapas, though tolerated for years, eventually became problematic for the Mexican government. Both sides began to view the documentation process as bureaucratic and unprofitable. The Guatemalan government and public opinion started to periodically denounce occasional and not-so-occasional labour conflicts. The irregular status of migrant workers and muddled labour arrangements with employers, among other things, hampered the resolution of conflicts.

By the mid-1980s, when the refugee issue was included in political considerations of the southern border, Mexican migration authorities shifted their attention to temporary migration. Initial attempts to regularise the situation sought to enhance the control and supervision of migrant workers in production units in the region. But major employer resistance coupled by social constraints revealed the difficulties of enforcement.

Migration authorities soon understood that the best way to achieve their objectives was to sway both employers and workers. Direct negotiations with producer organisations were a success and, in light of rapid changes in regional patterns of immigration, demonstrated the advantages of regularising the status of workers. One decisive argument was that regular and more clearly defined periods of stay and working conditions for cyclical migrants would raise confidence in both employers and workers.

Steps were taken to implement more efficient mechanisms, thereby avoiding difficulties in the documentation process. Employers met the costs of issuing documents and the requisite paperwork, and financed the investment of important infrastructure. Temporary dwellings were built at recruitment points to shelter workers until they reached an agreement with employers or contractors.

For a long time, authorisations issued by migration authorities consisted of collective permits granted to employers in a very *ad hoc* manner. Only two years ago did the Mexican government decide to change the procedure and issue individual permits. These personal documents offer more of a guarantee against potential human rights abuses and enable the migrant to travel throughout Mexican territory more confident that human rights will be respected.

6. ACHIEVEMENTS AND LIMITATIONS OF CURRENT MIGRATION POLICY

The Mexican government has recently taken positive steps to regularise and provide better conditions for Guatemalan migrant temporary agricultural workers entering and working in the southern border region. New procedures require employers to obtain migration authority permission to allow migrants to enter and work in Mexican territory in a specific unit and authorised activity. Recruiters, hired by employers as intermediaries, participate in the process and are required to have explicit and formal authorisation from their employers.

Although current statistics are partial since the new procedures do not cover the entire population of migrants, more and more figures show that the documentation process is fulfilling its objectives. Major efforts have been made to extend policy implementation and operation to all migrant crossing points, thereby ensuring their documentation.

Another area in need of major improvement is the status of family members. Women and children, and other relatives accompanying migrant workers should also be appropriately documented in accordance with their condition and nature. The Mexican government's recent ratification of the UN International Convention on the Rights of Migrant Workers and Their Families helps fulfil a series of responsibilities and duties and obliges authorities and society to comply with them. Just how far Mexico respects these obligations and duties should be the focus of extensive reviews.

The scope of migration authorities is limited by the capacities and obligations formally outlined in current legislation. A specific topic for review in this area is legislation on the authorisation and documentation of temporary agricultural workers. Current law pertains to non-immigrant (visitor) workers in Mexican territory who have a more urban profile, employed in traditional industrial and service activities. A specific and practical category could be considered by parliamentarians in the near future that would change the law, such as those adopted as a result of the enforcement of the NAFTA agreement.

The scope of migrant worker labour rights goes beyond the responsibilities of migration authorities, forming an area that is perhaps ill defined and complex. Periodic tensions with the Guatemalan government arise as a result of conflicts between employers and employees, largely due to the non-fulfilment of obligations and commitments by employers. The Mexican government should pay close attention to this relatively neglected area, which falls within the scope of labour authorities at all levels. Federal labour authorities have a major responsibility in this region given the nature of international flows of migrant workers across the border.

To pass appropriate legislation and formulate adequate policies, governments must clearly be knowledgeable of their countries' social phenomena. Shaping social sensitivity and public opinion requires the objective recognition of the nature of migration trends and their contribution to regional development. Advances in record keeping and policy making stem from research results, which have proven to be of higher quality and more reliable when based on agreements between scholars and public agencies. Promoting joint research can therefore engender a better understanding of the reality of the border region.

The existence of cross-border links and migrations, such as the temporary movement of workers, is evidence of positively accepted regional labour markets that may benefit people in the countries involved (Ordóñez Morales, 1990, 1993). But for this process to reach favourable levels, governments must offer clear terms within the law for every actor involved in labour and migration processes, especially workers, who need policies and actions for their protection. A stronger policy of dialogue between governments of neighbouring countries is another requirement for creating trust and understanding.

It is clearly possible to develop and establish favourable conditions for the movement and labour insertion of immigrant workers through regularisation processes. Countries should not bow to persistent pressures to combat the irregular employment of immigrants; and persecution must never replace humanitarian treatment and negotiation. Lobbying with employers and demonstrating the advantages of regularisation to employees form the best response to the demands of increasing cross-border markets in a world of growing economic integration and globalisation.

BIBLIOGRAPHY

CASTILLO, M.Á. (1990), "Población y migración internacional en la frontera sur de México: evolución y cambios", *Revista Mexicana de Sociología*, México: Instituto de Investigaciones Sociales-UNAM, Vol. 52, No. 1 (January-March), pp. 169-184.

CASTILLO, M.Á (1992), "Migraciones laborales en la frontera sur: ¿Un fenómeno en proceso de cambio?", in H. Muñoz (ed.) *Población y sociedad en México*, Las ciencias sociales, Coordinación de Humanidades, UNAM-Grupo Editorial Miguel Angel Porrúa, June, Mexico City, pp. 173-192.

CASTILLO, M.Á (forthcoming), "Tipos y volúmenes de la inmigración en la frontera sur de México", draft prepared for the *Estudio Binacional México-Estados Unidos sobre Migración*.

CASTILLO, M.Á and CASILLAS, R. (1988), "Características básicas de la migración guatemalteca al Soconusco chiapaneco", *Estudios Urbanos y Regionales (9)*, CEDDU-El Colegio de México. Vol. 3, No. 3 (September-December), pp. 537-562.

FÁBREGAS, A. *et al.* (1985), *La formación histórica de la frontera sur*, Mexico City, Cuadernos de la Casa Chata No. 124. Serie: Frontera Sur, Centro de Investigaciones y Estudios Superiores en Antropología Social (CIESAS) del Sureste/Programa Cultural de las Fronteras, Mexico.

GARCÍA DE LEÓN, A. (1981), *Resistencia y utopía, Memorial de agravios y crónica de revueltas y profecías acaecidas en la Provincia de Chiapas durante los últimos quinientos años de su historia*, 2 Vols., Ediciones ERA, Mexico City, Mexico.

INSTITUTO NACIONAL DE MIGRACIÓN (1991), *Estadística migratoria sobre visitantes agrícolas guatemaltecos*, Coordinación de Planeación e Investigación, Instituto Nacional de Migración, Subsecretaría de Población y Servicios Migratorios, Secretaría de Gobernación, Mexico City.

MARTÍNEZ VELASCO, G. (1994), *Plantaciones, trabajo guatemalteco y política migratoria en la Frontera Sur de México*, 1st. ed., Gobierno del Estado de Chiapas, Instituto Chiapaneco de Cultura, Ocozocuautla de Espinosa, Chiapas, Mexico City, Mexico.

MOSQUERA AGUILAR, A. (1990), *Los trabajadores guatemaltecos en México. Consideraciones sobre la corriente migratoria de trabajadores guatemaltecos estacionales a Chiapas,* México, 1st ed., Editorial Tiempos Modernos, Guatemala.

ORDÓÑEZ MORALES, C.E. (1990), "Migraciones de trabajadores guatemaltecos y crecimiento económico en el Soconusco, Chiapas", *International Migration*, Vol. 28, No. 2, pp. 229-239.

ORDÓÑEZ MORALES, C.E. (1993), *Eslabones de frontera. Un análisis sobre aspectos del desarrollo agrícola y migración de fuerza de trabajo en regiones fronterizas de Chiapas y Guatemala*, 1st ed., Universidas Autónoma de Chiapas, Tuxtla Gutiérrez, Chiapas, Mexico.

SOLÍS CÁMARA, J.C.F. (1998), *México: Una política migratoria con sentido humanitario*, 1st ed., Instituto Nacional de Migración, Secretaría de Gobernación, Mexico City, Mexico.

PART II
Analysis and Evaluation of Measures Undertaken to Combat the Employment of Illegal Foreign Workers

CHAPTER 5

Review and Evaluation of the Measures Implemented in OECD Member Countries

Analysis of the Responses from Certain Member Countries
to the Questionnaire Prepared by the OECD Secretariat
by
Sophie Robin and Lucile Barros
(Consultants to the OECD)

1. INTRODUCTION

In June 1996 a questionnaire dealing with foreigners' access to employment, sanctions against their illegal employment and enforcement results was submitted to the OECD Working Party on Migration. It was then sent out to Member countries to obtain material for comparative analysis (Table 1). This paper focuses on preventive measures and sanctions relating to the illegal employment of foreigners. It is based on the replies obtained and therefore only selected legislative frameworks are considered. Moreover, the particularities of the regulatory approaches and attitudes to the employment of foreigners has also resulted in replies being somewhat disparate, and our analysis reflects that. Finally, despite the wealth of information supplied, the difficulties of fully presenting and explaining the legal, political and economic systems within which illegal employment is being tackled led us to adopt the simplest and clearest approach possible. Accordingly, we first analyse the ways in which efforts to curb the illegal employment of foreigners (types of sanctions, administrative organisation, preventive measures) are structured, and then highlight the practical difficulties encountered and the developments in the methods being employed.

Table 1. **Measures to curb and sanction the illegal employment of foreigners in selected OECD countries**

Recapitulative table presenting the measures undertaken at the national level to combat the employment of foreigners in irregular situation

Country	Applicable sanctions				Responsible authorities	Preventive measures (in addition to border controls)	International co-operation
	direct employer	indirect employer	employees	those abetting illegal immigration or employment			
Australia	maximum fine of AUD 10 000 (but only applicable for a person who is aiding and abetting a person to commit a crime against the Commonwealth of Australia)	as with direct employer	removal to the border, bar on re-entry	as with employers	the Department of Immigration and Multicultural Affairs, police, customs and security forces	information campaigns aimed at employers; a review of current measures is under way	there may be approaches to relevant authorities in other countries in particular cases
Austria	fine, withdrawal of trading licence, ineligibility for public contracts, managing contractor liable, back-payment of taxes and social security contributions	managing contractor may also be held responsible	expulsion, bar on re-entry for a given period	information not available	labour inspectorate, police assistance for inspection operators	information not available	co-operation within the framework of the European Union
Belgium	fine and imprisonment, closure of the company, confiscation of equipment, suspension of activity, regulatory fine, payment of living expenses and the cost of repatriating the illegal worker	information not available	order to leave the territory in the case of irregular residence status	same sanctions as those on employer	labour inspectorate (employment and labour ministry); structured and institutionalised co-operation between inspectorates which are more or less in charge of the combat against illegal employment (common controls between labour inspectorates and security forces)	press campaigns aimed at employers; distribution of brochures	co-operation within the framework of the European Union
Finland	fine or imprisonment fulfillment of civil responsibility	as with direct employer if the direct employer is foreign	fine	fine or imprisonment in case of assisting the entry and stay of illegal immigrants	immigration department, police, border control officers, employment services, co-operation between authorities	information disseminated to employers and workers	co-operation within the framework of the European Union
France	fine and/or imprisonment, disbarment from activity, ineligibility for public contracts, confiscation of equipment, closure of premises, publication of the judgement, regulatory fine (special contribution), fulfillment of civil responsibility	criminal sanctions, jointly liable for costs and fines imposed on direct employer	minor criminal and regulatory sanctions, removal to the border in the case of irregular residence status	fine and imprisonment in case of assisting the entry and the stay of illegal immigrants, disbarment from activity, bar on re-entry, ineligibility for public contracts for companies	labour inspectorate police, gendarmerie,customs officers, co-operation between authorities	information disseminated to workers and employers, partnership agreements concluded between central government and employers' organisations, financial incentives to encourage the employment of documented workers	co-operation within the framework of the European Union, special bilateral co-operation with the UK and Germany
Germany	regulatory and criminal fine, imprisonment in the more serious cases, ineligibility for public contracts, payment of the cost of repatriating the illegal worker, payment of taxes and social security contributions	high regulatory fines	regulatory fine	fine or imprisonment in the case of illicit brokerage of labour, in the case of assisting illegal entry or stay under certain conditions; regulatory fine in the case of assisting illegal employment	illegal entry or stay: border control police, local authorities concerning foreigners; police illegal employment: federal labour office, customs officers, both with the support of tax, social security, health and safety authorities as well as the local authorities responsible for foreigners and moonlighting; co-operation between authorities co-ordinated by the federal labour office	information campaigns, financial incentives to encourage the employment of documented workers	co-operation within the framework of European Union, bilateral co-operation especially with France, UK, Netherlands, Portugal; sometimes (on a regional basis or limited to certain subjects) limited cooperation with certain countries of Central and Eastern Europe and Turkey on work contracts

Table 1. **Measures to curb and sanction the illegal employment of foreigners in selected OECD countries** (continued)
Recapitulative table presenting the measures undertaken at the national level to combat the employment of foreigners in irregular situation

Country	Applicable sanctions				Responsible authorities	Preventive measures (in addition to border controls)	International co-operation
	direct employer	indirect employer	employees	those abetting illegal immigration or employment			
Greece	fine (regulatory and criminal) and imprisonment	fine and imprisonment	fine and imprisonment, payment of departure tax	fine and imprisonment in case of assisting the entry and the stay of illegal immigrants, confiscation of means of transport, payment of living expenses and the cost of repatriating the illegal worker	labour inspectorate, police, customs services, co-operation between authorities	press campaigns	co-operation within the framework of the European Union
Japan	fine and/or imprisonment	fine and/or imprisonment	removal to the border, fine and/or imprisonment	fine and or imprisonment	regional immigration offices, police, co-operation between authorities	information campaigns aimed at employers and workers	bilateral co-operation with neighbouring states
Netherlands	fine and/or imprisonment, disbarment from carrying on business, closure of the company, fulfillment of civil responsibility	managing contractor may also be held responsible	removal to the border in case of irregular residence status	fine or imprisonment	police, ministry of justice, labour inspectorate, co-operation between authorities	information campaigns aimed at employers and foreign workers, financial incentives to encourage the employment of documented workers	co-operation within the framework of the European Union, bilateral agreement with China
Norway	fine (criminal or regulatory) or imprisonment	fine or imprisonment	removal to the border, fine and/or imprisonment	as with employers	immigration services (immigration, justice and police departments)	information pamphlets for workers	no measures implemented
Portugal	regulatory fines, ineligibility for public contracts, disbarment from accessing Community funds	information not available	disbarment from working, removal to the border in the case of irregular residence status, regulatory fines	imprisonment in the case of abetting illegal immigration	labour inspectorate and immigration services	information not available	co-operation within the framework of European Union, readmission agreements with France, Spain, Bulgaria, Poland and Romania, agreements with Brazil, Cape-Verde, Guinea-Bissau and Spain
Spain	regulatory fine, expulsion if foreign civil responsibility in certain cases	possible fine (reluctant jurisprudence)	fine or expulsion, possibly with bar of re-entry	regulatory fine	labour and social security inspectorate, security forces	information disseminated to workers	co-operation within the framework of the European Union, re-admission agreements with Morocco and Portugal
Switzerland	criminal sanctions (fine and imprisonment), regulatory sanctions (refusal of work permits for foreign employees)	information not available	fine or expulsion, possibly with bar of re-entry	fine and imprisonment	cantonal labour offices., regional labour inspectorates, cantonal police for foreigners, federal office for foreigners, police, customs authorities ; co-operation between authorities (tax and social authorities), but limited due to data protection	ad hoc police controls, roadside checks, social partners controls	bilateral cooperation (exceptional)
Turkey	no sanction	no sanction	expulsion, fine	fine and imprisonment, specific sanction for illicit brokerage of labour	police, action possible by the labour inspectorate and the employment authorities	no preventive measures	no measures implemented
United Kingdom	fines since January 1997	information not available	removal to the home country, fine or imprisonment	sanction in the case of assisting the entry and the stay of illegal immigrants	police and immigration services, co-operation between authorities	information sent to employers concerning the new legislation	co-operation within the framework of the European Union, special bilateral co-operation with France
United States	regulatory fine, criminal sanctions in the more serious cases fulfilment of civil responsibility	considered as direct employer (same sanction therefore)	removal to the border	increased enforcement targeting the smuggling of aliens	department of immigration and naturalizations, labour and employment department, local police officers, co-operation between authorities	information campaigns aimed at employers required employment eligibility verification	bilateral co-operation with Mexico

2. FRAMEWORK FOR CURBING THE ILLEGAL EMPLOYMENT OF FOREIGNERS

The approach is two-pronged: to curb illegal immigration, and to curb non-compliance with labour law. These two facets shape the regulatory framework, the sanctions imposed and the role of enforcement bodies. They are present together in most legal systems, offering a variety of approaches to illegal employment.

Categories of sanctions

Sanctions on persons working without due authorisation

Forced departure

Foreigners who work without due authorisation face sanctions in most OECD countries. This policy to curb illegal employment, which is in fact focused largely on illegal immigration, includes forced departure measures applicable to foreigners who breach immigration rules because they lack authorisation to work or reside in the country. The regulatory framework in a few countries provides for further sanctions, in many cases criminal sanctions, including imprisonment or fines for persons in illegal employment.

Australia is one country whose legislation provides for forced departure. Foreigners who work in Australia when their visa does not allow this, or overstay their visa, may have their visas cancelled; they will then be illegal immigrants and may be detained and forced to leave. They may also be barred from re-entering Australia for a period of up to three years. In all cases, obtaining a subsequent visa first requires repayment of detention and expulsion costs.

Regulations in Norway similarly provide that any person who breaches immigration law, including foreigners who illegally take employment, may be forced to leave, expelled or barred. In Japan a foreign worker who does not comply with the procedure for obtaining a work permit may also be expelled. The same applies in the United States. Foreigners working without permits in Turkey are again liable to expulsion. In Austria, the immigration legislation provides for the expulsion of illegal foreign workers found to be residing illegally in the country or whose residence has become illegal as a result of their illegal employment. In the event of repeated detection as an illegally employed foreigner, the person may be banned from entering the country for up to five years.

In the United Kingdom, forced departure is the most common sanction for foreigners in illegal employment; this measure involves escorting the foreigner to his country of origin. Dutch and Spanish regulations do not include any sanction for illegal workers, but foreigners without residence permits may be forced to leave. In France, foreigners without residence permits face up to one year in prison and fines of up to FRF 25 000. These penalties may be combined with bans from the country for up to three years, in which case the persons concerned are automatically escorted to the frontier. In Germany also, foreigners without a residence permit face up to one year in prison or a fine; besides these penalties, foreigners who illegally entered the country have to leave or else face expulsion. Should a foreigner who has been expelled enter the country illegally once more he may be fined or sentenced to up to three years in prison.

Penalties for foreigners working without due authorisation

Prominent among those countries which impose penalties on illegal workers is the United Kingdom. Under the 1971 Immigration Act, it is an offence to knowingly fail to comply with any condition of residence, such as a ban on employment. The offence carries a fine of up to GBP 5 000 or imprisonment for up to six months. In Switzerland, workers in an irregular situation are subject to a fine or forced departure, which may be combined with a ban on re-entry. In Portugal, the worker is sanctioned by an administrative fine which can be accompanied by a ban on working and, in the case of irregular residence status, forced departure.

Other countries take similar approaches. In Finland, foreigners working without a permit are liable to fines. In Norway any person who breaches immigration law is liable to a fine and/or up to six months in prison. In Japan a foreign worker who fails to comply with the work permit procedure faces criminal sanctions (fine of up to JPY 300 000 and/or imprisonment for up to three years). Greece provides for fines and imprisonment for any foreigner working without a permit, and illegal residents are required to pay on leaving an administrative charge proportionate to the length of unauthorised residence. Foreigners who work without a permit in Turkey are liable to fines.

France considers the employer to be the leading party in illegal employment, but illegal foreign workers face administrative fines or penalties, and criminal sanctions when fraud has been committed to secure a work permit. In Germany, a foreigner working without a permit is liable to an administrative fine of up to DEM 10 000.

Sanctions for employers of illegal foreign labour

The principle of penalties for employers is found in most of the regulatory systems considered. Sometimes designed as a necessary counterpart to penalties for workers, those for employers reflect the concern to place liability on those who allow or promote illegal employment, thereby taking advantage of the insecure circumstances of foreign workers. The gains from illegal employment, the exploitation of foreign workers and the resulting competitive distortions warrant penalties for employers.

Penalties for the direct employer

In the Netherlands the employer alone is liable for illegal employment, facing criminal sanctions of up to six months in prison and/or a fine of NLG 25 000 under the Employment of Foreigners Act. Sentencing guidelines recommend a fine of NLG 2 000 per illegal worker, in the case of a first offence. For subsequent offences, and when terms and conditions of work are poor and tax and/or social charges have not been paid, the judge is recommended to order a month's imprisonment and closure of the firm. Since 1994 an employer is also liable to criminal sanctions under the Penal Code for employing a foreign worker who is illegally resident in the Netherlands. The penalties here are imprisonment for up to a year and a fine of up to NLG 100 000. In addition, habitually employing illegal workers or making illegal employment a source of income is punishable by up to three years in prison and a fine of up to NLG 100 000. Committing any of these offences in the course of one's occupation may further mean disbarment from that occupation. In Austria, the law on the employment of foreigners is based on the principal that only the employer of the illegal worker may be punished. If convicted, the employer and/or the personnel responsible for hiring the illegal worker must pay a fine. This fine varies according to the number of foreigners illegally employed and whether the person had previously been convicted. Other sanctions which may be imposed against employers include withdrawal of their trading license (in the case of repeated offences), the refusal of further permits for foreign workers, exclusion from public contracts and the payment of surcharges for unpaid taxes and social security contributions as well as unpaid wages to the foreign worker (this latter in the form of a compensatory payment).

In Spain employing foreigners without work permits is a very serious offence, and the firm faces an administrative fine of between ESP 500 000 and ESP 15 000 000, for each illegal worker. In France the penalties for illegal employment bear largely on the employer, either a physical person or, since 1993, a corporate body. Any person who hires or retains someone who lacks due authorisation to work faces a penalty of up to three years' imprisonment and/or a fine of FRF 30 000, for each illegal foreign worker. The penalties are doubled for subsequent offences. Further penalties are also available: disbarment from carrying on business, ineligibility for public procurement, confiscation of items involved in the offence, publication of the ruling, and the closure of premises or businesses where the offence took place. In addition to criminal sanctions, administrative penalties apply to the employment of foreigners without work permits, in the form of a special penalty in respect of each illegal employee, independent of any criminal proceedings or penalties. The fixed penalty, of around FRF 19 000 in 1999, is doubled for subsequent offences.

In Belgium any person who employs a foreigner without permission to do so is liable to eight days to a year's imprisonment and a fine of between BEF 170 000 and BEF 600 000 for each worker. When the worker's authorisation to stay in Belgium is of less than three months, the penalties increase (a month to a year's imprisonment and/or a fine of between BEF 600 000 and BEF 3 000 000). The court may also order closure of part or all of the business, permanently or temporarily. Items involved in the offence or which served to commit it may be confiscated. Via further proceedings in the commercial courts, an employer convicted of employing foreign workers without a residence permit may be obliged to cease one or more of his activities. Substantial administrative fines may also be imposed on employers, when criminal proceedings are not taken. The employer is moreover obliged to pay the cost of detaining and repatriating any worker who is illegally resident. In Portugal, the direct employer is liable to administrative fines, exclusion form public contracts and denial of access to public funds.

German regulations on illegal employment of foreigners include sanctions for foreign workers without work permits, but the focus is on employers. They first face a regulatory fine of up to DM 500 000, which may be increased if need be to cancel out the gains from illegal employment. An employer who supplies false information on wages or conditions of employment in order to secure a work permit is also liable to a regulatory fine of up to DEM 50 000. Employment of foreigners without work permits may also give rise to criminal sanctions (fine or up to a year in prison), when over 5 foreign workers are involved, when they are employed for a period of 30 days or more, or when the offence is deliberate and repeated. In particularly serious cases, imprisonment of up to three years may be ordered. In order to prevent the exploitation of unauthorised workers, employers may also be fined and imprisoned for up to three years when the terms of employment differ substantially from those for German workers. In serious cases, imprisonment of between six months and five years may be ordered, to protect the labour market in the public interest. Whether the offence is serious or not, the employer is further bound to pay the cost of returning the foreigner to his home country. Employers may be ineligible to bid for public procurement contracts if sentenced to more than three months' imprisonment or a fine of DEM 5 000 or more. Social charges and taxes relating to illegal employment must also be paid.

In Finland an employer or his representative who recruits or retains a foreign worker without a work permit is liable to a fine or up to one year's imprisonment under the Aliens Act. Fines can be imposed on people who supply the authorities with false information about wages, terms of employment and the functions performed by foreign workers. If the offence is repeated, the employment services can refuse a work permit to an employer who has supplied false information, even prior to a court ruling. In Norway anybody who employs a foreigner without a work permit or procures employment for him, deliberately or through gross negligence, is liable to a fine or up to two years in prison. The authority concerned may decide on an administrative sanction (fine or confiscation) rather than bring proceedings in court.

Greece imposes prison terms or fines (GRD 30 000) on anybody employing a foreigner without a work permit. The employer must pay an administrative fine within 15 days of the offence being reported, at the order of the labour inspectorate or the local police, depending on which authority determines the offence. In Switzerland, the direct employer of a foreigner in an irregular situation is liable to both administrative and criminal sanctions. Should he repeatedly or seriously breach the laws relating to foreigners, the cantonal employment office may partially or totally reject his applications for foreigners' work permits. If the employer negligently or intentionally hires foreigners in an irregular situation he is liable to a fine ranging from between CHF 3 000 to CHF 5 000. Repeat offenders are liable to up to six months in prison.

In Japan a person employing a foreign worker who has not complied with the procedures for obtaining a work permit may incur a criminal sanction (a fine of up to JPY 2 000 000 and/or up to three years' imprisonment). A fine may also be imposed on the firm where the illegal employment occurred. The United States has since 1986 imposed penalties on people who knowingly employ an ineligible foreigner. For each worker hired, whether native or foreign-born, the employer has to complete an employment eligibility verification form setting out the worker's identity and eligibility for employment, under penalty of an administrative fine or, in more serious cases, criminal proceedings. Penalties also apply to employers who require workers to provide financial safeguards against fines or proceedings. Intentional use or attempted use of forged papers regarding a foreign worker's status is also an offence.

In the United Kingdom employers were until recently liable to prosecution only for assisting an illegal worker's entry or residence. Direct penalties were introduced in the Asylum and Immigration Act, which came into force on 27 January 1997, making it a criminal offence to employ any person subject to immigration controls who is not authorised to reside or work in the United Kingdom. Employers are liable to fines of up to GBP 5 000. Unlike in other regulatory systems, the penalty is less than that which can be imposed on workers.

Sanctions for indirect employment

In some countries indirect employment (i.e. via an intermediary) of a foreign worker without a work permit is a criminal offence. This means that the actual offender can be prosecuted, most notably in such cases as staff swapping or lending. French regulations are one example of this. Since 1997 French law provides that the final recipient of a service, the customer or main contractor, may be held liable for the financial consequences of illegal employment by suppliers or sub-contractors. He can thus be required to pay the payroll costs, including social charges and tax, left unpaid by the direct employer, under the rule of "financial solidarity" between co-contractors. The customer or main contractor may escape liability, however, if he can prove that he monitored the co-contractor's compliance with rules on the employment of foreigners.

In Austria, the sanctions which may be imposed on employers may be extended to apply to the managing contractor of a project, in so far as he can reasonably be expected to have knowledge of the legal status of his sub-contractors' employees. In the Netherlands the main contractor whose co-contractor employs people without work permits may be held liable in those sectors where illegal employment is common, such as the construction industry and the garment trade. In Germany the indirect employment, deliberate or through negligence, of foreigners without work permits can lead to substantial regulatory fines, which can be imposed on individuals or on corporate bodies or groups of individuals. In Finland a firm whose foreign sub-contractor employs foreigners without work permits faces the same penalties as an actual employer. In Japan and in Greece, the indirect employer is liable to a fine and/or a prison sentence. In the United States any person who knowingly makes use of an undocumented foreigner under a sub-contracting agreement is regarded as the employer and hence faces the same penalties.

Civil liability of employers

In some systems the criminal or administrative sanctions on an employer are combined with civil sanctions to protect the worker and to ensure that illegal employment does not generate improper benefit for the employer. In France an illegally employed foreigner is on the same footing as a properly hired worker with regard to the employer's obligations under labour regulations. For the period of illegal employment, for instance, he is entitled to payment of proper wages and related benefits, together with a month's wages for termination of employment. In order to assist civil sanctions against employers, employees' organisations can conduct proceedings arising out of the illegal employment of a foreigner, without having to show that the foreign worker authorised them to do so.

In the Netherlands labour regulations apply to illegally employed foreigners, and they can thus seek enforcement of their rights. In addition, since September 1995 an illegally employed worker is assumed to have been employed for six months, and can bring a civil action for payment of sums due for that period; the onus is on the employer to prove that employment was for a shorter period and/or that wages were actually paid. There is also an administrative sanction in that authorisation to hire may be withdrawn if the information on which it was based is not correct, which would seem to cover the employer's non-compliance with labour legislation.

In Finland the fact that employment is illegal is no bar to enforcement of regulations covering remuneration and other terms of employment. The same is true in the United States. Employment services ensure that illegal workers who have received insufficient wages are paid the balance, and not just the minimum wage, to which they are entitled, even when they have returned home. In Spain an employment contract is considered invalid if the employee has no work permit. Under labour regulations, however, the corresponding wages can in some cases be claimed, to ensure that an employer does not improperly benefit from the work performed by an illegal foreigner.

Sanctions for assisting illegal employment

In a number of countries proceedings can be taken not simply against the employer of an undocumented foreigner but, more broadly, against any person who assists or abets illegal employment. Until recently the United Kingdom imposed no special penalties on employers, but had a general offence of assisting or abetting entry or residence by an illegal worker. In Belgium any person who brings in a foreign worker without a proper work permit, for purposes of employment, faces the same penalties as an employer who, without authorisation, employs a worker without a residence permit. These penalties extend to any person who receives or seeks remuneration for bringing foreign workers into Belgium, for finding or procuring employment for them or for carrying out the formalities required to obtain permission to work, or for behaving as an intermediary in acts calculated to deceive the worker, the employer or the authorities. Such persons are bound, like the employer and possibility jointly with him, to pay for the upkeep and repatriation of any illegally resident worker.

In Turkey the rules are similar to those pertaining in the United Kingdom before the recent reforms. There is no specific penalty for employers: any person who assists the illegal employment of a foreigner is liable to one year in prison and heavy fines. People who bring in foreign workers are liable to imprisonment for up to three years and heavy fines. It is an offence to promise employment, a visa or a residence permit, punishable by two to five years' imprisonment and fines of up to twice the gains from the offence. Carriers who bring in illegal workers may have their licences cancelled. In Switzerland, those who intentionally place foreigners or who hire them in order to then rent their services to other companies without observing the regulations governing the employment of foreign labour are liable to a fine of up to CHF 100 000. In Australia, anybody who aids and abets the illegal immigration and employment of foreigners is liable, as are direct and indirect employers, to a maximum fine of AUD 10 000; this is however only in those cases where a crime against the Australian state has been committed.

In Spain, abetting or assisting the illegal employment of foreigners is a very serious offence, punishable by an administrative fine of between ESP 500 000 and ESP 15 000 000. In Norway, people who abet the employment of foreigners without work permits face the same penalties as the employers of such foreigners. Japan has penalties for people who assist illegal employment, keep foreigners under their control in order to have them work illegally, or act as professional middlemen. Here the police concentrate on offences related to illegal employment, such as prostitution, which involve organised gangs, middlemen and employers. Middlemen face up to three years in prison and fines of up to JPY 2 million. A middleman's actions abroad are also punishable in Japan. In the case of illegal provision or dispatching of workers, the penalties can be combined with sanctions under the Employment Security and Worker Dispatching Laws.

In Germany too it is an offence for firms without a recruitment licence to supply foreign workers without work permits, punishable by fines or imprisonment for up to three years. In more serious cases, prison terms of between six months and five years can be imposed. The illegal placement of foreign workers and unauthorised recruitment abroad are offences punishable by up to three years in prison or a fine. Again, in more serious cases the penalties are higher. In addition, the workers concerned will not subsequently be issued with work permits. Any person who assists the illegal employment of foreign workers may be subject to the same regulatory fines as the employer. Aiding or abetting foreigners' illegal entry or residence renders the person liable to up to five years in prison or a fine if it is done either repeatedly, for several foreigners or with the intention making a financial gain. In those cases where the offences are committed professionally by an organised gang, the prison sentence can range from one year to ten years.

Alongside those which prohibit assisting or abetting illegal employment, some systems prohibit assisting illegal entry and residence. In Finland, for instance, the Aliens Act prohibits abetting illegal entry. Any person who, to obtain financial benefit for themselves or others, brings or seeks to bring an undocumented foreigner into Finland, arranges or provides transport, or issues a forged document for entry, is liable to a fine or up two years' imprisonment. In Portugal, facilitating illegal immigration is sanctioned by a prison sentence.

In France penalties for "abetting illegal immigration" can be imposed on any person who assists the entry, movement or residence of undocumented foreigners. This includes middlemen who take money to supply employers with labour that they have illegally brought in. The penalties imposed are a maximum of five years' imprisonment and fines of up to FRF 200 000 for individuals and up to FRF 1 000 000 for corporate bodies. Additional penalties can also apply: disbarment from an occupation for up to five years, a ten-year ban on entry if the person convicted is a foreigner, or ineligibility for public procurement contracts in the case of corporate bodies. The Act of 11 May 1998, dealing with entry, residence and asylum, introduced an aggravating circumstance, for offences committed by organised gangs. The maximum penalties in such cases were raised to ten years in prison and fines of up to FRF 5 000 000.

Similarly, people who bring unauthorised foreigners into Greece, transport them within the country, assist their movements or provide them with housing face prison terms and fines. The involvement of transport companies is an aggravating circumstance, and courts can order the confiscation of vehicles. People convicted of these offences are also required to pay the upkeep and repatriation costs of the foreigners involved. In Switzerland, any person who facilitates the entry, exit or illegal residence of a foreigner (for example, by providing he or she with work or with accommodation) is liable to up to six months in prison and a maximum fine of up to CHF 10 000.

Administrative framework for curbing illegal employment

Most countries assign a central role to the police and the immigration service. Agencies enforcing labour and employment regulations may, in certain states, struggle to have the more prominent role. In many cases a number of departments are involved in curbing illegal employment, and the separate powers that they hold encourage joint action which appears more effective.

Police and immigration service only

The police and the immigration service are the sole agencies concerned in some countries. This is so in Norway where the immigration service, involving the police, the immigration department and the Justice Ministry, checks foreigners' work permits. Similarly, in the United Kingdom the police and the immigration service enforce asylum and immigration regulations. Since employers have become liable, the police and the immigration authorities have been considering joint actions against offending employers. In Turkey the police (General Directorate of Security in the Interior Ministry) investigate illegal employment and start legal proceedings. In addition, the police services must be notified within 15 days of a foreigner being hired; failure to do so is punishable by withdrawal of the work permit, fines and expulsion. When the labour inspectorate, which monitors compliance with regulations on working conditions, finds evidence of illegal employment, this must be reported to the Interior Ministry. In such cases, when the foreigners concerned are eligible for work permits the employment authorities (the Public Employment Institution) set the permit issuance procedure in motion.

In Australia the Department of Immigration and Multicultural Affairs enforces the immigration law. It operates via inspection services in all the States and territories. The police, customs and protection services also have powers to enforce immigration rules. In Japan the regional immigration offices have immigration control officers who are responsible for forced departure procedures. For investigations authorised by a magistrate, they can make inspections, investigations and seizures. They may place a foreigner in detention, prior to his forced departure, with a written order from the supervising immigration inspector. The police may also arrest undocumented foreign workers and middlemen, and conduct investigations.

Police and immigration services together with labour and employment services

In some OECD countries power does not lie solely with the police and the immigration service. Employment and labour services also play a role – either complementary, identical or predominant – in curbing the employment of undocumented foreigners. In the United States the Immigration and Naturalisation Service in the Department of Justice (INS) has inspectors who visit firms to check compliance with immigration rules. The inspectors can impose penalties, in particular fines, for non-compliance. Some jurisdictions have recently empowered local police officers to assist the federal authorities in immigration matters. Only a very small number of officers are involved, however. The Employment Standards Administration (ESA) in the Department of Labor monitors compliance with rules on wages and working hours, and at the same time inspects registers of papers authorising the employment of foreigners. ESA inspectors have no powers to impose penalties.

In the Netherlands the police and the labour inspectorate are responsible for curbing illegal employment. They have powers to inspect (requesting information, obtaining documents and information regarding a business, checking identity papers, entering premises except private residences) and to conduct investigations (seizing items, inspecting documents, entering premises apart from private residences, stopping vehicles, etc.). The law on the employment of foreigners requires people to co-operate with the police and the labour inspectorate. The latter intervenes on its own initiative, at the request of other services, the police in particular, or following complaints. But its powers are insufficient in some cases, because it cannot pursue people who run away from identity checks or enter private homes. In Portugal, the Employment Inspectorate and the Immigration Services are principally responsible for combating illegal employment.

In Finland the immigration department, the police, passport officers at entry points and the employment authorities have responsibility for monitoring the employment of foreigners, in other words enforcing the Aliens Act, and in particular monitoring compliance with the rules on the employment of foreigners in Finland. The employment authorities can enter places of work to check that foreign employees have work permits. In addition, the labour protection district offices in Finland monitor the application of social regulations to foreigners, under the Act on the Supervision of Labour Protection and Appeal in Labour Protection Matters. In Switzerland, a number of agencies are involved, notably the Cantonal Employment Offices, the Regional

Inspectorates, the Cantonal Police for Foreigners, the Federal Office for foreigners, the police services and customs. Co-operation between these agencies remains limited, however, due to data protection legislation.

In Spain, the labour and social security inspectorate is the agency with the powers to enforce the legislation on the employment of foreigners. It has administrative sections in every province and has the support of employment inspectors. It can conduct checks in firms, summon employers to the labour inspectorate or require them to produce documents or reports to clarify employment matters. It draws up reports on offences, which go to the appropriate body for settlement or proceedings. Since 1994 the "State security forces" have acted in support of the labour and social security inspectorate in immigration-related matters and in actions against the illegal employment of foreigners. The administrative structure is similar in Austria. Under the leadership of the Central Labour Inspectorate, nine specialised groups have been set up in the federal states. These groups are charged with the task of investigating the illegal employment of foreigners. They carry out inspections in factories, on construction sites and other outside workplaces, for example on farms. The police have a duty to assist the officers of the Labour Inspectorate if requested. Such assistance may be necessary when their is an accumulation of offences (both employment and residence are illegal) and also when the site to be inspected is too large to be properly covered by the small number of personnel at the disposal of the Labour Inspectorate.

In Belgium, curbing the illegal employment of foreigners is the responsibility of the social legislation inspectorate. These inspectors have substantial powers. They investigate illegal employment and make reports on the basis of which criminal proceedings may be launched. At the same time, the Employment and Labour Ministry has powers to impose administrative fines on employers who hire foreigners without authorisation. Likewise, in France the labour inspectorate is the main agency enforcing the work permit procedure. It has powers to enter places of work and inspect the work permits of employees and the relevant information held in the staff register. When an offence has been committed, inspectors draw up reports which are the starting point for criminal proceedings against employers. French police, gendarmerie and customs officers are empowered to check that foreigners are employed legally. Police operations are backed by a central directorate in the Interior Ministry, dealing with immigration and illegal employment.

In Germany, the local labour offices and the customs authorities are the main agencies responsible for combating the illegal employment of foreigners. As the federal labour office grants work permits for foreigners, the customs authorities are bound to their legal opinion in matters of principle. Both authorities have the right to enter premises without specific suspicions in order to examine that foreign workers are in possession of a valid work permit and that they are not employed under working conditions poorer than for comparable German employees. All the information they consider necessary has to be given to them. The local labour offices only have the power to impose administrative fines for illegal employment; in those cases where criminal offences have been committed the file is transmitted to the Public Prosecutor.

Co-operation among services

In most countries where a number of departments share responsibility for curbing illegal foreign employment, the services co-operate, formally or less formally and in various ways. The Netherlands has particularly extensive co-operation among services. Concerted action by police and labour inspectors is needed for inspectors to enter certain places and overcome some restrictions on their powers. The aim of co-operation here is greater efficiency, as shown by a drive in 1995 to ensure compliance with rules on the employment of foreigners, co-ordinated by the Public Prosecutions Department of the Ministry of Justice: before it started, as well as establishing judicial policy guidelines, efforts were made to clarify which services should be involved, the powers available to them and how these powers should be used. In 1996, the labour inspectorate reached agreement with the tax and social security agencies on exchanging information, to enable information to be passed on without prior permission from the Public Prosecutions Department. Meetings are regularly held between the Ministry of Justice, the Ministry of Social Affairs and Employment and the employment authorities on matters concerning the implementation of the law on the employment of foreigners. Public prosecutors preside over regional committees bringing together labour inspectors, immigration services and law officers concerned with proceedings.

Co-operation among the various agencies responsible for curbing the illegal employment of foreigners is also a major concern in France. The labour inspectorate, the police and the gendarmerie are combining their efforts. The police do not have the same powers as labour inspectors to enter workplaces and check work permits. At the local level, co-ordination rests with departmental boards to curb illegal employment (CODELTIs), with the Prefect as chairman and the area Chief Prosecutor as vice-chairman. The boards bring together the relevant government services and agencies, consular chambers (*chambres consulaires*) and the other social partners. They consider the situation in the area and set guidelines for action. An operational committee for curbing illegal employment (COLTI) is set up from among its members, chaired by the Chief Prosecutor. It is made up of local officers in the services concerned, and their respective powers and duties can thus be pooled. Consultations take place and information can be exchanged to prepare the ground for joint action. At national level, co-ordination rests with an interministerial delegation for curbing illegal employment (DILTI); it assists the control services, provides training for their staff and gives impetus to co-ordinated action.

In Finland the employment authorities work closely with the police in identifying cases of illegal employment. When the employment authorities find that foreigners lack work permits, they request the police to make enquiries as necessary. They also report to the labour protection and tax departments, when action on their part would be appropriate. The Interior and Labour Ministries work together in framing legislation and supervising operations and decisions by the employment authorities and the police. But there is no special body co-ordinating government action at national or regional level. By contrast, in Belgium a collaboration agreement was signed in July 1993 between the responsible Federal and regional ministers. This agreement helps the relevant inspectorates involved in combating illegal employment to increase the effectiveness of their inspections and promotes cohesion and co-ordination between the responsible agencies.

In Japan, national or international information campaigns and joint operations between the national police force and the Justice and Labour Ministries covering various aspects of illegal employment are co-ordinated in the Illegal Employment Prevention Council. There is also a Liaison Conference for Ministries Concerning Foreign Employment Issues. It runs yearly campaigns on illegal employment issues. Exchanges of information among government services have been stepped up to curb the forging of documents and visa overstaying, and to secure the information needed to take steps against undocumented foreign workers. Efforts are also being made to combat the forging of papers through simplifying the exchange of information between border control services and those responsible for issuing visas in embassies and consulates abroad.

In the United States, INS and ESA signed an agreement in 1992 to share information and co-ordinate inspections and sanction procedures, but it has not been brought fully into effect. Both services have close relations in high immigration areas such as New York and Southern California. In Australia the immigration, tax and employment services regularly compare their records on undocumented foreigners, to identify those who are working and those improperly receiving social benefits and services. The United Kingdom has local co-operation between the police and immigration services, often leading to joint operations. Nationally, there is co-operation between the Overseas Labour Service of the Department for Education and Employment and the Home Office on work permit arrangements and exemptions thereto.

Where necessary, the German federal labour office co-ordinates investigations and oversees inter-agency co-operation. In their proceedings, the local labour offices and the customs authorities are supported by the tax, social security, health and safety authorities as well as the local authorities responsible for foreigners and for combating illegal employment. Besides these authorities, whose powers and responsibilities are set out in the social law, other authorities, especially the police and the border control police also co-operate in combating the illegal employment of foreigners. The police often provide assistance when inspections are made of large unenclosed areas, for example construction sites.

Preventive measures

Preventive measures are relatively modest, when compared to the range of penalties in most countries' legislation. In most countries they are confined to information, sometimes targeted at the victims of illegal employment or those responsible for it. Some countries attach great importance to border controls, whereas others, taking a very different approach, offer financial incentives for legal employment.

Information campaigns

In the Netherlands information campaigns concerning employers' obligations under the law on the employment of foreigners have targeted organisations in a number of sectors. Agreements have been reached with the sectors concerned on the issue of work permits and training for new employees. This policy covers inland shipping, the garment trade, market gardening and Chinese restaurants. Information brochures dealing with labour regulations in the Netherlands are also passed out to employers and foreign workers. In Greece, press campaigns have been undertaken.

Preventive action in Finland has largely consisted of informing employers about procedures and rules to be observed, as well as informing foreign workers about their rights and obligations. The Norwegian immigration authorities produce information brochures on immigration rules and the conditions for obtaining work permits, which are sent out to organisations involved in international exchange programmes and to Norwegian embassies and consulates. Articles on illegal employment in the national press are also regarded as preventive steps. In December 1996 employers in the United Kingdom were fully informed about the provisions of the new Asylum and Immigration Act.

Australia runs an employer awareness campaign to encourage them not to employ undocumented foreigners. A community campaign for the general public stresses the importance of voluntary compliance with the Immigration Act. A revision of preventative measures is currently underway. The United States runs information drives, chiefly for employers. After the bill introducing sanctions for employers was passed, a detailed paper set out the new obligations of employers. Moreover, employers are obliged to verify the work permits of their foreign workers.

In Spain the provisions on the status of foreigners which took effect in 1996 were widely publicised. More generally, the provincial directorates for labour and social security and the corresponding information bureaux are responsible for informing and advising foreign workers about their rights and obligations. In Belgium, the Ministry for Employment has since 1994 undertaken a number of press campaigns in order to inform employers, their personnel managers and their agents of the penalties they face should they be found to be employing undocumented foreign workers.

In Japan the police liase with employers to prevent illegal employment. The government also runs an annual information campaign. In that connection the regional immigration offices provide detailed information, through the media and by distributing leaflets, to make the general public aware of the adverse effects of illegal employment. The Ministry of Labour holds information sessions for employers, and distributes leaflets and documents. The Immigration Office periodically issues statistics on illegal employment to foster greater understanding among the general public. Interviews in the press in sending countries help to provide information there. Japanese missions abroad also provide information on immigration rules in Japan. In France preventing the illegal employment of foreigners is one of the concerns of the departmental boards to curb illegal employment (CODELTIs) which bring together the relevant government services and agencies, consular chambers and the social partners. Partnership agreements are also concluded between central government and representatives of the sectors where illegal employment is most prevalent, one aim being to prevent the use of undocumented foreign labour.

Border controls

In the United States, border enforcement is the most important of the strategies used to curb illegal migration and illegal employment. Similarly, Japanese policy to curb illegal employment is focused on restricting the entry and settlement of foreigners likely to take up illegal employment. There are intensive controls on persons entering and leaving the country for this purpose, at ports and airports.

Financial incentives to employ documented workers

In the Netherlands, a law containing provisions exempting employers from social charges for temporary jobs of less than six weeks took effect in March 1997. The purpose was to encourage the employment of documented workers for seasonal jobs. In France the possibility for private employers to obtain tax rebates and reductions in social charges for certain domestic jobs (gardening, child care, household help, etc.) promotes the employment of documented persons, as does the simplified payment of wages and employer's social security contributions via the *chèque emploi-services* (employment-services chequebook). In Germany, under certain conditions households have the possibility to obtain tax rebates for certain domestic jobs. The German employment-services chequebook system only simplifies the payment of employer's social security contributions, however.

Those receiving unemployment benefit may obtain financial incentives (DEM 25 net per day) from the labour offices should they accept seasonal jobs of a maximum three months duration, for example in agriculture. This incentive is exempt from social security contributions and taxes and therefore encourages the employment of documented workers.

3. THE LIMITATIONS AND THE DEVELOPMENT OF MEASURES TO CURB THE EMPLOYMENT OF UNDOCUMENTED FOREIGNERS

Governments encounter many difficulties in implementing measures to curb the employment of undocumented foreigners, due to under-staffing and scrupulously framed regulations and to a lack of information and data. Paradoxically, the need to respect the fundamental rights of undocumented foreign workers or other persons under investigation may restrict the scope of action to curb illegal employment. These difficulties, coupled with the development of new and more sophisticated forms of illegal employment, have shaped changes in methods to curb the employment of undocumented foreigners. Some OECD countries have strengthened existing measures, or have introduced fresh ones, and have incorporated their operations against illegal foreign workers in the broader framework of curbing illegal employment. Other countries are seeking to develop forms of international co-operation to curb the employment of undocumented foreigners.

Difficulties encountered in implementing measures to curb the employment of undocumented foreigners

Several OECD countries referred to the difficulties which their enforcement services face in conducting operations in the field. In Austria, staff shortages in the inspection services compel them to select sites for investigations. They are unable to inspect all the firms under suspicion, to make systematic and comprehensive inspections, and to visit the more remote locations regularly. As a corollary of selection, the inspections which are carried out generally yield results. In France the main difficulties encountered concern the pooling of the powers and procedures assigned to individual enforcement services. Police officers report that their powers of investigation are in some cases unsuited to inspection procedures under labour law.

In the Netherlands the powers of labour inspectors are not always adequate, which has led to co-operation among the various agencies involved. In addition, legislation protecting personal privacy and the home substantially restricts the powers of labour inspectors, given that garment workshops, for instance, are often in people's houses. The free movement of persons promoted by the Schengen Agreements further complicates controls on foreign workers. For instance, lack of controls at internal borders makes it impossible to check that a Polish worker has taken up a job in the Netherlands while he has legal employment in Germany under the quota system. The United Kingdom reports that, once detained, undocumented workers apply for asylum, thereby suspending expulsion while the application is processed. Inspection services in the United States report the proliferation of forged papers and refer to the need to check that a permit has been renewed on expiry, and discriminatory practices by employers when they themselves conduct these checks.

In a number of OECD countries the enforcement services lack information to conduct operations. The lack of information is inherent in the employment of undocumented foreigners, which by definition is concealed. The Finnish authorities consider that the lack of data on the employment of undocumented foreigners demonstrates that illegal employment of this kind is not a major problem. Only a few such cases have been reported. Norway also lacks data on the employment of undocumented foreigners.

Some control services also lack data to assess the effectiveness of inspection and reporting procedures. In Germany, for instance, there are no data on illegal employment by sector or by the nationality of the employees. However, the federal labour office considers that the information derived from practical experience allows them to identify the key areas of illegal activities, the current trends and the nationalities of the persons most involved. In Switzerland, up to date data on the dissuasive effects of sanctions are not available, nor are they indeed on the severity of the criminal penalties imposed. On the basis of limited surveys, it would appear that the powers of inspection have not been sufficiently used and that the penalties imposed by the courts have been quite light and therefore, in all likelihood, of little dissuasive effect.

Countries including France, the Netherlands, Japan, Spain, the United Kingdom and the United States do record the number of offences reported, by sector and nationality, and the levels of fines imposed. France has established two special computer programmes for enforcement data, one national and the other departmental (TADEES system, COLTI application). While they do not gauge the full extent of illegal work and employment, they provide a set of indicators describing the wide range of offences, the characteristics of the employers and workers concerned, and the sectors where it is most frequently detected.

Stricter enforcement

A number of countries are tackling the persistent employment of undocumented foreigners and the development of new forms of trafficking in manpower. Japan, the Netherlands and the United Kingdom report organised networks which bring in, house and place foreigners in illegal employment, as well as middlemen specialising in the placement of undocumented foreigners. As a result, most Member countries have decided to step up enforcement against illegal employment of foreigners, and to introduce penalties for traffickers and middlemen.

In Austria, discussions on how illegal employment might be more effectively combated have focussed notably on the necessity of implementing more efficient control measures in order to curb organised illegal employment. In Belgium, the Act of 13 April 1995 contains provisions which, during proceedings for offences under social legislation, allow penalties for trafficking in human beings to be imposed as well. Particular targets are clandestine workshops producing garments where foreign workers are confined. In Switzerland, in order to respond to the specific difficulties linked to the employment of foreigners in an irregular situation, new measures are to be adopted in the context of the revision to the Federal Law on the residence and settlement of foreigners. Most notably, the existing sanctions are likely to be increased, a minimum sentence for employers and traffickers is to be introduced and the responsibility is to be extended from direct employers to *de facto* employers, service providers and principals.

In France it is now an offence to compel a person, by abusing his vulnerability or dependence, to work or live in conditions that are incompatible with human dignity. At the same time, curbs on the employment of undocumented foreigners have recently been extended. Penalties have been stiffened considerably, corporate bodies can now be charged, and the scope for charging middlemen involved in labour trafficking has been widened. The numbers of officers engaged in curbing the employment of undocumented foreigners has been increased, and their enforcement powers extended. Since 1997, for instance, police officers have been empowered to enter a firm's premises to check that the business conducted there and the employment of workers complies with provisions on concealed employment and the employment of undocumented foreigners. Customs officers also now have such powers.

In recent years the German Parliament has increased penalties against employers. Regulatory fines on direct or indirect employers have been raised and now apply to corporate bodies or associations as well. Fines on offending foreign workers themselves have been increased tenfold. In accordance with the intentions of the *Bundesrat* (chamber representing the *Lander*) to increase the efforts made to combat all forms of illegal employment, further increases in regulatory fines are under discussion. In Japan the May 1997 amendments to the Immigration Control Act included a new offence of arranging for collective stowaways. Provisions in the 1997 Asylum and Immigration Act in the United Kingdom made it an offence to employ a foreigner without a residence and/or work permit.

In March 1999 the United States Immigration and Naturalisation Service (INS) announced changes in its approach to curbing the employment of undocumented foreigners. It had found that the system in force since 1995 for inspecting and monitoring firms and penalising employers was not yielding the expected results. The INS consequently decided to devote greater attention to networks trafficking in foreign labour and to the forging of papers, as well as expelling foreigners who have committed offences. It thus hoped to dismantle the recruiting and trafficking networks which assist the entry and employment of illegal workers, rather than sanction employers who may have negligently hired undocumented foreigners.

Incorporating curbs on the employment of undocumented foreigners into the broader fight against illegal employment

In a number of countries curbs on the employment of undocumented foreigners are becoming part of a broader policy covering all forms of illegal employment. This includes both illegal lending or seconding of staff and concealment to avoid paying social charges and taxes. It is becoming clear that employing undocumented foreigners is only one of the ways in which firms can obtain cheap, flexible labour. When local workers or foreigners with permits will accept employment on the same terms as undocumented foreigners, employers have no need to risk hiring the latter. When jobs are scarce, local workers or foreigners with permits are more willing to accept poor conditions. To combat the damaging effects of illegal employment – exploitation, tax and social insurance fraud, distorted competition – operations have to be extended to cases which do not involve foreign workers.

This approach has been taken in Germany, where curbs on illegal employment extend to unlawful lending of staff, social insurance fraud and undeclared work. In Belgium the main problem is to see that employees are properly reported, and it is now compulsory to report hiring immediately. Unlawful employment of foreign workers is only one form of illegal work. A comprehensive approach is also taken in France, as the ongoing extension of regulations covering illegal or concealed employment demonstrates. The regulations make any form of concealment an offence, whether or not it involves undocumented foreigners. In Austria, concern to reduce the budgetary cost of illegal employment has taken the debate beyond the issue of undocumented foreigners to focus on measures designed to ensure that tax and social charges are paid on all employment. To this end, a draft law currently under consideration defines illegal employment not simply as employment of undocumented foreigners but also as non-payment of tax or social security charges, and conducting business without due authorisation.

International co-operation to curb the employment of undocumented foreigners

International co-operation with regard to the employment of undocumented foreigners is by no means extensive at present. Norway sees no immediate need for it, as illegal employment is very marginal there. It would, however, be ready to participate in international co-operative efforts if these were put in place. Australia has no form of international co-operation on these matters. Turkey would be ready to co-operate with other countries in exchanging data on foreign employment, but has not yet established co-operation.

Other countries have become aware of the need for co-operation, and are seeking to establish it in various ways, mostly via bilateral agreements. There are a number of reasons for governments to co-operate in curbing the employment of undocumented foreigners. The many offences related to such employment, including assisting illegal immigration and residence, forging papers and trafficking in labour, take advantage of the limitations on government powers, differences in regulations from one country to another, lack of co-ordination between government services, and difficulties in monitoring international operations, particularly cross-border services. Co-operation among Member countries would enable such offences to be tackled more effectively. In addition, lack of co-ordinated policy to curb employment of undocumented foreigners may result in distorted competition among firms in different countries.

Last, in any regional system allowing free movement for goods, capital and services, and freedom of movement for individuals and freedom of establishment for firms, one country's policy on curbing the employment of undocumented foreigners may have repercussions on employment in the other countries in the system. This could well be the case, for instance, for the European Union countries; in recent years they have decided to consult on this matter and to draw up joint resolutions and recommendations.

The first EU Council Recommendation on harmonising means of combating illegal immigration and illegal employment and improving the relevant means of control, approved in December 1995, places emphasis on the need to check that a foreigner is qualified for residence and employment on entering the country, when he applies for benefits, or when he is hired. The Council further encourages Member countries to introduce penalties against persons employing unauthorised foreigners, to establish a register of foreign nationals, and to secure the residence documents issued to foreign nationals against forgery and fraudulent use.

The Council Recommendation of September 1996 sets out common principles for residence and employment authorisations, penalties for employing persons without authorisation, co-ordination and collaboration between enforcement agencies, and exchange of information. A resolution was adopted in April 1999 to establish a code of conduct designed to promote co-operation among authorities in Member States to curb benefit fraud, avoidance of social security charges, and undeclared work with regard to cross-border secondment of workers. The European Commission has advocated co-ordinated operations across the European Union to combat undeclared work.

A number of OECD Member countries have entered into bilateral agreements relating to the employment of undocumented foreigners. Some are preventive, such as Germany's agreements with various Central and Eastern European countries. They compel CEEC firms carrying out projects or providing services in Germany with their own employees to observe the minimum general conditions set in collective wage agreements. Germany has special bilateral co-operative relationships with France, the United Kingdom, the Netherlands and Portugal, sometimes on a regional basis or limited to certain subjects. In conformity with the aforementioned code of conduct, the German government intends to conclude bilateral agreements with the other EU member states. In order to facilitate international co-operation, the German law on social data protection has been changed and allows the exchange of this information to corresponding foreign control agencies.

The Dutch employment service has concluded a special agreement with the Chinese Ministry for Social Affairs on the regular temporary employment of Chinese catering staff. This measure may help prevent illegal employment of foreigners in catering. Japan has procedures for bilateral consultation with neighbouring countries, and hopes to extend co-operation of this kind. For a number of years the Immigration Office has arranged joint seminars dealing with immigration controls and checking of entry, residence and employment papers.

Spain seeks co-operation with neighbouring countries on both prevention and enforcement. Like many Member countries, it has concluded agreements on the re-admission of undocumented foreigners, with Morocco on 1992 and with Portugal in 1993. In addition to this agreement with Spain, Portugal has also concluded numerous other re-admission agreements, most notably with France, Bulgaria, Poland, and Romania, as well as with Brazil, Cape Verde and Guinea Bissau. France and Germany decided in 1995 to pool their experience regarding illegal cross-border employment and to examine ways and means of enhancing co-operation between their respective services. The United Kingdom and France have exchanged liaison officers dealing with illegal employment. The arrangement enhances the exchange of information and also assists joint operations, in particular against networks of immigrant smugglers.

The United States focuses its bilateral co-operation with Mexico on curbing illegal immigration and strengthening border controls. The United States does not have any bilateral employment programmes. For more than three decades, it has practised a non-discriminatory migration policy which opposes single nationality legislation. Nonetheless, Mexican workers can and do participate in all United States agricultural worker programmes. In fact, they predominate in them.

4.   Conclusion

This analysis of preventive and enforcement measures in OECD countries highlights both the country's shared concern to curb the employment of undocumented foreigners and the disparities in the regulations currently in force. The policy directions share a number of common features: the strengthening of enforcement measures and penalties, greater co-ordination among services, and in some cases awareness of the need to work more broadly against all forms of illegal employment. Although these policy directions indicate that Member countries are aware of the challenges posed by illegal employment, paradoxically the steps to tackle it have tended to neglect measures which could make them more effective, such as preventive measures and enhanced international co-operation.

CHAPTER 6

Preventing and Combating the Employment of Foreigners in an Irregular Situation in the United States

by

John Fraser

(US Department of Labor)

1. DIMENSIONS

The United States estimates its resident illegal population at about 5.5 million, with an average annual increase of about 275 000. Nearly 60% entered the US illegally – officially, "without inspection" - while just over 40% initially entered legally but then illegally overstayed their authorised period of stay as tourists, business visitors or for temporary residency. Available data indicates that the resident illegal population is economically active in roughly the same proportion as the rest of the US population. About two-thirds of the illegal population is economically active.

This resident illegal population includes only those who have resided in the US for at least one year, excluding the seasonal flow of illegal migrants – principally from Mexico and Central America – who enter for employment purposes, mainly in agriculture, or to work enough to achieve target earnings. Estimates of the size of this temporary, seasonal, population vary considerably, especially at different times of the year. A reasonable estimate would be about 1 million, though it is probably somewhat higher during peak seasons; given the nature of this type of migration, workforce participation is quite high.

The US has a civilian workforce of about 140 million, with more than 133 million employed. Illegal foreign workers total about 4.5 million, representing approximately 3.5% of the employed workforce.

Illegal workers are active in all parts of the US economy. But immigrants, both legal and illegal, are concentrated mostly in low-skill, low-wage sectors, such as agricultural production, garment manufacturing, food processing (fruit and vegetable packing), meatpacking, poultry processing, food service (restaurants), hotels/motels, landscaping and increasingly in the construction industry. For example, the US Department of Labour estimates that illegal foreign workers account for approximately 40% of the 1.6 million hand-harvest agricultural workers.[1]

2. US STRATEGY

The United States clearly recognises that employment is the primary impetus for illegal immigration. In addition to border controls, the US employs two basic strategies to prevent and combat illegal employment: generous legal immigration for employment purposes and worksite enforcement.

Generous legal employment-based immigration

In recent years, the US has annually admitted an average of more than 850 000 legal permanent immigrants for four principal purposes: family reunification, employment, refugee resettlement and diversity. Employment-based immigration accounts for 11 to 14% of total legal, permanent immigration, including both workers and their immediate family members. Each year, 140 000 employment-based immigrant visas are available for workers and their families in five "preference" categories:
- Individuals of extraordinary ability, outstanding professors and researchers, and multinational executives and managers.
- Members of professions holding advanced degrees or persons of exceptional ability.
- Skilled workers (and no more than 10 000 unskilled workers).
- Religious workers.
- Investors ("employment creation").

Between 1992 and 1997 (the last year for which data are available), an average of about 113 000 employment-based permanent immigrant visas were issued annually (about 80% of available visas). A total of nearly 700 000 foreign workers (and their immediate family members) was admitted or had their status adjusted to that of "permanent residents"; 270 000 of these were sponsored workers.

Even more are legally admitted to the US each year for *temporary* employment. In fact, the large majority of those granted permanent resident status for employment purposes each year are simply having their temporary visa status adjusted; it is not as if they are being admitted from outside the US.

The US admits more than 22 million people each year on temporary visas (nearly 25 million in 1996), but the vast majority – some 90% – are tourists and professionals (though they account for a large portion of visa overstayers). Each year, between 750 000 and 1 million people are admitted to the US for temporary employment purposes in an eclectic mix of different visa categories. They include "professional" workers in "speciality occupations", unskilled workers for agricultural and other temporary jobs, entertainers and athletes, cultural exchange visitors, inter-company transferees, and treaty traders and investors.

---

1. Based on the National Agricultural Survey.

The generous US legal immigration system for both permanent and temporary admissions includes substantial provisions for employment-based migration. US employers thus gain access to and meet their employment needs in the international labour market, while foreign workers gain legal entry to the US labour market, thereby helping to limit illegal migration for employment purposes. The legal employment-based immigration flow, of course, is regulated and, to some (increasing) extent, gives preference to higher-skilled jobs and workers. It obviously does not prevent, but well may ameliorate, the scope of illegal migration for employment purposes, at least in some (higher-skill) sectors of the US economy. On the other hand, it is well recognised in the US that immigration flows – both legal and illegal – can serve to establish migration pathways and networks that maintain and even expand migration flows, despite regulation. Whether the generous US legal immigration system for employment (and other) purposes actually helps reduce illegal migration – as it should in theory – or promote it remains a subject of speculation.

Worksite enforcement

Effective control of borders and ports-of-entry is a principal strategy for preventing illegal immigration. Border control is supplemented in the US by a comprehensive three-pronged approach to addressing illegal employment at US workplaces: employer sanctions, labour standards and immigration law enforcement.

For more than a decade, since 1986, US immigration law has required employers to verify the employment eligibility – the legal status –of all workers they hire.[2] This new approach explicitly recognises that employment is the primary reason for illegal immigration to the US and was therefore intended to engage employers, whose jobs are the principal lure for illegal migrants, on the "front line" in preventing and combating illegal employment.

The law requires employers to follow certain procedures when verifying a person's eligibility to work legally in the US – mainly by examining documents that establish the identity and employment eligibility of their new hires. The law also subjects employers to sanctions (civil fines and, in the most egregious cases, criminal penalties) if they fail to follow these procedures, knowingly hire illegal workers, or discriminate in employment based on a worker's citizenship status or national origin. Enforcement staff from the Immigration and Naturalisation Service (INS) and the US Department of Labour inspects employer compliance with these requirements. The US Department of Justice enforces the law's anti-discrimination provisions. The Department of Labour alone has inspected nearly 375 000 employers on their compliance with employment eligibility verification obligations.

This new legal requirement of employers was very controversial and has been extensively monitored since its enactment. These monitoring studies – and the illegal population and employment data already cited - clearly indicate that employer sanctions have been ineffective in preventing the illegal employment of unauthorised workers, principally due to the widespread availability of low-cost, high-quality false or fraudulent documents. As a result, the INS has refined its employer sanctions compliance strategy to focus increasingly on manufacturers and purveyors of false/fraudulent documents, and to develop an alternative mechanism for some employers to

---

2. The law also protects workers against potential citizenship or national origin discrimination in the process.

verify workers' employment eligibility through access to an automated verification database. This pilot verification system has been operational, for limited use, for more than two years, but has revealed deficiencies that produce both "false positive" and "false negative" verification results.

The second prong of the US worksite enforcement strategy involves targeted enforcement of basic labour standards, such as, minimum wage, overtime and child labour requirements. This approach is based on the theory that – coupled with the relatively small risk of being sanctioned - US employers have strong economic incentives to risk sanctions by hiring illegal workers. Illegal workers are often hard working, docile and compliant (fearing exposure, apprehension and deportation) and are often willing to work long hours for less than legal minimum wages. Simply ensuring that workers are paid legal wages and afforded minimally decent working conditions certainly does not discourage illegal workers from coming to the US to take qualitatively better jobs. But effective labour standards enforcement – particularly targeted to low-skill, low-wage sectors of the economy - may change employers' willingness to risk sanctions and may reduce the economic incentive to employ illegal workers. The US Department of Labour has increasingly been focusing on employer compliance activities in low-wage sectors where both legal and illegal immigrant workers tend to be concentrated.

The US Department of Labour has, in some circumstances, co-ordinated its labour standards enforcement activity with INS worksite enforcement efforts or with other law enforcement agencies. Some critics, however, point out that the Department of Labour's activities and joint efforts may discourage vulnerable, exploited immigrant workers – both legal and illegal – from filing complaints against workplace abuses. Consequently, the Labour Department and INS have recently revised their joint worksite enforcement efforts to avoid giving immigrant workers (subject to workplace abuses) the impression that they are at risk of exposure to the INS when reporting abuses to the Labour Department.

The third prong of the US worksite enforcement strategy involves targeting workplaces that employ large numbers of low-skill, low-wage workers. In the recent past, immigration enforcement interventions – not including employer sanctions enforcement - primarily consisted of INS worksite raids intended to identify, apprehend and deport illegal workers. Employers whose businesses are raided by the INS are seldom sanctioned, but their business operations are often significantly disrupted as a result of the immediate and unexpected loss of large numbers of illegal workers.

This intervention method has provoked criticism as well. In some cases, employers have threatened their illegal workers with exposure to the INS – or actually informed the INS – in order to elude demands for improved wages or working conditions, or when efforts are underway to organise (unionise) the workforce. In other cases, employers have complained about the disruption to their business operations when they ostensibly did not or could not know that workers were illegal because of false documents.

These criticisms – and assessments of the effectiveness of this approach – have led the INS to carefully review its worksite enforcement approach and recently to announce a new worksite enforcement strategy. The new strategy will enhance the agency's enforcement focus on the manufacture and purveyance of false/fraudulent documents and the organised smuggling of illegal migrants specifically for US employment/employers. Another new tactic is to examine employers' employment eligibility verification documents against the verification database and to inform employers which workers are falsely documented, thereby requiring them to dismiss these workers or be subject to inspection and eventually sanctions.

3. CONCLUSION

The lure of employment in the United States is a powerful incentive for illegal migration. Low-cost, motivated, docile, compliant, unorganised, and disposable workers are highly desirable to some US employers, as are highly skilled or promising workers who do not have legal authorisation to work in the country. These two poles create a powerful attractive force that has so far defied attempts by law enforcement to bring illegal employment in the US under control.

Despite massive increased investment in these comprehensive law enforcement efforts, and continuing elaboration and adjustments in the law enforcement strategy and tools employed, the illegal population and employment in the US continues to increase, though hopefully at a lower rate than would otherwise occur. The effectiveness of our increased investment and evolving, improved strategies in turning around this unacceptable situation must continuously be evaluated.

CHAPTER 7

Measures Taken to Combat the Employment of Undocumented Foreign Workers in France
Their Place in the Campaign against Illegal Employment and their Results
by
Claude-Valentin Marie
(Chargé de mission, Responsable des Etudes et des Statistiques, Délégation interministérielle de Lutte contre le Travail illégal – DILTI –, Paris)

1. INTRODUCTION

In beginning this report, it should be noted that combating the illegal employment of foreigners in France is not a matter of autonomous, institutional management. It is part of a comprehensive legislative scheme aimed at all illegal employment practices, the victims of which may be employees who are French citizens, citizens of EU member states, or foreigners from third countries who have the requisite work permit. The term, "illegal employment", refers to this broader field of investigation (Box 1).

The present analysis adopts and builds on this specificity, which resituates the employment of "undocumented" foreigners relative to illegal forms of employment as a whole. It helps one better understand the changes in employer practices of the last decade.

2. FOREIGNERS IN THE JOB MARKET: A REALITY GOVERNED BY A WELL-DEVELOPED SYSTEM OF REGULATIONS

Since the mid-1970s, restrictions in France on job market access for foreigners who are nationals of third countries have constituted one of the major tools for immigration policy making. Following the lead of all Member States of the European Union, the rule is to reduce the number of new

---

Box 1. **Illegal employment: a multifaceted offence**

The generic term, "illegal employment", is used to designate not just a particular violation, but a panoply of unlawful practices, each with its own specific elements as defined in the Employment Code.

The most prevalent violation is clandestine employment (*travail dissimulé*). This occurs when a company executive fails to declare his company or its employees. In so doing, he harms the entire system, engages in unfair competition and deprives his employees of their social welfare benefits. The employee who is not declared by his employer cannot be charged with this offence, which is defined in Articles L.324-9 and L.324-10 of the Employment Code. As a victim of the concealment, the employee may not be held responsible or jointly responsible for the offence.

Clandestine employees may be French nationals or foreigners. If the employee is a foreigner and does not have a work permit, the employer compounds the offence of clandestine employment with a second offence for employing an undocumented foreigner, thereby violating another specific article of the Employment Code (Article L.341-6). Here again, it is not the foreign employee who is held accountable, but rather the employer, thereby exposing himself to two charges: one for clandestine employment and another for employing an undocumented foreigner.

For other offences within the purview of illegal employment, the employer may find himself hauled into criminal court: these include the unlawful lending of personnel (*le prêt illicite de main-d'œuvre*) or bartering in personnel (*le marchandage*).

Unlawful lending of personnel occurs when one company supplies workers, for a lease fee, to another company that treats them as though they were its own employees. In this case, both companies are implicated in the prohibited activity; one doing the illegal leasing of the worker, the other using him. The prohibition does not apply to temporary employment agencies, modelling agencies or other brokerage or personnel agencies governed by special regulations authorising their activities.

Bartering in personnel occurs when a worker is supplied in exchange for some form of profitable consideration that harms an employee on assignment or allows the circumvention of statutory provisions, regulations or collective bargaining agreements designed to benefit the worker.

Illegal employment also encompasses violations committed by employees. This occurs, for instance, when a person receiving unemployment benefits, by virtue of having been registered as actively seeking work, holds an off-the-books job at the same time. These persons expose themselves to penalties for defrauding the Unemployment Office. This violation is codified in Article L365-1 of the Employment Code. It is separate and distinct from the violation of clandestine employment.

entries accorded permanent work authorisation to an absolute minimum.[1] This rule emerges from two crucial policy imperatives: protecting the national job market and giving priority to employees who live in the country in question (nationals or foreigners with legal status). In the last fifteen years, EU governments have geared their legislation, together with controls, to achieving these two objectives.

A foreigner wishing to work in France thus faces two major constraints: obtaining a work permit prior to entry into the country and the possibility that the desired permit is precluded by actual job market conditions.[2] But regardless of the level of enforcement of existing law, work-related immigration has never been halted, and the illegal employment of foreigners has never been stamped out. This observation applies to France as well as to its EU partners.

This situation is reflected in the resolution of the European Union's Justice and Interior Ministers on "the restriction on entry of nationals of third countries for purposes of employment" (1994) and their corresponding recommendations. The same applies to the White Paper on "European Social Policy" (1996). All of these documents attest to the continuing impact of work-related immigration in all its manifestations (legal and illegal) and, most especially, to the ongoing interest in this phenomenon. In its document, the European Commission clearly voiced its willingness to offer "proposals concerning illegal employment including its links to illegal immigration". To that end, it envisaged encouraging "the sharing of experience among the Member States with a view to giving renewed impetus [to the fight against illegal employment] and the identification of possible solutions".

Concern over whether primary perpetrators of illegal employment are dealt with accordingly has not, however, deafened the ear of government to appeals from companies or dampened official willingness to promote, where needed, the renewal of legal forms authorising the temporary employment of foreigners. Various provisions have offered a response to this desire for flexibility in dealing with work-related immigration.[3] This means that while the two principles, protection of the job market and job priority for the available labour force, continue to be reaffirmed, their implementation is subject to a whole host of exceptions.

Public authorities in recent years have generally taken a dual track approach in developing their initiatives. On the one hand, they have strengthened legislative controls, expanded the authority of responsible agencies and stiffened penalties for violation. On the other hand, they have facilitated the recruitment of certain categories of foreign workers, particularly through more flexible application of regulations.

Prior authorisation and preclusion by actual conditions on the job market

Any foreigner[4] wishing to take salaried employment in France must secure prior approval from relevant authorities, who in turn are required to review the employment situation in the

---

1. The FRG and Denmark were the first to take this decision, in 1973. They were soon followed by France (circular of 5 July 1974) and Belgium (governmental decision of 1 August 1974).

2. These requirements are standard throughout all countries of Western Europe. This explains the close similarity of their laws.

3. By means of labour agreements with certain third countries (Belgium, Germany), restricting the access of new migrant workers (Italy, Luxembourg) or quotas (Spain and Italy).

4. Here the term, "foreigner", refers to persons from countries that are not members of the European Economic Area.

country. These are the basic principles to achieving job market protection. The principle of preclusion based on the situation of the job market is one of the most common in EU countries. It requires the issuing of each new work permit to depend on the job market situation in the industry, region or occupation sought by the applicant. This is considered the most satisfactory means of controlling temporary job migration and of guaranteeing a kind of hiring preference for nationals and foreigners who already have work permits. Consequently, relevant authorities must check that their files do not already contain the résumé of an out-of-work employee who is able to fill the job mentioned on the work permit application. The local labour department has five weeks to conduct its investigation.

If the application for work authorisation is denied, the grounds for denial must be stated, and the decision may be appealed within two months after notification. The employer who signed the employment contract is also notified of the denial, as well as of the penalties he will incur if he employs a worker whose application has been denied. France also has regulations governing the engagement of non-salaried personnel. Persons intending to start a business must first obtain an entrepreneur's identity card. The application, accompanied by an abstract from police records, is forwarded to the prefect of the department where such persons wish to set up business; a decision is made at the same time whether to issue the applicant a temporary residence permit.

Applications from independents are evaluated on the basis of occupational qualifications, financial solvency and moral character. Officials solicit input from the chambers of commerce, relevant trade unions, and sometimes from the mayor of the community in question.

Exceptions to the principles

The principle of advance authorisation is subject to numerous exceptions. The latitude shown may consist of either a preferential issuance or of an outright waiver. The grounds vary. Most often, the applicant's treatment is justified by the presence of family members, by the type of activity involved (its nature and/or duration), by the specificity of the law as it affects the applicant or by humanitarian considerations. To a greater degree than with work permits, real "pragmatism" enters the picture when taking into account job market conditions in light of each particular set of circumstances. Here again exceptions are justifiable based on the legal status of the applicant and especially on the kind of job involved. Strong preference goes to very high-skill, high paying jobs, for which a work permit is almost never denied and rarely precluded because of job market conditions. This point is illustrated by the circular of 16 July 1998 from the Population and Migration Department (*Direction de la population et des migrations (DPM)*)[5] which waived the job market preclusion principle for computer engineers earning an annual salary of at least FRF 180 000.

This flexibility is also confirmed by the Act of 11 May 1998,[6] which introduced two new categories of temporary residence permits that allow the holder to practice his profession: one for scientists (teachers and researchers) and the other for artists.

---

5. DPM Letter No. 42 of December 1998 clearly states that this circular was in response to complaints received from companies stating that they were having problems recruiting personnel.

6. Law dealing with foreigners' rights to visit or stay in France and the right of asylum.

3. EFFORTS TO COMBAT ILLEGAL EMPLOYMENT OF FOREIGNERS WITHOUT WORK PERMITS

Direct criminal sanctions against employers

In France, it is the employer who is held responsible as instigator or beneficiary of fraud. The employer alone is subject to prosecution for failing to obtain authorisation before employing a foreign employee. Any person who hires a foreigner or retains a foreign employee who does not have a work permit is guilty of an offence. He is liable to 3 years imprisonment and/or a fine not to exceed FRF 30 000 for each count of employing "undocumented" foreigners.[7] For repeated offences, penalties may be doubled. Concomitant penalties may be added, such as, posting the judgement on the doors of the offender's business, publishing notice of the offence in newspapers, confiscating tools, machinery, equipment, and vehicles used to commit the offence, together with articles produced by the "undocumented" foreign labour. The judge may also bar the offender from practising his trade or profession for up to five years and exclude him from tendering for public procurement contracts for a like period.

The offender must also make a special contribution to the Office of International Migrations (OMI) in an amount equal to 1 000 times the minimum time-based rate, which in 1999 was nearly FRF 19 000. This contribution is multiplied for each count of illegal hiring of foreigners.[8] In the case of repeat offences, the contribution increases to 2 000 times the minimum time-based fee. This penalty also applies if a foreign employee is kept on after withdrawal or non-renewal of the work permit. Penalties also apply when one fails to adhere to the restrictions (geographic and/or industry-specific) specified in the permit as issued. In all cases, the severity of the penalty increases for repeat offences.

Direct civil penalties against employers

Under French law, a finalised employment contract between an employer and a foreign employee who has no work permit is void, as it's illegal. The problem with the rule is that it makes the employee suffer all of the consequences of the contract's illegality. The Act of 17 October 1981 seeks to remedy this situation. It essentially states that the unauthorised foreigner is compliant as of the date of hire and thus accords him the status of a normal employee, entitled to benefits and responsible for performing the obligations provided for under the contract, the most important being his salary and his seniority rights.

If the employer breaches, the foreign employee is entitled to one month's salary as a lump-sum indemnity, unless the contract itself provides for something more. The employee is entitled to enforce his claim before the competent labour court (Article L.341-6-2). He may be represented in that proceeding by an institution (union or association). He may even claim damages in court

---

7. The term, "undocumented foreigners", as used in this report, refers to foreigners who carry on some kind of paid activity without the requisite administrative authorisation. This category exceeds that of foreigners who merely do not have authorisation to visit or stay in the country. While such persons obviously are not allowed to work, there are others who have the requisite authorisation to visit or stay, but not to work.

8. A circular from the Minister of Justice of 30 September 1983 invites the courts to notify OMI of the cases on their dockets that involve this area of the law so that OMI can appear as a civil party in the case.

for additional losses incurred, provided he furnishes the requisite evidence showing that the statutory relief alone was not insufficient.

France is therefore one place where (however rarely implemented) the possibility of civil sanctions does exist. Based on a theory of unjust enrichment, the employer is penalised, having to bear the consequences of an unenforceable contract from which he benefited. The underlying goal of legislation concerning the employment of foreigners is to dissuade employers from hiring those without work permits.

Liability of principals

Current legislation is not limited to only charging the employer who directly hires the unauthorised foreign employee. French law expressly authorises indicting a person who, in full knowledge of the unlawful activity, derives an indirect benefit from it. The concept of "employment through an intermediary", expressly introduced in Article L.341-6 of the Employment Code, attempts to address this kind of situation (Act of 10 July 1989). It permits action against the real principal, who benefits from services rendered under unlawful circumstances. This provision also authorises action against a person who uses workers provided by an employee lending operation. It is a veritable showcase of the difficulties involved in trying to control the activities of service companies operating from outside the country.

In an effort to offer a more forceful response to abuses committed through the systematic use of middlemen, the Act of 11 May 1997 on illegal employment extends the principle of joint and several liability to the employment of "undocumented" foreigners (Box 2). Originally applicable only to the offence of concealing employees, this provision makes all those connected liable, thereby sanctioning all perpetrators of the fraud.

Anyone (individuals excepted) who upon signing a contract does not receive confirmation that the other party to the contract is in compliance with the rules regarding employment of foreigners also becomes jointly and severally liable for payment of the special contribution to the OMI. The rule applies to any contract with a value of FRF 20 000 or more. Enforcement officials may increase these sanctions against those who orchestrate the wrongdoing. An employer who hires a foreigner without a work permit typically does not report the hiring to the social welfare authorities. By this omission, he immediately incurs two violations: employment of an "undocumented" foreigner and concealment of an employee. Prosecution of these two offences thus brings the aspect of joint and several liability into play twice against the principal, inasmuch as the detriment incurred and the claimants on these respective offences are different.

This example illustrates the benefits of an integrated approach that addresses the multifaceted nature of illegal employment. Because it encourages the consideration of several offences provided for under the Employment Code, this approach creates an incentive to track down all perpetrators of the fraud, and increases the chances of prosecution and penalty. The first few judgements that have used the joint and several liability remedy against principals appear to have had a positive effect on contracting agencies and on business people. Many are consequently more alert to the practices of sham intermediaries and ostensible independent contractors.[9]

---

9. In the event that "bogus independent workers" are used, only a court-ordered re-qualification with regard to work would allow the employer to be sanctioned for employing an "undocumented" foreigner and for non-compliance with employment regulations.

> ### Box 2. **Joint and several liability**
>
> The provision on joint and several liability is intended to impose financial consequences on the ultimate beneficiary of services rendered by unlawful means (the immediate customer, the principal or project owner). From this ultimate beneficiary, it permits the recovery of salaries, payroll taxes and taxes left unpaid or unremitted by the perpetrator of the concealed employment. This mechanism provides employees and social welfare and tax authorities with an additional guaranty that amounts owed to them will be paid. When all the elements of a claim are present, claimants can look directly to the person placing the order or to the government contractor, especially in those cases – which are common – where the perpetrator of the illegal employment is broke, has gone out of business or has simply disappeared.
>
> In order to avoid the often onerous consequences of this law, anyone who signs a contract with a businessperson must, upon signing the contract, demand from him documented proof that he is conducting his activities in compliance with the law. If this confirmation is not sought, the customer will be subject to joint and several liability.
>
> The provision on joint and several liability therefore obliges every company, every contracting agency, every individual to exercise care in choosing the business person to whom it entrusts a project. Lack of vigilance could make him liable for the social contributions and tax debts of another who operates his business on the fringes of the law. An inter-ministerial memorandum of 30 December 1994 went out to judges and enforcement authorities reminding them of the existence of this regulation and urging them to use it whenever possible.

Liability of juridical persons

Enforcement received a major boost with the passage of the 5-year Employment Act on 20 December 1993. With this statute, French law recognised, for the first time, the principle of criminal liability for juridical persons who trade in personnel. All penalties for natural persons are now applicable to juridical persons, except that the maximum fine has been raised to FRF 150 000. Penalties include a ban against tendering for public procurement contracts, a fine of FRF 150 000, the closing of the place of business and a ban against doing business for a maximum of five years.

Sanctions against intermediaries

Also under closer scrutiny are intermediaries who accept payment for providing employers with personnel who they know do not have proper papers. These third parties are likewise liable to criminal penalties. The offence, denoted by the concept, aiding unlawful immigration, is codified in Article 21 of the Order of 1945 as amended. The maximum penalties are 5 years imprisonment and a maximum of FRF 200 000 in fines for natural persons, and FRF 1 000 000 for juridical persons. Added to this are a variety of concomitant penalties, in particular, a bar for up to 5 years on conducting business or practising a profession, a 10-year bar on re-entry into France if the person convicted is a foreigner, and a bar against tendering for public procurement contracts in the case of a juridical person.

The Act of 11 May 1998 on the entry of foreigners into France for purposes of residence and the right to asylum added an aggravated count when the violation is committed through the efforts of an organised group. In this case, maximum penalties increase to 10 years imprisonment and FRF 5 000 000 in fines.

Box 3. **Preying on vulnerability**

Apart from these offences, in a proper case, a claim for illegal employment can result in incrimination for subjecting a person to inhumane working or housing conditions by preying on his or her vulnerability or situation of dependence, or for obtaining services from such persons for no payment or for a wage which is manifestly disproportionate to the value of the work performed.

These offences, defined in Article 225-13, 14 and 15 of the Penal Code, are punishable by 5 years imprisonment and a maximum fine of FRF 1 000 000 for natural persons and FRF 5 000 000 for juridical persons.

Sanctions against employees without work permits

Under the French scheme, it is the employer who bears primary responsibility for illegal employment. The foreign employee without a work permit may be punished for an administrative violation or for an infraction. Criminal prosecution is however possible when the work permit is obtained by fraud (Art. L.364-2, Employment Code) or through forgery or uttering a forgery (Art. L 441-1 *et seq.*, Penal Code).

But the biggest risk for a foreigner who has neither a work permit nor a residence permit is deportation. Being in France without either, the foreigner becomes liable to imprisonment for one year and to fines of up to FRF 25 000. The court also has the discretion to bar re-entry for up to 3 years, which automatically leads to deportation. These penalties, however, are the jurisdiction of the police responsible for foreigners[10] and not included in the rules governing employment.

New agencies and new areas of authority

Three series of measures have boosted efforts to control and combat the employment of "undocumented" foreigners. Sanctions are now stiffer, juridical persons are now subject to criminal prosecution and the possibilities of indicting intermediaries who trade in labour are now enhanced. There are also the provisions aimed at controlling and preventing illegal employment in general. One such is the notice in advance of hire (déclaration préalable à l'embauche, DPAE). Officers of the criminal investigation branch of the police (gendarmes and police officers) also now have the

---

10. Article 19 of the Order (Ordonnance) of 1945, as amended.

authority to enter business premises without the predicate of exigent circumstances or a warrant[11] to check that business and employment practises do not violate prohibitions against clandestine employment and the employment of "undocumented" foreigners.

Introduced to the Penal Code in 1997,[12] this authority is not tantamount to a right of entry for purposes of inspecting employment conditions. It is more strictly circumscribed. It is available only upon the written request of the Public Prosecutor. It may be exercised only at the premises identified in the request, only for a limited time, and solely for the limited purpose of investigating two specified offences. In parallel with these legislative improvements, the institutional legislation has undergone numerous modifications, focusing on three avenues: creation of new agencies, broader authority for police to report cases of illegal employment and the development of internal co-operation. The number of officials authorised to combat the employment of "undocumented" foreigners has thus increased, chiefly by extending this authority to agencies that did not previously have it, such as, customs officials.

The national police are in charge of the more specific battle against trafficking in labour and illegitimate immigration. It operates this battle through two specialised units: the central office of the border police (PAF) and the general information bureau whose domain is the entry, residence and employment of foreigners. The PAF is also responsible for co-ordinating action among all branches of the national police in combating illegitimate immigration. The idea behind creating new agencies simultaneously responsible for policing foreigners and for employment law was to increase the chances of combating illegal immigration, employment of "undocumented" foreigners and illegal employment in general. Each of these two branches of the national police has a unit specifically in charge of these matters. For PAF, this is OCRIEST,[13] while the 12th section of the general information bureau performs this function for the prefecture of Paris.

Efforts to better co-ordinate available resources

Growing co-operation between enforcement agencies is undoubtedly the most significant change of the last decade. The objective was to make them more efficient, and make large-scale operations feasible, thanks to their combined authority, power and legislative influence. That these agencies join forces is a major asset in efforts to control illegal employment – their combined efficiency grows due to their individual strenghts. The innovative aspect of this legislation against illegal employment in France lies in the willingness of enforcement officials – whose traditional duties, priorities and "culture", in particular, are by definition worlds apart – to co-ordinate their action.

Article L.324-12 of the Employment Code is the main tool used in this co-ordination. It contains an exhaustive list of agencies authorised to take action (Box 4) and seeks to avoid conflicts

---

11. This constitutes an extension of the existing police powers of the criminal investigation branch of the police: crime in progress (flagrant délit) (Article 53 et seq. of the Code of Criminal Procedure), order (ordonnance) from the chief judge of the District Court (Tribunal de Grande Instance) (right to enter and search including inhabited premises, Article L.611-13 of the Labour Code), with a warrant signed by a judge (Article 14 of the Code of Criminal Procedure).

12. Act of 24 April 1997.

13. Central Office for the Prevention of Illegal Immigration and the Employment of Undocumented Foreigners.

---

between their areas of responsibility, without encroaching on their prerogatives. In practice, their co-operation is furthered either by the increased authority of each agency or the implementation of new controls. It has the added advantage of enhancing the deterrent effects of penalties by allowing more than one to be imposed at the same time.

The Act of 11 March 1997 has boosted this co-ordination, by making it possible to incorporate new agencies, expand their jurisdiction, avoid friction over prerogatives[14] and enhance their authority. This concern for coherence and balance has, for example, further empowered officials within the Board of Customs, authorising them to investigate and record (verbaliser) instances of employment of "undocumented" foreigners.[15] The same law also facilitates the exchange of documents and records protected by professional confidentiality. But while the Act of 31 December 1991 eased regulations on professional confidentiality, experience showed that even greater flexibility was needed. It has therefore been expanded in two directions. First, it now applies to a larger variety of illegal employment offences. Second, it authorises exchanges between enforcement agencies vested with these powers and the social welfare officials responsible for recovering unremitted contributions and for delivering services.

Institutional co-ordinating regulations were amended by the Decree of 11 March 1997. An inter-ministerial commission to combat illegal employment (DILTI) was created and given responsibility for co-ordinating action under this regulation on a national level. DILTI develops

---

Box 4. **Control services vested with relevant powers**

The following enforcement officials have authority to act in cases involving illegal employment: senior and junior officers of the criminal investigation department of the police; officials of the chief bureau of taxes and customs; officials approved for this purpose and sworn officials of social security agencies and social and agricultural mutual insurance programmes; labour inspectors and enforcement officials; officials and sworn agents in maritime matters; sworn civil aviation officials; and land transport officers and officials. They must forward case reports directly to the public prosecutor.

The listed officials are obliged to use the powers of investigation granted them under the laws and regulations that apply to them. This is the case, for example, with respect to the right of entry into a company or other business premises. While labour inspectors are authorised to enter to perform their duties, the powers of officials of the criminal investigation branch of the police (police and gendarmes) in this area are more strictly circumscribed by the Code of Criminal Procedure (CPP). Likewise, inspectors and auditors of the French inland revenue service must exercise their powers of investigation in instances of illegal employment in a manner which comports with the Code of Tax Procedures.

---

14. For example, all agencies have an equal right to be provided with documents needed to record the offence.

15. The law also authorises them to report violations involving third persons who bring foreigners into France for purposes of seeking employment (Articles L.341-9 and L.364-6 of the Labour Code).

its activities along three main avenues: providing assistance to enforcement agencies, training their operatives and helping to co-ordinate their efforts, statistical analyses, studies, standardisation of procedures and prevention. To ensure the accuracy of its analyses and studies, DILTI receives copies of all reports of illegal employment filed by enforcement agencies that it subjects to anonymous, in-depth analysis with the aid of a specially designed computer system.

Co-ordination at the local level is achieved through departmental commissions to combat illegal employment, which report to the Prefect's Office or to the Public Prosecutor's departmental representative. These commissions are composed of representatives from all relevant government services, consultative bodies and social welfare agencies. The commissions observe local conditions and make recommendations on programme initiatives. Within each commission is an operational committee to combat illegal employment (COLTI) that reports to the Public Prosecutor. This infrastructure is specifically for local enforcement agencies. The relevant authority and powers are actually executed through COLTI, which co-ordinates joint actions and informational exchange among them.

4. IMPROVING KNOWLEDGE OF THE REALITIES OF ILLEGAL EMPLOYMENT

Current understanding of the economic, social and geographic aspects of illegal employment is still incomplete. The consequences are two fold: it makes enforcement more difficult and perpetuates false impressions about the situation. For now, the most sensible way of attacking the problem is to study the reports of violations filed by enforcement officials. Two specially designed computer systems are used to process this information: one at the national level (TADEES) and another at the departmental level (COLTI Application).[16] DILTI sees to it that they are coherent and co-ordinated to serve the needs of enforcement officials.

Processing reports at the national level: the TADEES system

This system addresses the need for reliable data on the incidence of illegal employment; information which to a large extent has been guesswork until now. Processing is done anonymously. The system is therefore not intended to keep files on violators or to track the outcome of prosecution.[17] Besides collecting reports as a quantitative matter, it permits qualitative analysis of illegal employment by organising figures by economic sector, region and violator nationality.

The results of this work, which has been available since 1992, provides unpublished information on:
- The annual number of reports of violations referred to prosecution.
- The incidence of each type of violation relative to all reports filed.
- What portion is made up of undeclared independent contractors and illegal employment of salaried personnel.
- The number of reports broken down by economic sector.

---

16. Act No. 91-1383 of 31 December 1991 and the Decree of 11 March 1997.

17. The information recorded includes: name of the agency filing the report, place and date of the occurrence; the number, activity, legal form and citizenship of the businesses or companies involved; the number and nature of violations reported; the number, citizenship, gender and marital status of the defendant(s); the number, marital status, citizenship and gender of the employee(s) victimised by the illegal hiring.

- A regional breakdown of the incidence of illegal employment.
- A breakdown by nationality, region and occupation of persons charged.
- Breakdown by nationality of employees who have fallen victim to such practices, by region and business sector.
- Details on the involvement of various enforcement agencies.

This direct information on the realities of day-to-day activities of enforcement officials is helpful when it comes to training and a boon to co-ordination efforts. It also helps to improve legislation aimed at controlling and preventing illegal employment. Analyses and studies based on these initial data may serve as an annual update of efforts to curb illegal employment. They also support the efforts of the national commission to combat illegal employment created by the Decree of 11 March 1997.

Despite significant results obtained thus far, procedures need improvement. The aim is to speed up the processing of data and use it in shaping national policy on illegal employment. To further this goal, DILTI has proposed a simplified procedure for collecting data to the agencies. Accelerating collection and analysis will permit it to offer the agencies it serves quarterly "control panels" of their action, which should in turn help each to adapt its programmes to real situations.

COLTI's permanent file

The Decree of 11 March 1997 stated that processing be done under the authority of the Public Prosecutor at the local level and thereby address an operational concern – making it possible to track reports of violations filed by authorities at the departmental level in real time, to keep records of the prosecution results in each case and thereby create a central file on violators (companies and individuals) in order to respond to the requirements listed in the new provisions of the Act of 11 March 1997. While it partially duplicates what the TADEES system does, the two systems differ in two important respects:

- TADEES is an anonymous data bank while COLTI identifies companies and individuals.
- The purpose of TADEES is to create a central record of reports of violations filed nation-wide for use in statistical analysis. The COLTI system's function is more operational; it keeps a record of reports of violations and the action taken on them but its scope is strictly local.

Three lessons emerge from the reports of violations processed between 1992 and 1997:

- A clear decline in the number of reported cases of foreigners being employed during this time period. This decline contrasts with the rise in reports regarding illegal employment as a whole, and particularly that of clandestine employee.
- A change in observed illegal practices by nationality prosecuted. Clandestine employment is therefore more common among French employers than among foreign employers. Conversely, foreign employers account for more than half of company executives who were reported to have been employing undocumented foreigners.
- Regionally, there is a wide disparity between clandestine employment and employment of undocumented foreigners. While the first is occurring throughout the whole country, the second is concentrated in the *Ile-de-France* and *Provence-Alpes-Côte d'Azur* regions. In fact, these two regions apparently account for more than two-thirds of the charges for employment of undocumented foreigners referred by enforcement officials to prosecution.

5. RESULTS OF ACTION BY ENFORCEMENT AGENCIES IN 1997

Key annual figures

In 1997, there were 10 049 violations reported and 10 663 companies cited. In all, 17 505 violations were reported of which 13 534 persons were prosecuted. Incidentally, there were 21 266 illegal hirings. These results obviously do not cover all of the instances of illegal employment, but rather only that portion that came to light through the action of enforcement agencies and their reports. Nonetheless, this processing remains very relevant. It provides a complete overview of tangible indicators that describe the diversity of illegal employment and point out the relative significance of its elements and profiling of violators.

Number of reported violations rising

The brisk rise of reported violations in the mid-1990s did not continue at the same pace in recent years. Results from 1997 show that enforcement activity stabilised: the total number of reported violations was 10 049, as compared to 10 020 in 1996. But reports of illegal employment increased by 76% in five years.

Nearly 60% of violations discovered in service industries

Breakdown by economic activity reveals a continuation of the prior trend. The service industry leads all others and its share of reported violations grows each year. In 1997, it accounts for more than two-thirds of violations.

Less than 6% of illegal hires are foreigners without proper papers

In carrying out their enforcement duties, authorised agencies found nearly 21 266 illegally employed persons. Here as well, existing trends continue in two key areas:
- A growing number of such employees are citizens (60% as opposed to 51% in 1994).
- Conversely, an increasingly noticeable decline in the number of foreign workers without work permits. In 5 years, their number has fallen by more than half. In 1997, these "undocumented" foreigners represented fewer than 6% of illegal hires, as compared to 17% of the total in 1992.

A growing concentration of reports of illegal employment in the service sector

The breakdown of violations reported in 1997 by economic sector shows no change from previous years. This figure remains stable or grows slightly in the most active sectors, in particular, the service sector. As the leading sector of employment creation, the service sector is also the one that appears most frequently in reports of illegal employment. Trade and hotels, cafes and restaurants invariably lead the pack in this sector. The sector as a whole accounted for 62% of total violations reported in 1997 compared with 59% in 1995. These results confirm that there is not necessarily a correlation between illegal employment and business sectors in decline. Contrary to what most people believe, it keeps pace with (or even anticipates) changes in economic activity and employment as a whole (Table 1 and Figure 1).

The construction industry, however, has retained its place in this contest. Its is the best represented activity in the reports of violations throughout the entire country and in every category of illegal employment (employment of undocumented foreigners, clandestine employment, bartering and unlawful labour lending). A detailed exam confirms earlier indications regarding the evolution of illegal employment practices. Despite a long tradition of using immigrant workers, unscrupulous employers in this industry now seem less inclined to hire undocumented foreigners or to conceal their employees (whether citizens or foreigners with requisite permits).

The garment industry, which is often cited as an example, was implicated in only 4% of prosecutions in 1997. This sector does, however, have a higher-than-average incidence of employment of "undocumented" foreigners.

Table 1. **Infractions detected in 1992, 1995 and 1997, by sector of activity**

	Total	Agriculture	Clothing industry	Construction	Other industries	Trade	Hotels, bars, restaurants	Other services
	Thousands	Percentages						
1992	11.4	8.0	4.5	31.4	4.3	16.2	13.2	22.4
1995	19.9	8.0	3.0	25.5	4.0	20.0	15.0	24.0
1997	17.5	7.0	4.0	24.0	3.0	21.0	15.0	26.0

Figure 1.   **Breakdown by sector of the infractions detected in 1997**

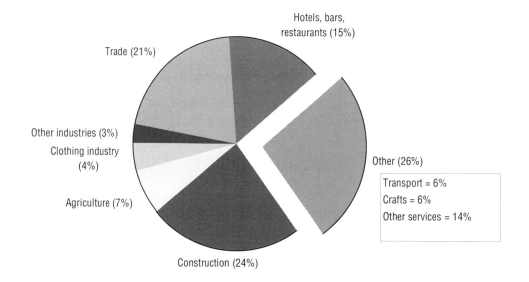

Transport = 6%
Crafts = 6%
Other services = 14%

Steady rise in concealment of employees

Clandestine employment was the most frequently reported offence in 1997. Its share of total violations has been climbing year after year, exceeding 65% in 1992 and 72.3% in 1997 (see Box 5).

Box 5. **Clandestine employment**

Clandestine employment as defined in the law covers a large variety of situations. The term refers, for instance, to cases where one performs work for which one expects payment, such as automobile repair, plumbing, painting and the like, without reporting it. Such persons are acting as independent contractors who evade their legal obligations (commercial, tax and social security). They engage in unfair competition with regard to others working in the sector and harm everyone by not paying income taxes, payroll taxes and social security contributions connected to this activity. These persons would be reported as concealing activity.

A second situation may be one where the executive of a company that has been duly registered but does not adhere to reporting rules for tax or social purposes. He also engages in unfair competition that is harmful to business persons in his sector and to the community as a whole. He would be reported for clandestine employment for failing to report to social services or tax authorities.

In a third situation, the employer is normally registered and known to tax and social service authorities but does not report employees. In this case, he would exacerbate the situation, for in addition to unfair competition, worsening tax and social deficits, he would deprive his employees of their social welfare benefits. This employer would be reported as concealing employees.

In defining clandestine employment, the law seeks to control three aspects of a company's existence: the propriety of its existence, the propriety of the business conducted, and where applicable, the propriety of the conditions of employment of its staff. In all of these cases, it is the company executive who is guilty of the offence of clandestine employment. His unreported employees may not be held responsible for an offence when they were the primary victims of that offence.

Efforts to combat clandestine employment thus have three objectives: defence of employees' rights, protection of companies against unfair competition, and deterrence of tax evasion and of the failure to make requisite social contributions.

The Act of 11 March 1997, which redefined clandestine employment (Box 5), also specifies the different categories of offences with greater clarity, clearly distinguishing the concealment of activities, the concealment of employees and the remedies against a company which (in the preceding two forms) engages in clandestine employment. Detailed analysis of the experience of enforcement agencies shows (Table 2) that, among all categories, there is a clear preponderance of concealment of employees; its share in statistics rose year after year (55% in 1997 as against 41% in 1993).

Table 2. **Details on clandestine employment 1993, 1995 and 1997**
Percentages

	Concealing activity	Concealing employees	Failing to report to social services or tax authorities	Use of an illegal subcontractor	Placing of advertisement intended to attract undocumented labour	Total
1993	38	41	3	16	1	100
1995	34	45	4	16	1	100
1997	33	55	not available	11	1	100

Box 6. **Notice in advance of hire (DPAE)**

Private employers are required to give advance notice of any employee they propose to hire. The declaration must be made to a social welfare agency no later than the first day on which the employee actually begins work.[18] The employer will supply the employee with a receipt indicating all the necessary DPAE information, which in turn goes into the national DPAE file. The file is available to designated enforcement authorities who may consult the file directly or electronically. It provides irrefutable proof of the date of hire of every employee. In 1997, agencies consulted the national DPAE system more than 80 000 times (compared to 62 000 in 1994).

This comes undoubtedly as a result of the newly implemented notice in advance of hire (*déclaration préalable à l'embauche*) (Box 6) which clearly reinforced the effectiveness of enforcement agencies' inspections by eliminating the employer's right to contest the date of hire of a particular employee. The Act of 11 March 1997 applies the offence of concealment of employees to any employer who deliberately fails to fulfil this obligation.

Enforcement agencies all agree that this file consultation service has made their work easier and more efficient. In fact, close to two-thirds (64%) of the prosecutions for concealing employees in 1997 were initiated once it was discovered that there was no DPAE on file; in 1994, the percentage was 55%.[19] The reports also indicate that the forms of clandestine employment (or rather their combined forms) vary noticeably depending on the activity under consideration. In the garment trade and hotel and restaurant industry, while fewer and fewer company executives are concealing their operations altogether (13%), they are increasingly concealing their employees (83%).

---

18. This formality is waived for individuals if the work involved is domestic or household work. However, it does apply when employing workers providing services in the home.

19. Use of this facility varies from one agency to another. Officials of employment departments (Urssaf and labour inspectors) use it most to support their charges of concealing employees. It seems to be used somewhat less by gendarmes and police officers (56,5%).

The situation is different in trade and in auto repair, where concealment of activity (46%) outweighs concealment of employees (31%), and where there is an especially high incidence of using concealed employees, at 22% twice the average (11%).

Development of illegal employment practices and insecurity of the available workforce

As in the past, the increase (measured by reports of violations) in the concealment of employees is paralleled by a continuing drop in reports of violations for employing undocumented foreigners (see Figure 2). In 1997, second offences only accounted for 4% of all those recorded, as compared to 13% five years earlier. This decline clearly must be ascribed to enforcement efforts; agencies' efforts have largely deterred employers. But this decline in the employment of undocumented foreigners also reflects a real evolution in illegal practices, which for several years now have caused employers to opt for concealing employees. Victims include citizens of France or other EU-member states or foreigners from other countries who have the right to work in France.

With regard to illegal employment in particular, this development reflects the growing imperilment of a portion of the available workforce. These persons are increasingly obliged to accept work that they would have refused a few years ago. This situation increases the pool of potential victims of illegal employment. Its probable effect – given the present set of economic circumstances – is to reduce the incentive to employ new immigrants without proper papers, though this largely depends on the region and industry involved.

Figure 2. **Illegal employment practices, 1992, 1995 and 1997**
Percentages

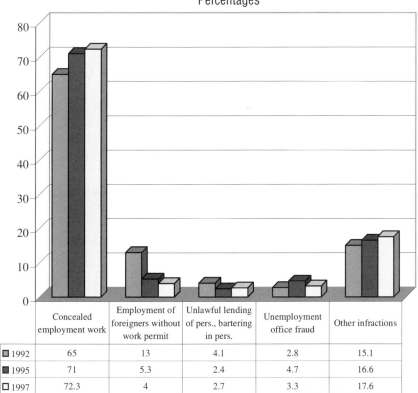

	Concealed employment work	Employment of foreigners without work permit	Unlawful lending of pers., bartering in pers.	Unemployment office fraud	Other infractions
1992	65	13	4.1	2.8	15.1
1995	71	5.3	2.4	4.7	16.6
1997	72.3	4	2.7	3.3	17.6

Figure 3. **Principal infractions of employment law, by sector of activity**

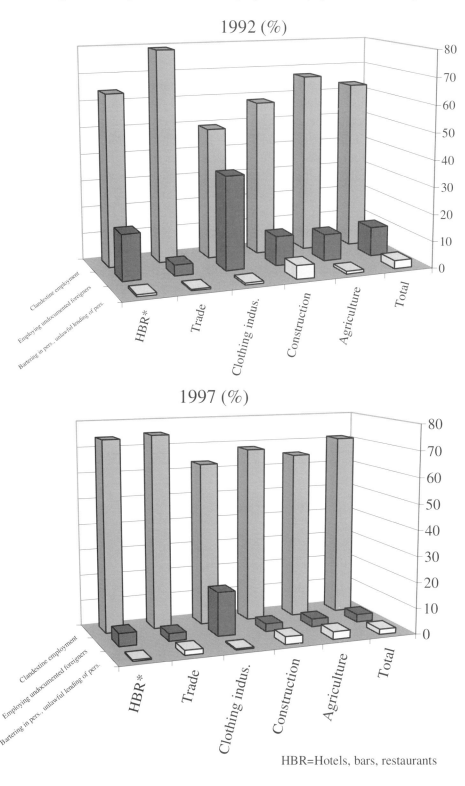

1992 (%)

1997 (%)

HBR=Hotels, bars, restaurants

Figure 3 sets forth the principal violations charged in 1997 and in 1992, and illustrates well this dynamic. It shows how the share of illegal employment practices (clandestine employment, employment of "undocumented" foreigners, bartering and unlawful lending of personnel) and their combinations vary from one period and activity to another. This chart indicates a clear evolution in the management of the available workforce. The case of the clothing industry is the most illustrative. One can clearly see the changes that took place between 1992 and 1997 in terms of the share of violations reported by category – clandestine employment and the employment of undocumented foreigners. The trend is similar in other industries.

Foreigners without work permits make up less than 6% of illegal hires

These changes naturally translate into profiles of employees who are victims of illegal employment. In reports of violations filed with DILTI in 1997, there were a total of 20 222 illegal hires. Compared to previous years, this total presents two key characteristics: a growing number of victims are French citizens and the number of foreigners without work permits continues to drop.

In 1997, enforcement agencies discovered that French citizens accounted for more than 65% of employees hired illegally. This percentage was 51% in 1992. Conversely, the share attributable to "undocumented" foreigners went from 13% to 6% during the same time period.

Based on reports of violations, illegal employment appears to harm primarily employees who are French citizens, and then foreigners who have permits to live and work in France. As with French citizens, these persons are usually victimised through concealment of their employment. These circumstances, which clearly support the evidence that illegal employment practices are changing, may actually be creating a pool of victims on which unscrupulous employers can draw.

French citizens are increasingly the ones charged

The increase in the number of French citizens charged squares with the number of persons charged with illegal employment by enforcement agencies. In 1997, these agencies referred a total of 13 534 cases for prosecution. In the vast majority of them, the defendants were company executives (non-salaried independents or employers) and, to a lesser degree, individuals and salaried employees, who were generally charged with defrauding the Unemployment Office or collecting benefits while employed. Here too, the trends of past years continue. Taken together, the share of French citizens continues to rise (78% in 1997 as against 74% in 1994), that of citizens of EU-member states remained constant at around 4%, while there was a further decline among persons from other countries (18% as against 22%).

Even in decline this foreign presence is remarkable, especially among employers, whose share increased slightly this past year, while it declined among non-salaried independents. It is important to note that those involved are company executives, charged with engaging in illegal employment and not with failure to have a visa or residence permit.[20] Compared to citizens, foreign employers are more often charged with employing "undocumented" foreigners. Mostly Turks, North Africans

---

20. Even if some of them may figure twice, these two areas need to be clearly distinguished. One originates in employment law, the other in the law applicable to police responsible for dealing with foreigners.

and Asians, they make up a little more than half of the company executives charged on these grounds. But, regardless, they do not contradict the overall trend already described: among these persons as well, this type of hiring is declining from year to year.

Ile-de-France, the region with the highest incidence of illegal employment

Review of reported violations by geographic zone confirms a very large dispersion of illegal employment throughout the country, with the notable exception of Ile-de-France, which accounted for 18% of the 17 505 infractions recorded nationally in 1997. This is a larger share than the 14% recorded two years earlier. In second place, one finds the areas of *Provence-Alpes-Côte-d'Azur* (11%), *Nord-Pas-de Calais* (9.1%), followed by *Midi-Pyrénées, Rhône-Alpes, Aquitaine, Languedoc-Roussillon, Lorraine* and the French overseas territories which each make up between 6% to 7% of the same total.

A cross-analysis of geographic zone and type of violation reveals a distinct difference between clandestine employment, which seems to be quite prevalent throughout the country, and employment of undocumented foreigners, reports of which are concentrated in a very small number of regions. According to the evidence, the employment of undocumented foreigners occurs primarily in urban areas while clandestine employment occurs in urban and rural areas alike. Here again, *Ile-de-France* is, so to speak, in a class by itself. Reports of violations indicate an incidence of clandestine employment of 67.4%, which is a bit below the national average of 72.3%, but there are decidedly more instances of employment of undocumented foreigners (11.4% against the national level of 4%).

This region therefore appears to be the centre for reported cases of this type of violation, accounting as it does for half of the incidences of employment of undocumented foreigners reported nation-wide. It is followed, though with quite a gap, by the region of *Provence-Alpes-Côte-d'Azur* (13%) and the rest of the French overseas departments (8.3%). Apart from this exceptional case, most violations commonly processed in other regions are for clandestine employment, which often accounts for more than three-quarters of the total. The figure is as high as 80% in some regions (*Auvergne, Basse Normandie, Bretagne, Franche Comté, Limousin*).

The incidence in sectors varies with the region

The intense concentration of undocumented foreign employment in *Ile-de-France* can be explained first by differences in illegal employment practises from sector to sector. The correlation is especially strong in the case of the garment trade. In terms of reporting, this sector demonstrates two prime characteristics: it is number one in the employment of undocumented foreigners (18% as against the national average of 4%) and, second, the businesses involved are almost all located in *Ile-de-France*, a good half of those in Paris proper.

Though not having the exclusively *Ile-de-France* character of the garment trade, every industry's share of reported cases of illegal employment varies by region and reflects the region's economic peculiarities and conditions.

Contributions of individual agencies are more complex than raw statistics would suggest

When viewing the case report figures as a whole, the shares attributable to each agency appear at first sight to be very lopsided (see Figure 4). In terms of raw numbers, the criminal investigation branch of the police (police and gendarmerie) and officials of the "social welfare agencies" (labour inspectors and URSSAF) appear unquestionably to have contributed the lion's share.

Figure 4. **The reporting of illegal work in 1997 by the reporting public service sector**

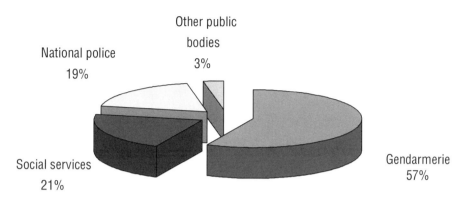

But two considerations prompt one to look beyond simple ranking and regard these results in more relative terms.

- The first is that not all officials in a particular agency have authority to take action or report on the whole range of violations constituting illegal employment, and of these, some have only recently been granted that authority.
- The second is that officials within each particular agency assigned to this function vary greatly from agency to agency. The gendarmerie has by far the largest number of officers who could potentially report such cases. Second to the gendarmerie are the national police, which have specialised units for immigration control and illegal employment. Then come the labour inspectors, third in terms of having personnel potentially available for this assignment.

The double pay-off through agency co-ordination

To fully appreciate the role of each participant in this campaign, it is necessary to bear in mind just how co-ordinated inter-agency action really works. Participation may consist of helping in the preparation of an enforcement action, which could entail direct involvement in its execution, but which could also entail sharing information used as evidence to support the charge. Such co-ordination is also demonstrated in follow-up action to enforcement (particularly by tax authorities and URSSAF), including that undertaken by other agencies. The double pay-off comes when violators can be cited for tax and/or social service obligations at the same time that criminal penalties are exacted. Progress has been made on all of these levels. Committing more resources to co-ordination will encourage further efforts.

It is true that co-ordination is one of the chief policy achievements in the campaign against illegal employment in France. But while the co-ordinated approach has led to more effective enforcement and better procedures, it tends to obscure the true contribution – in quantitative terms – of some agencies. Officials from one or more other agencies frequently intervene – perhaps through direct involvement in enforcement action or indirectly by assisting in its preparation – to support action initiated by the agency producing the report, but for which they are not accredited.

One must bear in mind this fact when attempting to evaluate the contributions of respective agencies in the campaign against illegal employment.

In terms of direct involvement, roughly only 12% of case reports filed in 1997 were the product of co-ordinated action involving officials from several agencies in the actual enforcement. While certainly encouraging, this figure needs improvement so long as significant disparities persist among agencies and/or regions. Applying the same criterion on a national level, officials of the national police and URSSAF, the agencies most inclined to using this modus operandi, posted figures of 21% and 20%, respectively. The practise is also most prevalent in the regions of *Nord-Pas-de-Calais, Ile-de-France, Languedoc-Roussillon* and *Provence-Alpes-Côte-d'Azur.*

Prevention

There is no internal system set up to specifically prevent employment of illegal aliens. Such prevention is simply part of the general strategy against illegal employment. Among the relevant measures in this context, two are worthy of mention: the partnership agreement and *chèque-service.* Introduced by a memorandum from the Prime Minister dated 24 January 1992, the partnership agreement is a pact between the government and business representatives (on national and departmental levels). It seeks to involve business people in all phases of the campaign against illegal employment. It even permits them to appear as civil complainants in criminal actions involving illegal employment. By the end of 1997, 11 such agreements had been signed on the national level and 183 on the departmental level.

Created on 1 December 1994, the *chèque-service* is a programme that simplifies hiring and compensation formalities. It can be used by anyone who wishes to employ domestic help (for child care, baby-sitting, housekeeping, home maintenance, at-home care of the elderly, domestics, and so forth). It exempts the employer from all administrative formalities (employment contracts,[21] pay slips, reporting to social welfare agencies). Combined with other tax measures, it creates an incentive for individuals to hire staff legally for those kinds of services. In fact, it allows a tax deduction of up to 50% for salaries paid to household employees, to a maximum of FRF 45 000.

The law's provisions were further relaxed by the Act of 29 January 1996, in favour of persons rendering services to individuals. The law extended the *chèque-service* programme to the performance of up to 39 hours of service, but requires that the employer sign a contract with any employee working more than 8 hours. The law also now extends to domestic help employed by industry, craftsmen and commercial firms able to offer this kind of work to individuals. It allows works councils to give financial assistance to employees who use *chèque-service.*

6.   OUTCOME OF PROSECUTION

Sharp rise in convictions for illegal employment over the last ten years

In 1995, nearly 6 800 persons were convicted of illegal employment. Since the law on clandestine employment was amended in the mid-1980s, sanctions imposed by the courts for illegal employment have steadily become harsher. In ten years, the number of persons convicted

---

21. When the employee works no more than 8 hours a week.

on this charge increased by over 800%, reaching 6 800 in 1995. This total represents more than 38% of all convictions on employment law violations handed down for the year (13 320) as against 31% in 1990. Clandestine employment is solely responsible for this increase.

Clandestine employment is by far the leading grounds for conviction on charges of illegal employment

Over 90% of convictions were for clandestine employment as against 5% for violations of the rules on employing foreigners. This trend in convictions corresponds closely to the trend in reported cases. Again, clandestine employment clearly dominates the field and its share of convictions handed down for illegal employment continues to grow. At the same time, there is a decline in convictions for the employment of undocumented foreigners, which again corresponds to the figures on cases reported.

Clandestine employment has led the list of grounds for conviction on employment law violations since 1993, far surpassing "health and safety" which led at the beginning of the decade. It alone accounts for the rise in convictions on employment law violations. As in prior years, there are few convictions for bartering, unlawful lending of labour, or for violating the rules on temporary employment. Year after year, convictions on these grounds seem to be declining. These figures attest to the difficulty that enforcement officials have in reporting such cases, and the courts in prosecuting them.

Heavier fines for employing undocumented foreigners than for clandestine employment

Employment law violations are usually punishable by fine, ranging from FRF 6 700 to FRF 8 600, depending on the type of case. While the average fine for clandestine employment falls within this range, the average fine for employment of an undocumented foreigner appears to be higher (between FRF 7 035 and FRF 9 641). But the best evidence that the courts are taking a harder line is the increase in past years of actual prison sentences and therefore the concomitant decline in fines.

Two types of cases attract the closest judicial scrutiny: illegal employment and work-related accidents. In these types of cases, the likelihood of a prison sentence is decidedly higher, mainly for illegal employment. In fact, in over 85% of cases involving employment law violations where the sentence includes imprisonment, the prison time is for illegal employment, especially "clandestine employment". But prison sentences wherein the sentence must actually be served are still rare. Fewer than 4% of persons convicted of employment law violations serve time in prison and then only for about 5 months on average. Eight out of ten times the sentence comes on a conviction of clandestine employment.

7.   CONCLUSION

Three outstanding lessons emerge from the preceding developments. All involve the commitment of enforcement agencies, broadening of their powers and co-ordination of their efforts.

Agencies still committed

That the various agencies are committed to being more than labour inspectors is evidenced not only by the increasing number of officials who are becoming involved in this area, but also by a change in their approach to the realities of illegal employment. In reading their reports carefully, one notices that even the so-called "generalists" are becoming more adept each year in dealing with illegal employment cases. They have proven their skills even in complex cases where unlawful activity may be veiled by a legal fiction. The same goes for the gendarmerie, the border police and the intelligence service (RG).

A multifaceted offence

This progress is all the more important since the types of offences officials must look out for have multiplied and the scope of their authority has expanded accordingly. Compared to the accomplishments of the late 1980s, the change is impressive. During that period, reports focused almost exclusively on the illegal employment of foreigners.

Today, most agencies deal with cases of foreigners hired by a company or construction project as well as violations in lending or bartering labour, along with all types of clandestine employment. This new approach is what accounted for the translation of reported violations into convictions in 1997, convictions that reflected the same trends evidenced in reporting figures from 1992 to 1997. The increased diversity of agency action has had a two-fold effect. On the one hand, it has highlighted the multifaceted nature of these offences; on the other, while not diminishing its importance, it has put the incidence of illegal aliens into proper perspective.

But whether conviction or case report, the incidence of clandestine employment is vastly greater than that of the employment of undocumented foreigners. One should therefore not automatically assume a nexus between unlawful immigration and illegal employment.

A more coherent system of regulations

Comparing these results with those of 10 years ago[22] would be meaningless without qualifying them. There has been a complete change of scope (the types of offences recorded) and of the reporting involved (the agencies included in the statistics). The comparison is nonetheless interesting. These changes and the two-fold evolution they evidence are themselves an indication of the commitment of French authorities in the past decade. That same political will is visible in the marked attitude change towards this phenomenon and the greater resources applied to it. Not only are more enforcement officials involved in the campaign against illegal employment, the target of their efforts has both expanded and become more focused.[23] The Act of 1987 marked a

---

22. There were 2 514 reports of violations for the years 1986-87, or four times less than in 1997.

23. There was particular concern regarding the term, "clandestine employment", the subject of a good deal of confusion that distorts views on the true significance and role of foreigners in economic offences. The confusion arises when clandestine employment is associated only with the employment of "undocumented" foreigners. It has again come into widespread misuse even (for a while) among some enforcement officials. It continues to be misunderstood by many elected officials. Clearly, the use of "undocumented" foreigners will continue to be the most commonly criticised practise, even though the facts prove that it is far from the most common.

turning point in attitudes toward illegal employment; a series of legislative amendments followed in support of this new attitude.[24]

All of these statutes, provisions and measures have aimed to strengthen the mechanisms used to combat the problem, broadening the scope of action against it, and making the system operate better by giving enforcement officials the means to deal with its changing realities. This was achieved through a three-fold change:

- The focus on illegal employment of foreigners has given way to a fuller appreciation of all the offences constituting illegal employment.
- The scope of enforcement efforts has been expanded accordingly.
- There is enthusiastic support for the co-ordination of those efforts.

This last point – that enforcement efforts be co-ordinated – is critical. When all enforcement agencies with jurisdiction combine their efforts, they can force the offender to pay a much heavier price: once for criminal sanctions and again for unremitted taxes and social contributions. The deterrent effect of sanctions is enhanced, so that they become a genuine aid to prevention.

---

24. The Act of 10 July 1989, in particular, created harsher sanctions for clandestine employment, the employment of "undocumented" foreigners and the illegal importation of foreign labour, and created a new violation: employment of an "undocumented" foreigner through a third person. The Act of 12 July 1990 amended the articles of the Employment Code that dealt with sub-contracting and the lending of personnel (L.125-1 and L.125-3), and increased sanctions. The Act of 31 December 1991 extended the power to report clandestine employment to officials of the agricultural mutual programmes, Urssaf and maritime matters authority. The Decree (décrét) of 11 March 1997 improved the operations of departmental commissions and co-ordination of agencies; co-ordination made possible through the relaxation of rules on confidentiality between enforcement agencies (the Act of 31 December 1991).

CONCLUSION

Policy Recommendations

The fight against the illegal entry, residence and employment of foreigners has become a priority of immigration policies in OECD countries. The persistence of irregular migration, albeit at different levels for different receiving countries, is at the heart of current policy debates. This is true both in countries that have expressed a political will to manage migration flows more effectively and to fight against the trafficking of labour, and in those that continue to receive a large number of immigrants as part of an active policy to recruit permanent migrant workers.

This seminar provided participants with the opportunity to draw the lessons from the results obtained and the difficulties encountered by many Member countries when implementing policies to combat the employment of foreigners in an irregular situation, and to examine in particular the preventive measures and the sanctions imposed against employers and, in some cases, workers. The role of trafficking networks was frequently underlined, as was their increasing involvement in international labour movements. This is why the penalties imposed against those who aid and abet illegal immigration and employment were the subject of particular attention and why participants discussed how national and international co-operation might be enhanced in order to more effectively prevent the illegal employment of foreigners.

During the seminar, many recommendations were made regarding the policies to be implemented. They are presented below and will be the subject of an annual monitoring process under the aegis of the OECD Working Party on Migration in order to evaluate the progress made in this area by the Member countries.

The employment of undocumented immigrants is just one element, and not necessarily the most important, of economic activity in the so-called "underground" or "undeclared" economy. Both immigrants and nationals participate in the underground economy. Whatever is done to combat the hiring of illegal immigrants, therefore, must address the problem of undeclared work in general rather than merely the employment of illegal immigrants. Nevertheless, policies that address this issue must take into account the fact that illegal immigrants are especially vulnerable because of their precarious situation – they do not have the legal right to work, nor do they have, in many instances, the right to reside in the receiving country.

Sanctions against the illegal employment of immigrants must be applied to the main actors involved in the relevant breaches of labour and immigration laws. This list includes direct employers and indirect employers (these latter outsource segments or phases of their operations to other firms); any persons who actively promote illegal immigration and/or the employment of illegal immigrants, be they intermediaries making a financial gain from providing accommodation or professional traffickers of illegal labour. It may finally include undocumented workers themselves.

Unless they form part of a broader policy framework to control and manage immigration flows, measures to combat the employment of immigrants in an irregular situation will not be effective. Punitive sanctions alone, without complementary measures, are of limited value. Several OECD countries have found that a combination of sanctions and non-punitive preventive measures is the most effective strategy against the employment of illegal immigrants. This involves, for example, informing employers, immigrants and sending countries about the existing legislation governing migrants' entry, residence and labour market access as well as about the risks associated with illegal employment.

Better co-ordination and coherence of administrative measures to tackle the employment of illegal immigrants is fundamental, both at national and local levels. It is important because labour markets and, therefore, illegal hiring practices, have a strong local dimension. A particularly important area of co-operation among agencies is the exchange of information about illegal practices, the measures taken to address them, and their results. This information should be accurate, and the government agencies concerned must have at their disposal effective and accurate methods to evaluate their interventions. This information, however, should not be collected at the expense of individual rights to privacy.

It is important to address the difficulties that government inspection agencies encounter when implementing measures against the employment of illegal immigrants. The jurisdictions and capacities of these agencies are in fact often insufficient, most notably in the case of undocumented work in private residences, to which these agencies have extremely limited access. Moreover, fines for illegal employment practices are in general low and therefore ineffective as deterrents. Several Member country representatives recommended that awareness-raising programmes be created for all those working in the judicial system thereby alerting them of the importance of following through with legal sanctions and of ensuring that all fines imposed are paid in full and in a timely manner. This sort of intervention would reinforce and strengthen the role of sanctions in combating illegal hiring practices.

The general public must be better informed about the risks and the penalties for using illegal labour. The main targets should be employers and workers in industries where illegal practices are prevalent, but also employers that resort to the use of undeclared labour only on an occasional basis.

Specific measures adopted in certain OECD Member countries might serve as models for others. Examples of best practices include instituting the obligation to notify the relevant government agencies prior to hiring; providing fiscal incentives for the employment of legal workers (by reducing or exempting employers from social charges and taxes in certain sectors and for certain types of jobs); and, streamlining contractual and administrative requirements associated with service sector employment (notably for domestic help). Another example is forging partnerships between relevant government agencies, on the one hand, and employers and business associations, on the other, in order to promote joint efforts to combat illegal employment.

A large number of OECD countries refuse to undertake regularisation programmes, citing primarily the risk of attracting new migrants who would seek to take advantage of the programme or to remain illegally in anticipation of a future regularisation. Regularisation programmes alone are insufficient to effectively combat illegal immigration and the illegal employment of foreigners. Some beneficiaries of regularisation programmes may slip back into illegality as a result of the precariousness of the legal status they are granted. Recent regularisation programmes implemented in a number of OECD countries do, however, present advantages. First, they provide vital information to the authorities regarding the number of migrants who fulfil the required conditions, the networks that enabled illegal migrants to stay in an irregular situation and the economic sectors most concerned. Second, regularisation is often an opportunity to grant legal status and rights to foreign workers and residents who settled in a country many years earlier but who remained in an irregular situation. Finally, if the situation of clandestinity attains in a country a critical dimension, regularisation programmes can help to fulfil public security objectives. They can help immigrants avoid excessive exploitation and/or illicit, even criminal, activities.

Whilst several OECD countries have already undertaken co-operative efforts, particularly with sending countries, international co-operation to combat the illegal employment of foreigners is very underdeveloped. Yet the need for international co-operation is becoming more urgent, especially to combat labour trafficking networks. European Union members have become aware of this necessity and the Council of the European Union has put forth several recommendations. Likewise, the Commission of the European Union has drafted a report on illegal employment in general which identifies four main groups of participants in the undeclared economy: multiple job holders, the "economically inactive" population, the unemployed and third-country nationals illegally resident in the EU. In other OECD Member countries, such as the United States, Canada and Mexico, international co-operative actions, when they have taken place, have been essentially bilateral and often very specific.

The expected benefits of greater international co-operation, however, are limited. Democratic societies do not prevent their citizens from emigrating in search of a better life for themselves and their families. The individual migrants have, in most cases, strong personal reasons to emigrate, even if such a decision requires that they live in an illegal situation. International co-operation could further be developed by:

- Improving the methods of information exchange between competent administrations.
- Improved training and greater exchanges of personnel specialised in control and repression, both those working at the borders as well as those involved in the fight against illegal employment.
- Strengthening co-operation with sending countries: measures to disseminate information to potential migrants on the regulations governing legal employment and on the sanctions they are likely to face in receiving country should they take up an illegal situation. A productive partnership can be forged with countries of origin to protect their most vulnerable categories of nationals, informing them that they run the risk of becoming victims of trafficking networks.

ANNEX
REVIEW OF THE RELEVANT LEGISLATION IN AUSTRIA, BELGIUM, GERMANY, JAPAN, THE NETHERLANDS AND SWITZERLAND

Measures Undertaken to Combat the Employment of Foreigners in an Irregular Situation in Austria

by
Viktor Riedel
(Federal Ministry of Labour, Health and Social Affairs, Austria)

All measures to combat the employment of foreigners in an irregular situation must be taken globally. Although individual measures, such as an efficient inspection system, may provide satisfactory solutions in certain areas, they do not tackle the root of the problem.

Attempts to draw conclusions about possible measures based on statistical surveys of the dimensions of the problem are also difficult.

All that is possible is to evaluate the social and economic effects of this phenomenon on the basis of reports and calculations from experts and scientists, and to draw appropriate conclusions. None of the standards used to assess the illegal employment and residence of foreigners is based on empirical, reliable data. It is impossible either to present the relevant economic figures and details or even to count the number of persons involved.

Any discussion of measures, and attempts to assess their effectiveness, spins off from observations and experience, and uses the meagre information provided by the state to combat this phenomenon as efficiently as possible.

1. THE ORGANISATION OF COMBATING THE EMPLOYMENT OF FOREIGNERS IN AN IRREGULAR SITUATION IN AUSTRIA

The Central Labour Inspectorate oversaw the establishment of small groups in the Labour Inspectorate of each of the nine federal states. Each of these groups contains at least two specialists and is deployed to investigate the illegal employment of foreigners. They inspect factories, construction sites and other external workplaces, for example, on farms, where it is suspected that foreigners are illegally employed.

Persons whose employment is of doubtful legality must identify themselves to the officers of the Labour Inspectorate and prove that their status is legal.

After investigation of all the details, in particular whether the foreigner is legally present in the country or not, the regional administration is summoned, if appropriate, to bring criminal proceedings against the person employing the foreigner. In this event, the company and/or responsible person in the company may be fined for illegally employing foreign workers.

2.   Sanctions in the case of illegal employment

The Austrian Employment of Foreigners Act is based on the principle that only employers of illegal foreign workers may be punished.

In the event of conviction, the employer and/or responsible personnel who arranged the hiring of illegal workers must pay considerable fines, for example:
- For a first offence with up to 3 foreigners: ATS 10 000 to 60 000.
- For subsequent offences (up to 3 foreigners): ATS 20 000 to 120 000.
- For a first offence with more than 3 foreigners: ATS 20 000 to 120 000.
- For subsequent offences (more than 3 foreigners):   ATS 40 000 to 240 000.

In each case, the fines apply per foreigner illegally employed.

In order to gather the necessary evidence, rights of access to construction sites, factories and external workplaces also exist under penalty of fine on refusal.

The police have a duty to assist officers of the Labour Inspectorate if required. This is necessary, on the one hand, in the case of accumulated offences (for example, if the foreigner is illegal) and, on the other, because it is impossible for a small team at the disposal of the Labour Inspectorate to properly inspect construction sites over a certain size. This police assistance also serves to protect the officers of the Labour Inspectorate, who are unarmed.

Other possible sanctions against the employer include:
- Withdrawal of trading license in the case of repeated offences.
- Refusal of further permits under the "Employment of Foreigners Act" for hiring additional foreign workers.
- Exclusion from public contracts.
- "Customer liability", extension of sanctions to include the managing contractor of a project, insofar as he is presumably knowledgeable of the legal status of workers employed by his subcontractors.
- Surcharges in the form of subsequent demands for unpaid taxes and social security contributions.
- Subsequent payment of unpaid wages in the form of "compensatory payment" to the foreigner (it is not possible to begin legal proceedings to recover unpaid wages from an employment agreement which is itself illegal).

Other legislation also provides for sanctions against illegal foreign workers, in particular laws concerning foreigners:
- Deportation, if residence in the country is illegal or has become illegal as a result of illegal employment.
- Ban from entering the country (up to 5 years) in the event of repeated offences as an illegally employed foreigner.

The penalties, occasionally criticised by legal experts, are unusually high in comparison to other areas of administrative criminal law. On the other hand, unions are particularly in favour of penalties large enough to skim off profits gained through illegal employment and are continually demanding larger fines and more efficient inspections.

In isolated cases, the size of penalties also leads to the delay of criminal proceedings in regional administrations or, in doubtful cases, their abandonment as a result of pressure from an important local business person. To prevent this outcome, the Labour Inspectorate has "right of representation" in such criminal proceedings and can itself appeal in the case of abandonment.

The "Independent Administrative Senates" (of which there is one in each federal state) decide on appeals both from the accused and from the Labour Inspectorate. These Administrative Senates have the status of a tribunal, in the sense of the European Convention on Human Rights.

The only possible recourse against decisions of the Independent Administrative Senates is an examination of the completed proceedings by the Administrative Court, to which an appeal may be directed either by the person found guilty or by the Federal Minister for Labour, Health and Social Affairs in the event of infringement of procedural or other statutory requirements in the course of the appeal proceedings.

3. AIM OF THE INSPECTIONS

Since the inspecting bodies have rather inadequate personnel resources at their disposal, areas for inspection are carefully chosen. In many cases, it is impossible to follow up every suspicion, but inspections must be chosen according to the weight of suspicions or the location (not too far) of the suspected offence. As a result, complete inspection is impossible and distant areas can be visited only sporadically. On the other hand, the pre-selection process does lead to a relatively high rate of results.

The probability of discovering illegally employed foreigners is especially high in the construction and allied building trades, catering, agriculture and private house building sectors. A random survey has shown that, on average, illegal foreign employees are discovered every eighth inspection; in the catering sector, every fifth; and in agriculture, over one in three. Most inspections (approximately half), however, involve the construction sector.

4. THE UNDERLYING REASONS FOR ILLEGAL EMPLOYMENT OF FOREIGNERS

Simple case observations reveal the following conclusions:
* The most frequent form of illegal employment of foreigners involves either unskilled or easily learned work.
* Seasonal peaks are often covered through illegal workers.
* Illegal employment of foreigners in sectors requiring higher qualifications is less frequent.
* Areas for which the labour market offers no workers or where work permits have reached their maximum possible level abet the rise of illegal employment.
* Legal residence requires ability to earn a living in the country. (Asylum seekers and students, for example, are not permitted to accept employment, especially when the maximum number of work permits has been issued or on grounds of legislation applying to foreigners).
* Wives or husbands want to contribute to the family income by working illegally.
* The difference in wage levels, compared with the former COMECON states, exerts pressure on the illegal labour market; unemployed persons, civil servants, and so forth,

want to earn an additional income "over the border" (working on weekends or during vacation, without any intention of settling).

5.   PROSPECTS FOR THE FUTURE

As a result of various studies, which have calculated losses in income to the state budget of up to ATS 230 billion due to illicit employment, politicians are facing increasing pressure to launch measures to combat illegal activities. Discussion of this issue is no longer restricted to illegal foreigners, but focuses on measures that must have fiscal consequences; it is no longer relevant if the illicit work is performed by foreign or by Austrian workers. The debate ignores the fact that the income of illegal foreigners hardly benefits the Austrian economy. In view of increasing unemployment figures, rising budget deficits and, above all, exploding state social expenditures, the main objective is to construct a proper market situation so that every form of paid employment is subject to statutory taxation and social security regulations. In other words, employment without tax deductions or social security contributions is no longer regarded as a trivial offence. An area of conflict nevertheless arises. On the one hand, the average person building a family home could hardly afford to do so without recourse to illicit working while, on the other, companies operating legally are less competitive. Such a situation in turn leads to unemployment.

Discussion on this topic will always be controversial. In addition to the above-mentioned penalties, those who pay their taxes the "proper" way are now demanding a tax relief ("Luxembourg model") – a demand which is dismissed as absurd by budgetary experts.

After a long series of discussions lead by the Federal Ministry for Labour, Health and Social Affairs, the government announced its intention to adopt a series of measures designed to combat illegal employment. These measures are comprised notably of the following regulations:

- Illicit working is defined not only as illegal employment of foreigners, but also as tax evasion, non-payment of social security contributions and working without a trading license.
- With the exception of trade and tax legislation, supervision of illegal workers is transferred to customs authorities (as is already the case in Germany).
- The administrative proceedings connected with those offences are no longer initiated by the regional administration but by the customs authorities themselves.
- Inspecting bodies' right of access to factories and construction sites are reinforced.
- Advertising for illegal employment is forbidden.
- Organised illicit working will be more vigorously investigated.
- Registration for social insurance must take place at the start of employment (otherwise it is impossible to check whether statutory social insurance requirements were met).
- The authorities involved must co-operate more fully.
- Co-operation and exchange of data are facilitated through amendments to data protection legislation.

Current Belgian Legislation on Sanctions against the Employment of Foreigners in an Irregular Situation

by
Jean-Claude Heirman
(Inspecteur social, Directeur, Ministère de l'Emploi et du Travail, Bruxelles)

The main task of the Employment Law Inspectorate (*Inspection des lois sociales*) of the Ministry of Employment and Labour (*Ministère de l'Emploi et du Travail*) is to monitor the application of employment legislation and, in particular, to ensure compliance with fundamental principles in this field. The department therefore sees the regular declaration of workers as fundamental, and accordingly supports the campaign against the fraudulent employment of unauthorised foreign workers.

This paper has two parts: there is a brief presentation of regulations that have been introduced to combat undeclared work, followed by an analysis of the main sanctions covering the employment of foreigners in an irregular situation.

1.   REGULATIONS APPLYING TO ALL EMPLOYERS IN THE PRIVATE SECTOR

Employment documentation

Royal Decree No. 5 of 23 October 1978 relating to the holding of employment documentation (*Moniteur belge*, 2 December 1978) and the Implementing Royal Decree of 8 August 1980 (*Moniteur belge*, 27 August 1980) provided the Employment Law Inspectorate with effective tools for combating illegal labour.

These Royal Decrees require all employers to hold a *workforce register* at the workplace. Those who employ staff at several places must, at all workplaces other than the one at which the workforce register is held, also have a *special workforce register* (a kind of simplified workforce register).

In cases where workers are normally employed for fewer than five consecutive working days in the same place (for example, drivers), or when they are employed on construction sites, the employer may replace this special workforce register with an *individual register* – a card issued to each worker containing information from the special workforce register.

An *attendance register*, which includes data on working hours and information from the special workforce register, may also be held for certain categories of workers in three economic sectors: the diamond industry, horticulture, and hotels, catering and cafés.

The workforce register must be available for inspection by the monitoring authorities; this also applies to the social workforce register and the attendance register. Registers consist of bound, numbered files, and each worker must be listed using a continuous numbering system and following the chronological order of when he/she started work; the starting date must also be noted.

The absence of a workforce register (or special register, individual register or attendance register) at the workplace and the non-registration of workers in one of these documents constitutes a serious breach in the eyes of the Employment Law Inspectorate. A report is normally drawn up each time an employer violates these rules.[1]

Regulations applicable to certain employers in the private sector

The Royal Decrees of 22 February 1998 (*Moniteur belge*, 18 March 1998) and of 24 September 1998 (*Moniteur belge*, 7 November 1998) have adopted a new provision since 1 January 1999: the immediate declaration of employment in three economic sectors: construction, public surface transport and temporary employment agencies.

Affected employers must provide the National Social Security Office (*Office national de sécurité sociale*)[2] with certain information relating to workers via electronic mail; and they must do so no later then the worker's commencement date. This new regulation, which will likely encompass all economic sectors in the near future, ensures the better and regular monitoring of the declaration of workers.

Foreign workers

Royal Decree No. 34 of 20 July 1967 on the employment of foreign workers (*Moniteur belge*, 29 July 1967) incorporates the principle of prior authorisation to hire. Its aim is to prevent migrant workers from being recruited without first determining whether Belgium's labour market needs them, and to ensure that those who are available for work in Belgium are given priority for employment.

This means that employers may not normally hire workers (blue-collar or white-collar) who do not have Belgian nationality or who are not a EEA nationals, unless they have obtained prior authorisation to hire from the regional Minster with responsibility for employment.

When an employer is granted leave to employ, the worker is automatically granted a work permit. But the fact is that the decision of the Council of Ministers on 1 August 1974 to put an end to immigration is still in effect.

Regulations on the employment of foreign workers not only cover persons under employment contracts but also foreign nationals with or without contracts, working under the authority of another person (for example, volunteers, young *au pair*, and trainees).

---

1. This is a measure whereby the Employment Inspector officially notifies the judicial authorities of a breach so that the judicial authorities can prosecute the alleged offender under criminal law.

2. A state body with responsibility for collecting social security contributions payable on behalf of employed workers. These contributions fund all social benefits such as unemployment and health insurance.

Royal Decree No. 34 of 20 July 1967 does not counteract regulations on self-employed foreigners, especially with regard to the issuing of employment cards by the Minister for the middle class.

Foreign workers without a work permit are generally employed without being registered in employment registers (see points a and b above).

Over and above these irregularities lies the additional problem that such workers do not have valid residence permits, as laid down in the Act of 15 December 1980 on the access, short-term stay, settlement and expulsion of foreigners (*Moniteur belge*, 31 December 1980).

2. SANCTIONS AGAINST THE EMPLOYMENT OF FOREIGNERS IN AN IRREGULAR SITUATION

Only those sanctions that specifically refer to the employment of foreigners in an irregular situation are examined here. The three types of "sanctions" vary according to the stage reached in the procedure.

The "inquisitorial" phase[3]

Employment inspectors do not have judicial powers but the Act of 16 November 1972 on employment inspection (*Moniteur belge*, 8 December 1972) accordingly gave them considerable powers to ensure they carry out their work effectively.

It is for this reason that the Act of 1 June 1993 (*Moniteur belge*, 17 June 1993) added paragraph 2 to Article 4 of the 1972 Act. It states that the Minister of Employment and Labour may introduce an action for suspension before the President of the Commercial Tribunal[4] at the request of the Employment Law Inspectorate.[5] It involves an emergency interim ruling which, at the Minister's request, enables the President of the Tribunal to suspend one or more activities of an employer guilty of breaches, such as, employing foreign workers illegally residing in the country or workers violating regulations on employment documentation or social security.

In concrete terms, irrespective of the legal procedure employed and prior to any ruling on the substance of the case, this type of procedure terminates the activity of an enterprise (or division thereof), a workplace or any other place where the employment of foreign workers residing illegally in Belgium has been established.

In this context, the Act of 13 April 1995 (*Moniteur belge*, 25 April 1995) is also important. It contains measures to curb the trading in human beings and child pornography. Article 9 empowers the Ministry of Employment and Labour to introduce an action of suspension, this time before

---

3. The "inquisitorial" phase should be understood to mean the administrative inquiry usually carried out by Employment Inspectors prior to any judicial procedure.

4. The President of the Commercial Tribunal has been given the task to rule on this action because it is based on Chapter VII of the Act of 14 July 1991 on commercial practices and on consumer information and protection (*Moniteur belge*, 29 August 1991), which outlaws unfair competition.

5. This procedure has been incorporated into the law on labour inspection because all departments of the Employment Inspectorate continue to be those most heavily involved in enforcing Royal Decree No. 34 of 20 July 1967 relating to the employment of foreign workers.

the President of the Court of First Instance[6] (another example of an emergency interim ruling), if employment inspectors have sufficient reason to suspect, or discover violations of employment legislation – especially in places where the trading in human beings (for example, sweatshops in the garment industry where foreign workers are forced to work against their will) and child pornography are present.

The judicial phase

All reports drafted by Employment Law Inspectorate are submitted to the Labour Auditor[7] who assesses the merits of the case according to employment law.[8] If the Labour Auditor decides to deal with breaches resulting from the employment of foreigners in an irregular situation, he/she must proceed with this action before the Criminal Court (*Tribunal correctionnel*) (criminal jurisdiction), since the labour courts, due to their composition, are considered incompetent in criminal matters.[9]

Sanctions under criminal law

Article 27 of Royal Decree No. 34 of 2 July 1967 on the employment of foreign workers provides for sanctions that vary according to the kind of breach committed. These are examined below.

i) The following persons (legal entities only)[10] are liable to a jail sentence of one month to one year and/or a fine of BEF 600 000 to BEF 3 000 000[11] (Article 27 of Royal Decree No. 34):

    a. Any employer, his/her appointee[12] or representative[13] who causes or permits the employment of non-Belgian or non-EU nationals, without previously obtaining authorisation from the regional minister for employment. To this is coupled the

---

6. A judge who "naturally" knows breaches of criminal law.

7. With regard to implementation, the work of the Labour Auditor and labour law itself are unique in the context of Belgian social legislation. The Labour Auditor's Office is a prosecuting department in the employment field - it specialises in pursuing legal action against breaches of employment legislation.

8. The Labour Auditor may therefore decide not to proceed with a report purely on the grounds of the case's merit. But in exercising this power, the Auditor must take account of the restrictive directives of criminal policy laid down by the Minister of Justice and *procureurs généraux* (senior judges in certain courts).

9. Labour courts are made up of professional judges (Presidents of Divisions) and non-professional judges, sometimes called "employment judges", who are appointed for a 5-year term.

10. Under Belgian criminal law, there are no criminal sanctions against individual entities.

11. Between euros 14 873.61 and euros 74 368.06 (conversion rate: euro 1 = BEF 40.3399).

12. Belgian social legislation uses the term prépose to identify only those employees (for example, directors of personnel) charged with overseeing others and, in a way, acting as their employer (the head of personnel, for example). The "appointee" must therefore have a managerial function, authority to make decisions that commit the employer and ensure compliance with employment legislation.

13. The "representative" (*mandataire*) is someone who stands in for the employer, is charged with carrying out one or more tasks on his/her own account, and ensures compliance with employment law on the employer's behalf (for example, a human relations department). The representative differs from the appointee in that the former is not dependent on the employer, and performs his/her job quite autonomously.

additional aggravation that the worker is neither allowed nor authorised to settle or reside in Belgium for more than three months. In such circumstances, the Criminal Court may impose not only criminal sanctions (as set out above) but also order the total or partial *shutdown* of the enterprise whose managers breached the law (a judge only resorts to this measure in serious cases).

b. Any person bringing into the country a foreign worker (from outside the EEA) who does not have a valid work permit but who seeks employment. This provision targets the numerous intermediaries who have set up often lucrative businesses that enable workers recruited in certain countries to enter Belgium even though they do not hold a work permit prior to entry.

c. Any person who has, in any way, either accepted or demanded payment for bringing foreign workers (from outside the EEA) into Belgium, for obtaining employment for them or for completing administrative formalities provided for under Royal Decree No. 34. It also applies to any person who in acting as an intermediary has sought to mislead workers, employers or competent authorities.

This provision mainly targets people who "act" as employers and who frequently apply for authorisation to employ a person without actually having a job opening. They demand money from foreign "workers" under the presumption that they will find them work. Foreigners who thus obtain a work permit subsequently discover that these so-called "employers" are unable to offer them any work at all and, as they usually have no money, quickly become victims of other exploiters.

Article 32 of Royal Decree No. 34 states that, with regard to the breaches set out above, the judge may take account of mitigating circumstances to reduce the scale of the punishment as long as the fine is no less than 80% of the statutory figure.

ii) The following persons (legal entities only) are liable to a *jail sentence* of between 8 days and 1 year and/or a *fine* of between BEF 170 000 and BEF 600 000[14] (Article 27 of Royal Decree No. 34):

a. Any employer, his/her appointee or representative who causes or permits the employment of non-Belgian or non-EU nationals without previously obtaining authorisation from the regional minister for employment.

b. Any employer, his/her appointee or representative who withholds work permits intended for workers or makes them cover the costs for which they are responsible.

c. Any employer who, without good reason, terminates a worker's employment prior to the date set out in the contract, and possibly enforced by the regulation on the granting of employment authorisation. In practice, when a worker does not normally reside in Belgium, granting authorisation to hire and issuing work permits depend on the employer and the worker signing the contract. The employer must ensure that the employee will have regular work during the employment period – usually 12 months from the point at which he/she begins work. This measure is intended to prevent foreign workers from being heedlessly recruited and dismissed shortly afterwards, thereby increasing the number of unemployed. An employer, therefore, though having abided by the regulation and without fear of infringing it, may be liable to criminal sanction.

---

14. Between euros 4 214.19 and euros 14 873.16 (conversion rate: euro 1 = BEF 40.3399).

d. Any person who interferes with the monitoring work of employment inspectors.

Article 32 of Royal Decree No. 34 states that, with regard to the breaches set out above, the judge may take account of mitigating circumstances to reduce the scale of the punishment as long as the fine is no less than 40% of the statutory figure.

iii) In the case of the breaches set out in i) and ii), the fine is imposed as many times as there are people who do not have Belgian nationality (and are not EU nationals) who are affected by the breaches committed. The employer is also responsible under civil law for fines imposed on his appointees or representatives.

A *special confiscation* measure (a penalty that is issued over and above the fine and/or imprisonment) may also be applied to movable property. This includes immovable property which by destination or incorporation constitute the object of the offence or which helped or were intended to commit the breach (such as, the vehicle used to bring the foreign workers into the country illegally) even where these goods are not the property of the guilty party.[15]

The criminal transaction

Article 216bis of the Code of Criminal Instruction contains a "judgement-free procedure"[16] for certain breaches of criminal law. This procedure, which is conducted by the Labour Auditor under criminal employment law, is usually referred to as a "transaction", and brings the public action to a close through the payment of a sum of money. This sum may be neither more than the amount of the fine under criminal law nor less than BEF 2 000.[17]

For certain serious breaches, including the illegal employment of foreign workers and the illegal trafficking in workers (for example, the breaches set out above in i), the transaction put forward by the Labour Auditor may not be less than the minimum for administrative fines [BEF 150 000[18] (see below)]. When extenuating circumstances are allowed, the transaction may not be less than 80% of the minimum administrative fine (BEF 120 000).[19]

The sum of the transaction shall be multiplied as appropriate by the number of workers for which the fine has been imposed.

The administrative phase

The Act of 30 June 1971 on administrative fines (*Moniteur belge*, 13 July 1971) punishes breaches of certain criminal employment laws with administrative fines. It acts as a kind of "check" on the power of Labour Auditors to discontinue proceedings under the criminal employment law.

When a Labour Auditor decides not to prosecute a breach concerning the employment of foreign workers in an irregular situation under criminal law,[20] a civil servant in the Ministry of

---

15. This is covered by an express dispensation in Article 42(1) of the Penal Code.

16. The guilty party is therefore not brought before the Criminal Court.

17. Euros 49.58 (conversion rate: euro 1 = BEF 40.3399).

18. Euros 3 718.40 (conversion rate: euro 1 = BEF 40.3399).

19. Euros 2 974.72 (conversion rate: euro 1 = BEF 40.3399).

20. Or institute a criminal transaction. It is not possible to institute a criminal sanction and impose an administrative fine simultaneously. Even where a criminal prosecution leads to an acquittal, it cannot trigger an administrative fine.

Employment and Labour [the Director-General of the Investigation Department (*Service d'études*)] may decide to impose an administrative fine, but only on the employer (the legal or natural person) or on those persons set out in i) b. c. and ii) d. Notification of a decision on an administrative fine halts the public action. The administrative fine must be paid within three months of notification of the decision. The employer, or person contesting the decision,[21] may appeal to the Labour Tribunal. This appeal suspends the implementation of the administrative decision except where it has been taken as a result of a breach set out in i). In these cases, because of the extreme seriousness of the breach, an appeal to the Labour Tribunal does not suspend the obligation to pay the administrative fine.[22]

Administrative fines for the illegal employment of foreign workers are extremely high:

- For the breaches examined in i), the fine ranges from BEF 150 000 to BEF 500 000[23] per illegally employed worker; this is multiplied by the number of people affected by the breach.

The civil servant referred to above may, in the event of extenuating circumstances, impose an administrative fine that is less than the minimum provided for by the law as long as it does not fall below a threshold of 80% of this statutory minimum. The purpose is to ensure that the administrative fine remains enough of a deterrent.

The administrative fine for breaches analysed in i) ranges from BEF 15 000 to BEF 100 000[24] and is multiplied by the number of illegally employed workers. There is a ceiling of BEF 4 000 000.[25]

Here again the Director-General of the Investigation Department may, in the case of extenuating circumstances, impose an administrative fine that is less than the minimum provided for in the law, as long as it does not fall below a threshold of 40% of the statutory minimum.

When there is more than one breach [for example, in the case of simultaneous breaches of Royal Decree No. 34 and of other employment laws, such as, the holding of employment documentation (see a) above)], administrative fines may be imposed together as long as they do not exceed a total of BEF 4 800 000.[26] No ceiling exists on simultaneous fines for breaches referred to in i).

3.   SANCTIONS UNDER CIVIL LAW

Article 6bis of Royal Decree No. 34 provides for a specific civil sanction in addition to the criminal and administrative sanctions referred to above.

Any worker illegally residing in Belgium who is detained in the course of an inspection will normally be ordered to leave the country. Article 6bis identifies who must pay the repatriation costs.

It affects all those guilty of breaches listed in i). They are jointly responsible for the accommodation, living, health care and repatriation costs of the worker concerned, as well as for the costs that the Belgian state has had to pay for family members illegally living with him/her.

21. The tax authorities are responsible for recovering the fine in question.
22. If the administrative decision is overturned by the Labour Tribunal, the fine is naturally reimbursed.
23. Between euros 3 718.40 and euros 12 394.68 (conversion rate: euro 1 = BEF 40.3399).
24. Between euros 371.84 and euros 2 478.94 (conversion rate: euro 1 = BEF 40.3399).
25. Euros 99 157.41 (conversion rate: euro 1 = BEF 40.3399).
26. Euros 118 988.89 (conversion rate: euro 1 = BEF 40.3399).

If these persons fail to pay the sums owed, tax authorities are responsible for recovering the sums concerned.

The expenses in question have been determined on a flat-rate basis in the Royal Decree of 4 August 1996 (*Moniteur belge*, 4 September 1996). They are BEF 1 290[27] per person per full day for accommodation, living and health care costs, and BEF 46 320[28] for repatriation costs.

---

27. Euros 31.98 (conversion rate: euro 1 = BEF 40.3399).
28. Euros 1 148.24 (conversion rate: euro 1 = BEF 40.3399).

Combating the Irregular Employment of Foreigners in Germany: Sanctions against Employers and Key Areas of Irregular employment

by
Rainer Irlenkaueuser
(Director, Ministry of Labour and Social Affairs, Bonn)

1. PRELIMINARY REMARKS

The employment of foreigners in an irregular situation is just one feature of the overall issue of illegal employment. While other forms of illegal employment (such as illegal hiring out of workers, benefit fraud and moonlighting) are often more extensive, the political debate often centres on the irregular employment of foreigners, especially citizens of non-EU/EEA countries who take up employment in Germany despite regulations on residence and work permits.

In principle, foreign employees seeking work in Germany require both a residence permit and a work permit, unless special rules apply. In this context, the issuance of a residence permit and a work permit does not necessarily go hand in hand; certain groups of persons whose presence in Germany is either permitted or tolerated can only legally take up employment after so-called "waiting periods".

Foreigners, however, who come under the EU or EEA regulations on free movement and who have a special legal entitlement to reside in Germany are not obliged to obtain the employment office's approval before engaging in dependent employment. Exceptions are permissible based on intergovernmental agreements, by laws or ordinances.

The Ordinance on Work Permits annuls the work permit requirement in a number of cases (including cross-border traffic, student internships, and for board members of legal entities and of partnerships and senior executives). There are also exceptions to the fundamental cessation of recruitment, which has existed since 1973, that allow for the granting of work permits – if the employment of foreigners does not negatively affect the German labour market; if no German or equivalent foreign worker is available; and if foreign workers are not employed on less favourable terms than comparable domestic employees. Apart from regional exceptions (including the US and Switzerland), the so-called Ordinance on Exceptions to the Cessation of Recruitment defines the prerequisites for and the duration of permitted employment for various occupational activities, which must be fulfilled in addition to the previously mentioned conditions. Work permits are granted in a number of cases, including for professional cooks, seasonal workers, contract workers and frontier commuters. Activities that do *not* require approval or work permits often provide a back door for illegal employment.

In Germany, the irregular employment of foreigners is considered socially harmful, undesirable from the point of view of labour market policy and as having a negative effect on fair competition. Owing to the large number of undetected cases, it is impossible to reliably estimate the exact extent of irregular employment and the resultant damage caused to the national economy and society as a whole. Calculations, however, reveal that 10 000 lost jobs - regardless of the practices involved - result in lost taxes and social insurance contributions amounting to DEM 310 million.

The constant rise in regulatory fines and warning charges imposed by the Federal Labour Office, which carries out a major proportion of the checks, indicates that this is a "growth market". Although the global figures for regulatory fines (1998: DEM 225 million; 1997: DEM 172.9 million; 1995: DEM 110.5 million) say relatively little, fines imposed for all forms of illegal employment of foreigners (1998: DEM 50.8 million; 1997: DEM 42.4 million) show a substantial increase. Regulatory fines imposed on employers for illegally employing foreigners amounted to DEM 47.4 million, while fines paid by illegally employed foreigners totalled DEM 1.9 million. Employers had to pay regulatory fines of approximately DEM 580 000 for illegally employing foreign temporary workers. Regulatory fines amounting to approximately DEM 910 000 were imposed on general contractors in cases of indirect illegal employment of foreigners.

2. SANCTIONS

In combating the irregular employment of foreigners, German legislators concentrate on sanctions against the employer. The reason is that employers often make a substantial profit from the irregular employment of foreigners, frequently exploit the illegal foreigners and distort competition. Without this demand, the irregular employment of foreigners would decline substantially. As the employer is often located in the country, the execution of regulatory fines and criminal prosecutions is possible without great difficulty. Germany has greatly increased sanctions, against employers in particular, in recent years. A further tightening of regulations is currently in debate.

Illegal employment of foreigners

Sanctions against employers

Regulatory fines

The maximum regulatory fine for an employer who hires a foreigner without the necessary work permit was raised from DEM 100 000 to DEM 500 000 on 1 January 1998. This increase is intended to draw attention to the particular social harm caused by the illegal employment of foreigners. To ensure that the offender will not benefit from the economic advantage sought in hiring illegal foreigners, the amount imposed may also exceed the range of the regulatory fine.

Cases of indirect illegal employment of foreigners are also subject to a regulatory fine of up to DEM 500 000. If a general contractor knowingly or negligently allows subcontractors to employ foreigners without work permits, he is guilty of indirect illegal employment of foreigners. In contrast to the previous law, where gross negligence was the decisive aspect, any form of negligence is now sufficient and the range of fines has been increased. A regulatory fine can also be imposed on legal entities and associations of individuals.

A regulatory fine of up to DEM 50 000 can be imposed on an employer if he obtains a work permit for a foreign employee under false pretences, by providing erroneous information on wages, working hours, or other working conditions.

Based on bilateral intergovernmental agreements and the Act on the Posting of Workers, companies in CEE countries which employ their own workers to carry out work and services on behalf of a domestic company (for example, the building of a house) must comply with the general conditions of the collective wage agreement or, at least, the minimum conditions (in this case, the minimum wage in the construction sector). Companies may face a regulatory fine of up to DEM 1 million if they violate minimum working conditions. General contractors who knowingly or negligently allow subcontractors to employ foreign workers in violation of minimum working conditions may also be fined DEM 1 million.

Foreigners employed in Germany as contract workers require a work permit, for which the employer must pay a fee. If this fee is reimbursed either by the foreign worker or by any third party, the employer can face a regulatory fine of up to DEM 50 000.

An employer who refuses to co-operate with regulatory checks or denies entry to business premises may be subject to a regulatory fine of up to DEM 50 000.

Criminal offences

To protect foreign illegal workers against exploitation, Germany imposes a three-year maximum prison sentence or a fine on employers if working conditions deviate substantially from those of comparable German employees. A prison sentence of between six months and five years is possible in particularly serious cases. This provision is also intended to maintain order on the labour market.

Germany imposes a prison sentence of up to one year or a fine for employing a substantial number of illegal foreigners (more than five) for an extended period (at least 30 calendar days) and also for the repeated, wilful employment of foreigners without work permits. A prison sentence of up to three years or a fine can be imposed in particularly serious cases.

Other sanctions

An employer who hires foreign workers without the necessary work permits must bear the often substantial costs of repatriation and may be excluded from all public contracts for a two-year period if sentenced to more than three months in prison or fined more than DEM 5 000.

As neither social insurance contributions nor taxes are usually paid in the case of the illegal employment of foreigners, the corresponding duties and taxes have to be paid in arrears.

Contracting companies from CEE countries that violate the prescribed working conditions may be excluded from further work in Germany. The strict liability of the general contractor under the Act on the Posting of Workers is now, as of 1 January 1999, also applied to companies from CEE countries performing contracts for work and services. This new regulation is intended to incite general contractors to be more careful when selecting and monitoring subcontractors. If they fail to pay, the general contractor must accept responsibility for their obligations (such as, minimum wage and contributions to holiday funds).

Sanctions against the worker

Foreign workers employed in the Federal Republic of Germany without a work permit can be fined up to DEM 10 000, which is far more stringent than the previous law that stipulates a maximum regulatory fine of DEM 1 000.

Illegal hiring out of workers

In Germany, the professional hiring out of workers requires a licence from the Federal Labour Office. Agencies for the provision of manpower from the EU or the EEA can obtain a licence on the same conditions as German nationals.

Sanctions against agencies for the provision of manpower

Regulatory fines

An agency licensed to hire out workers that hires out a foreign worker without a work permit is threatened by a regulatory fine of up to DEM 500 000, just as any other employer who hires an illegal foreigner.

Criminal offences

An agency for the provision of manpower that hires out illegal foreigners without a hiring out licence faces a prison sentence of up to three years or a fine. A prison sentence of between six months and five years is possible in particularly serious cases.

Sanctions against the user firm

Regulatory fines

A user firm that employs an illegal foreign temporary worker commits a regulatory offence which is punishable by a fine of up to DEM 500 000 (previously DEM 100 000).

Criminal offences

As with the illegal employment of foreigners, a user firm that hires an illegal foreign temporary worker under working conditions that deviate substantially from those of a comparable German temporary worker is liable to a prison sentence of up to three years or a fine. A prison sentence of between 6 months and 5 years may be imposed in particularly serious cases.

A user firm that employs illegal foreign temporary workers on a major scale (more than five illegal foreign workers for at least 30 calendar days), or repeatedly, also faces a possible prison sentence of up to one year or a fine. A prison sentence of up to three years may apply in particularly serious cases.

Other sanctions

Even if the temporary work contract between the temporary work agency and the temporary worker is invalid, an employment relationship nevertheless exists between the user firm and its temporary worker. The latter has a claim on the user firm, at least for the wage agreed upon with the temporary work agency. The user firm is also liable for taxes and social security contributions.

Illegal employment placement or recruitment from abroad

The unauthorised placement or recruitment of non-EU/EEA foreigners constitutes a criminal offence subject to punishment in the form of a prison sentence of up to three years or a fine. The prison sentence ranges from six months to five years in serious cases. The Federal Labour Office has made it clear that no work permit is to be given to workers from non-EU/EEA countries if their employment came as a result of unauthorised employment placement or recruitment

3. CHARACTERISTICS OF FOREIGN WORKERS IN IRREGULAR EMPLOYMENT SITUATIONS AND KEY AREAS FOR ACTIVITIES OF THIS KIND

Business sectors

Foreigners are illegally employed in virtually every sector of the economy. The key fields – with different regional and seasonal weightings - are the construction and associated industries, the hotel and restaurant sector, cleaning services, agriculture and forestry, horticulture and landscaping, food production, passenger and goods transport, metalworking companies, brochure distribution and funfairs. Businesses in the entertainment sector and door-to-door sales teams are also particularly susceptible to the use of illegal foreign workers. There is growing illegal employment on private building sites and in private households. Key areas also include sectors that use subcontractors.

Violations primarily occur in small and medium-sized companies, whereas large companies try to comply with the provisions on residence and work permits.

Regional key areas

In regional terms, the employment of illegal foreign workers is prevalent in major cities, because of greater anonymity. But the situation also often depends on the *type* of work – for example, seasonal work in agriculture.

Qualifications

Illegally employed foreigners are predominantly given work as helpers, performing activities that require few technical qualifications. But there are also signs of a growing trend towards the employment of skilled or trained personnel, for example, in construction or nursing.

Qualified skilled workers, such as, electricians, butchers, bricklayers, plumbers and welders, as well as highly specialised engineers, are often employed in addition to plain helpers.

The great majority of illegally employed workers originate from the CEE countries, including the former Yugoslavia and Turkey.

Special forms of perpetration

In addition to the forging of passports to feign EU citizenship and the forging of work permits, illegal foreigners constantly circumvent restrictions imposed by the law on work permits.

Foreigners with work permits for seasonal agricultural work, for example, have built dwellings and renovated agricultural buildings. Persons with permits to work as helpers in the restaurant sector have also been employed on building projects.

Foreigner nationals often claim that the work they are performing is private or unpaid help for friends, or that it is done for their own use. For instance, many have claimed that they were renovating their own accommodation and presented corresponding rent agreements as proof. Investigations, however, revealed that they were sham rent agreements designed to conceal their illegal work.

In other cases, groups of foreign nationals claimed that they were members of a partnership and thus exempt from the Ordinance on Work Permits. Partnerships of this kind purportedly signed contracts with third-party companies for the construction of houses, the contracts being fulfilled by the partnerships. In reality, however, it was purely a matter of circumventing the law, because the circumstances constituted the illegal employment of foreigners.

In the context of purported contracts for labour and materials, the restricted field of activity often is not respected: other work is performed that is not covered by the law on work permits.

On the basis of a bilateral intergovernmental agreement, foreign computer specialists are allowed to execute certain contracts for work and services in this sector. But inspectors discovered that the limitations were not observed, thereby revealing that these specialists worked illegally.

Illegal Migration, Overstay and Illegal Working in Japan Development of Policies and their Evaluation

by

Yasushi Iguchi

(Professor, Faculty of Economics, Kwansei-Gakuin University, Japan)

1. INTRODUCTION

This paper reviews the development of illegal migration, overstay and employment in Japan and the countermeasures by authorities, which include juridical and administrative sanctions and inter-ministerial and international co-operation. Economic developments in East Asia and the labour market situation in Japan are essential to any re-examination of illegal immigration, illegal overstay, illegal employment, trafficking (and prevention efforts), inter-ministerial co-operation and the process of deportation.

2. GENERAL BACKGROUND

Economic development, labour market and international migration in Asia

Thailand's monetary crisis in July 1997 proved to be highly contagious on other economies in the region. The hardest hit was Indonesia, which remains a source of concern given the severe poverty and political instability. There are signs that the economies of Thailand, Malaysia and Korea are improving, although the labour market situation is still deteriorating. The reverse movement of workers from urban to rural areas continues. Poverty is increasing, especially in countries hardest-hit by the crisis (Lee, 1998). It is true that China has been relatively unaffected by the crisis, but it too suffers from the restructuring of state enterprises and rising unemployment (Iguchi, 1998).

The Japanese economy was further deteriorating as a result of the negative impact of both domestic and international financial crises since the second half of 1997. Bankruptcies soared in the first half of 1998 and unemployment rose to 4.6% in January 1999, as further restructuring of large enterprises ensued. Fortunately, several measures were taken to stabilise and revitalise the financial sector. The Japanese yen has appreciated to around 115–120 JPY per USD while the Tokyo stock exchange rose to JPY 16 000 of the Nikkei average in April 1999.

In East Asia as a whole, unemployment may have reached 20 million in 1998 and is still increasing. As a result of negative labour market tendencies, the potential for illegal migration may be growing.

Basic framework for accepting foreign workers in Japan

The framework for accepting foreign workers is stipulated, on the one hand, in the Economic Plan (1996) and Employment Counter Measures Plan (1996) and, on the other, in the Immigration Control and Refugees Recognition Act. The former prescribes basic policy for accepting foreign workers, while the latter prescribes concrete criteria and measures.

Japan accepts, as much as possible, foreigners who posses technology-related skills and knowledge; unskilled foreign workers, however, are carefully examined, according to the present Economic Plan and the Employment Countermeasures Plan decided by the Cabinet.

The Immigration Control and Refugees Recognition Act classifies two categories of foreigners. Table 1 indicates the numbers of foreigner workers and their professional activity. The government's basic policy is applied only in Table 1 of the Act (Iguchi, 1999).

Recent development of foreign workers in Japan

According to Ministry of Labour estimates, the total number of foreign workers in Japan rose by almost 5% in 1997 to 660 000 or 1.2% of the total workforce (Table 1).

First, based on Alien Registration Statistics, foreigners who have residence status for work purposes amounted to 107 000. Second, the number of foreign workers of Japanese descent (second and third generation) was 234 000. Their rise in numbers is mainly attributable to the influx of Latin American *Nikkeijin*. Third, students and pre-college students working part-time on a non-designated activities permission may amount to around 32 000. Fourth, overstayers working illegally are estimated around 276 000. The share of overstayers among foreign workers as a whole may be 42%.

Table 1. **Estimates of foreign workers in Japan, 1993-1997**
(in thousands)

	1993	1994	1995	1996	1997
Qualified workers	95	106	88	98	197
Workers of TITP/WH	5	6	7	9	12
Student workers	39	33	32	30	33
Workers of Japanese descent	175	181	194	211	234
Illegal workers	300	294	287	285	277
Total, excluding permanent residents	**610**	**620**	**610**	**630**	**660**

Note: TITP: Technical Intern Traineeship Programmes. WH: Working during holiday.
Source: Ministry of Labour with some revision by author.

3. ILLEGAL MIGRATION TO JAPAN IS RAPIDLY INCREASING

The deterioration of East Asian economies since the middle of 1997 brought about higher illegal migration pressures (Table 2). As a result of tighter immigration controls and tough surveillance of Japanese coastlines, illegal migration has reverted to more sophisticated methods, advanced technology and complicated manoeuvrings. It often involves traffickers and organised crime groups, among which the Snake Heads of China are the most notorious. But other organised crime groups come from Hong Kong and China while several Japanese groups are also active (NPA, 1998*a*).

Illegal entries by boat are also on the rise. The Maritime Safety Agency (MSA) and the police have reported increasing cases of indictment, from 29 cases (679 persons) in 1996 to 73 cases (1 360 persons) in 1997. According to the MSA, instead of using Chinese fishing boats, many are increasingly reverting to cargo boats or Korean fishing boats as disguise. Just over 90% of illegal entrants were Chinese (MSA, 1999).

Some bilateral practical co-operation was finally reached between the MSA in Japan and the Maritime Police in Korea and between national and local police agencies in Japan and China to exchange information on smugglers (NPA, 1998*b*; MSA, 1999).

In May 1997, criminal sanctions against collective smuggling were introduced to the Immigration Control and Refugees Recognition Act (Art. 74-2–4). Illegal entries have since apparently been declining. Case studies indicate that illegal migrants and workers must pay enormous fees to intermediaries: approximately JPY 2 million (USD 16 500) for a trip from Thailand to Japan. According to information from the National Police Agency (NPA), the Snake Heads demand approximately JPY 2 to 3 million in advance. The conditions in which such illegal trafficking takes place are not yet clear.

Table 2. **Estimates of illegal entries, 1993-1997**

	1993	1994	1995	1996	1997
Total	**5 227**	**5 598**	**4 863**	**4 827**	**7 117**
Of which:					
China	541	799	812	1 068	3 045
Thailand	3 273	2 953	1 832	1 488	1 487
Philippines	624	815	973	1 087	1 089
Korea	154	104	144	181	323
Pakistan	101	217	311	348	321

Source: Ministry of Justice.

4. OVERSTAYERS: STABILISING IN NUMBER

The number of overstayers, which soared until 1993, has since stabilised (Table 3). The majority entered Japan with a tourist visa. The suspension of a visa-exemption arrangement has led to a decline of overstayers from certain Asian countries (MOJ, 1998*a*).

Table 3. **Overstayers by nationality, 1993-1998**

	1993	1994	1995	1996	1997	1998
Total	**298 646**	**293 800**	**286 704**	**284 500**	**282 986**	**276 810**
Of which:						
Korea	39 455	43 369	47 544	51 580	52 387	52 123
Philippines	35 392	37 544	39 763	41 997	42 547	42 608
China	33 312	39 738	39 511	39 141	38 957	37 590
Thailand	55 383	49 992	44 794	41 280	37 096	38 193
Peru	9 038	12 918	15 301	13 836	12 073	11 606

Source: Ministry of Justice.

Measures to tighten controls of visas for pre-college students, mainly from China and Korea, and entertainers, from the Philippines, have been effective to a certain degree. There is an increasing number of runaway trainees or technical intern trainees who become overstayers. In certain cases where Chinese state enterprises have undergone severe restructuring, some Chinese trainees ruin their prospects of being re-employed even when they leave Japan. Today, more than a half of overstayers remain in Japan for more than two years. When they are indicted, a higher percentage of them demand hearing and filing of objections after immigration examination according to the Act. This is because more overstayers are marrying Japanese nationals. As a result, the Minister of Justice now issues more and more special permissions for residence (MOJ, 1998*a*).

In February 1999, the Immigration Control and Nationality Act was amended to include a new criminal sanction against overstaying, and the re-entry prohibition after deportation was extended from one to five years (Art. 5).

5.   PROBLEMS OF ILLEGAL EMPLOYMENT

Measures against illegal employment

The crackdown on illegal workers, intermediaries and employers intensified in the 1990s. The legal basis of the crackdown was strengthened in the Immigration Control and Refugees Recognition Act in 1989. At that time, sanctions on employers (also applicable to intermediaries) were introduced (Art. 73-2) in addition to sanctions against illegally working foreigners (Art. 73).

The number of employees caught violating regulations has slowly been declining since 1994 (Table 4). The National Police Agency has made efforts to hire special staff to cope with increasing crimes committed by foreigners, especially overstayers (NPA, 1998*a*). But indictment of foreigners is complicated, time consuming and costly. The Immigration Bureau of the Ministry of Justice (MOJ) has established special task forces in the Immigration Bureaux in Tokyo, Osaka and Nagoya. Also, the Team for Special Measures against vile cases was set up in the Tokyo Immigration Bureau.

New detention houses built near international airports seemingly take human rights into consideration (MOJ, 1998*b*). An intensive crackdown on foreigners violating the Immigration Control and Refugees Recognition Act has been introduced in every local Immigration Bureau since 1997 (MOJ, 1998*a*). In October 1998, the headquarters to promote the intensive crackdown of illegally residing foreigners was established in the Ministry of Justice. For example, immigration authorities implemented an intensive crackdown in 28 prefectures resulting in the indictment of 1 018 illegal stayers and entrants. The Ministry of Labour, which is responsible for the Labour Standard Administration and Public Employment Service (PES), has different functions. Labour standards inspectors have the right to investigate an establishment at any time and to protect workers, including foreigners. The PES conducts placement services for foreign workers permitted to work, especially second or third generation ex-emigrants from Japan (*Nikkeijin*).

Another important issue for the PES is to combat illegal intermediaries and protect workers from vile brokers. The basis of such activity is the Employment Security Law and Worker Dispatching Undertakings Law. But the power of the PES is limited to inspection of intermediaries and it can only report vile intermediaries to police when they have several kinds of information.

Situation of illegal workers

It is not easy to grasp the situation of illegal workers. Statistics on illegal workers who violate the Immigration Control and Refugees Recognition Act, however, do indicate some common features of illegal workers. Other analyses provide the results of case studies (Yorimitsu, 1997; Tokyo Labour Institute, 1996). According to a 1997 study on numbers of illegal workers by nationality, Korea had the largest share (25%), followed by China (18.8%), the Philippines (12.2%), Thailand (10.8%) and Iran (5.35%) (MOJ, 1998*b*) (Table 4).

Men account for 62% of illegal workers. Women's proportion, however, continues to increase, though the number of illegal workers (both men and women) dropped in 1997. The activities of illegal workers by sex show that men are principally found in construction (35.2%) and production (28.2%), while women work mainly as hostesses (40.2%) and waitresses (15.5%) as well as factory workers (14.0%).

Table 4. **Illegal workers by nationality, 1993-1997**

	1993	1994	1995	1996	1997
Total	**64 341**	**59 352**	**49 434**	**47 785**	**40 604**
Of which:					
Korea	11 865	10 730	10 529	11 444	10 346
China	4 989	7 311	7 595	7 401	7 810
Philippines	4 617	5 260	5 476	5 646	5 067
Thailand	12 685	10 654	6 948	5 561	4 483
Iran	8 886	5 628	3 246	3 180	2 225

Note: Illegal workers are foreigners indicted by the Immigration Control Bureau because of illegal employment.
Source: Ministry of Justice.

The residence status of illegal workers breaks down into "temporary visitors" (64.5%), "pre-college students" (11.5%) and others. The average daily pay of illegal workers is not particularly low: 62.5% of all illegal workers receive more than JPY 7 000 per day (approximately USD 58) (MOJ, 1998*b*). Illegal work is generally concentrated in and around the Tokyo Metropolitan Area and the region from Tokyo to Osaka. The regional distribution, however, is widening and illegal work can now be found in every prefecture.

The distribution of illegal workers by industrial sector may depend on the general distribution of foreign workers and the substitution and complementarity between legal and illegal workers. There are different reasons why Japanese workers do not work and foreign workers do in specific sectors: low wages (textile), poor working conditions (fabrication of metal) and irregular working time (food and drink). Some sectors, such as textiles, introduce trainees more intensively than others, while the food industry accepts foreigners of Japanese descent.

6.   CO-OPERATION AMONG THE THREE MINISTRIES

The three ministries mentioned above have been co-operating since 1992 to combat illegal working and overstay. Under this scheme, local immigration bureaux and police agencies collaborate to crackdown. For example, in January and June 1998, enormous and intensive crackdowns took place under such joint action, especially in and around the Tokyo Metropolitan Area: 2 617 foreigners were found to be violating the ICRR Act (MOJ, 1998*b*; NPA, 1998*a*).

Joint action between the Labour Standards Bureau and the other two authorities is a rare occurrence. In reality, the Japanese labour administration has no power to indict illegal workers, according to the Immigration Control and Refugees Recognition Act. But there have been cases where a local labour standards bureau and a local police agency have acted jointly to crackdown on the illegal dispatching of foreign workers.

In early 1999, the high-level committee of the three ministries agreed to play a more active role in the fight against illegal employment. Their co-operative efforts have gone hand in hand with a new framework to co-ordinate foreign worker policies among 17 ministries.

7.   ALTERNATIVES TO ILLEGAL WORKING

The Japanese government has encouraged companies to abstain from hiring illegal workers and to hire foreigners of Japanese descent or introduce Technical Intern Trainees (TIT) (Iguchi, 1998). The employment of foreigners of Japanese descent, such as Japanese-Brazilians or Japanese-Peruvians, has been facilitated by the Immigration Control and Refugees Recognition Act of 1989. Without the possibility of hiring foreigners of Japanese descent, it might have been almost impossible to reduce the country's dependency on illegal foreign workers.

The PES has a network with the Japanese-Brazilian Employment Centre in Sao Paolo in Brazil that helps to place foreign workers of Japanese descent all over Japan. The foundation of the centre is recognised as legal by the Brazilian government. Another way to avoid illegal employment is to promote the Technical Intern Traineeship Programme, which started in 1993. Those trainees who have passed an official skill test are permitted to change their status of residence from "trainee" to "designated activities" and to be employed by the same firm under an employment contract. Under the TITP, they may be employed with this status for a maximum of three years. The Japan International Training Co-operation Organisation (JITCO) co-ordinates the acceptance of foreign trainees, implements skill tests and encourages the proper acceptance of trainees.

Japanese embassies in several Asian countries have launched campaigns to discourage emigration to Japan for illegal employment.

8. DEPORTATION

Foreigners found violating the Immigration Control and Refugees Recognition Act are either prosecuted in accordance with the Act or deported to their home countries. When immigration control officers suspect someone of violating any of the items of Article 24 of the Act, they are to conduct a thorough investigation. If grounds of suspicion are sufficient, it is normally possible to detain the foreigner with a written detention order. The Immigration Inspector examines whether the suspect's actions fall under any item of Article 24 of the Act. If there is no objection to the findings, a written deportation order is issued and executed.

Illegal entrants from China are generally deported as a group, because many of them do not have any money and the number of deportees is so large. After consultation with the government of China, they are deported by ship or plane chartered by the Chinese government. The majority of deportees are sent back at their own expense. As it takes time to collect such expenses and to obtain visas from consulates, the detention period is often prolonged.

9. TRAFFICKING AND INVOLVEMENT OF CRIMINAL ORGANISATIONS

The trafficking of women and children has become an international concern. In Asia, the IOM reports the trafficking to Japan from Asian and Latin American countries. The OECD Ministerial Meeting in 1998 also recognised the importance of combating trafficking following the decision by the Stockholm Conference of NGOs in 1996. The main concern with trafficking in Japan is the growing number of commercial sex workers from Thailand, the Philippines, Korea and Colombia. According to information from the National Police Agency, foreign women engaged in entertainment businesses are often highly in debt, are sometimes deprived of their passports and do not receive full remuneration. In many cases, they are forced into prostitution. The phenomenon of street prostitution has been spreading from the Tokyo Metropolitan Area to other nearby cities (NPA, 1998*b*).

The number of foreign women used as prostitutes was 1 425 in 1997. According to the National Police Agency, the largest numbers were from Thailand (452), Korea (243), the Philippines (225) and Columbia (224). It is also noteworthy that, according to the Ministry of Justice, gangsters play an important role as intermediaries in the case of illegal female workers from Thailand and the Philippines (MOJ, 1998*b*; NPA, 1998*a*). The Employment Security Law (improper placement), the Prostitution Prevention Law and the Immigration Control and Refugees Recognition Act provide a solid legal basis for the crackdown on traffickers

A draft law to prevent the abuse of children in sex businesses was recently presented to the Japanese Parliament. In Tokyo, some NGOs have concluded agreements with embassies of Thailand and the Philippines to organise the rescue of trafficked women from those countries. This network may fill the vacuum between the government of Japan and the Asian embassies and meet the needs of foreign workers.

10. CONCLUDING REMARKS: GENERAL EVALUATION

Japanese policies to combat illegal employment are characterised by the implementation of consistent (and preventive) measures and sanctions. Preventive measures include the possibility to hire foreign workers of Japanese descent or introduce Technical Intern Trainees; they are complementary to sanctions. Sanctions include those against collective smuggling, illegal entry, overstaying, non-designated activities as well as illegal employment, hiring of illegal workers and serving as an intermediary.

Another characteristic of Japanese policy is that it does not allow for the regularisation of overstayers or illegal foreign workers. Instead, special permission of stay granted by the Minister of Justice allows foreigners in the process of deportation to acquire legal status for humanitarian reasons. Irrespective of improvements and the successes of measures taken by the government of Japan, several problems remain.

First, measures against illegal intermediaries have not been successful. In reality, illegal migration does not usually take place without illegal intermediaries or similar international networks. To tighten control of intermediaries, there should be more effective legal bases and co-operation among different administrations.

Second, international co-operation for information exchange with agencies in neighbouring countries is still very limited. Successful co-operation between agencies in Japan and China or Korea remains *ad hoc* and piecemeal. In general, bilateral co-operation should be expanded and based on the multilateral monitoring of progress and policies.

Third, sanctions on employers are not very flexible and theirs effects are very limited. In Japan, the imposition of sanctions on employers is a juridical measure, not administrative. Since the legal process is very burdensome and does not cover a large number of violations, the possibility of imposing administrative sanctions on employers of illegal workers should be considered.

It seems that the legal basis for inter-ministerial co-operation should be re-examined to encompass more effective joint action. The challenge to Japanese policy is whether it can reduce the country's dependency on foreigners in an irregular situation, without adopting regularisation measures. The Japanese government should seek, develop, and improve its current policies and strengthen international co-operation.

BIBLIOGRAPHY

CORNELIUS, W. and KUWAHARA, Y. (eds.) (1998), *US-Japan Comparative Study on Foreign Workers.*

GOVERNMENT OF JAPAN (1998), SOPEMI Japan Report, Tokyo.

IGUCHI, Y. (1997), *International Migration and Labour Market* (in Japanese), Japan Institute of Labour, Tokyo.

IGUCHI, Y. (1998), "Challenges for trainee programmes for foreigners in Japan: Growing importance of Technical Intern Traineeship programmes", *Japan Labour Bulletin*, October.

IGUCHI, Y. (1999), "Developments in the Japanese economy and their impacts on the labour market and migration" in *Labour Migration and the Recent Financial Crisis in Asia*, OECD, Paris.

LEE, E. (1998), *The Asian Financial Crisis*, ILO, Geneva.

MARITIME SAFETY AGENCY (MSA) (1999), "Crackdown on human smuggling by boat in 1998", *Immigration News Magazine*, Vol. 142, March.

MINISTRY OF JUSTICE (MOJ) IMMIGRATION CONTROL BUREAU (1998*a*), *Immigration Control 1998,* Tokyo.

MINISTRY OF JUSTICE (MOJ) (1998*b*), *White Paper on Crimes,* Tokyo.

MINISTRY OF LABOUR (MOL) (1998), *White Paper on Labour Economy*, Japan Institute of Labour, Tokyo.

NATIONAL POLICE AGENCY (NPA) (1998*a*), *White Paper on Police,* Tokyo.

NATIONAL POLICE AGENCY (NPA) (1998*b*), *Situation of foreigners and measures taken in the first half of 1998*, Tokyo.

TOKYO LABOUR INSTITUTE (1996), *Communication and Human Relationship of Foreign Workers*, Part 2, Tokyo Labour Institute, Tokyo.

YORIMITSU, M. (1997), "Troubles of illegal workers and labour consultation", *Troubles of Foreign Workers and Problems*, Employment Promotion Centre, Tokyo.

Current Dutch Legislation and Policy towards Preventing and Combating the Employment of Foreigners in an Irregular Situation
by
The Dutch Ministry of Social Affairs and Employment and the Dutch Ministry of Justice

1. INTRODUCTION

This document is a summary of the main aspects of policy and its implementation on this issue. This paper covers three items:

- The Aliens Employment Act and its implementation (including the need for interdisciplinary actions in practice).
- An overview of developments and the current state of affairs in relation to police supervision.
- A brief outline of the policy on aliens staying in the Netherlands for extended periods without having a valid residence permit.

2. THE ALIENS EMPLOYMENT ACT

Introduction

The Aliens Employment Act provides for the employment of foreign nationals within the Dutch labour market, to the extent that foreign nationals do not already have access to the Dutch labour market on some other grounds (such as asylum or family reunification). The Aliens Employment Act is aimed at the employer, who may only employ a foreign national if he – the employer – is in possession of an employment permit to be issued to the employee concerned.

The Aliens Employment Act came into effect on 1 September 1995, replacing a similar act dating from 1979. There has, in fact, been some form of legislation providing for the employment of foreign nationals since the 1930s.

The Dutch Minister of Social Affairs and Employment is responsible for the policy adopted in the field in question. Thus the Dutch Ministry of Social Affairs and Employment is specifically charged with the task of formulating the policy that applies with regard to access to the Dutch labour market as well as with upholding the Aliens Employment Act. The actual implementation of the Aliens Employment Act has been delegated to the (independent) Public Employment Service. Nevertheless, the ultimate political responsibility rests with the Dutch Minister of Social Affairs and Employment.

Policy regarding the entry of Foreign Nationals to the Dutch labour market

The objective of the Aliens Employment Act

Entry into the Netherlands with a view to engaging in some form of employment is, in principle, only possible if Dutch interests are thereby served. Dutch interests are considered to be served if there is no possibility of filling the vacancy with domestic labour or labour considered to be equivalent (so called "priority labour", or, in other words, EEA citizens and foreign nationals resident in the Netherlands who have free access to the labour market). Thus the policy regarding the admission of migrant workers is a restrictive policy.

The Aliens Employment Act has four objectives:

1. To restrict the entry of labour from outside of the EEA.
2. To improve the allocation within the labour market.
3. To counter illegal employment.
4. To allow foreign nationals who have been admitted to the Netherlands on a permanent basis the greatest possible choice of employment.

Objective 1: The restricted admission of labour from outside the EEA

A central principle of the Aliens Employment Act is that if priority labour is or can be expected to be available for a vacancy for which an employment permit is requested, the said request will be refused. Furthermore, the act also stipulates that the Public Employment Service must be notified of the vacancy at least five weeks before a request for a work permit is submitted, in order that optimal use may be made of the supportive function of the Public Employment Service.

Finally, the employer in question is required to pay at least the statutory monthly minimum wage. These grounds for refusal are mandatory – an employment permit will automatically be refused if any of these conditions is not met.

In addition to these mandatory grounds for refusal, there are also a number of optional grounds for refusal. The employer can be called to account for the effort made to recruit priority labour; if insufficient effort has been made in this respect an employment permit may be refused. Furthermore, the possibility of filling a vacancy with priority labour may not be hindered by the fact that the employer is offering an excessively low wage (a wage which is in line with the market is the norm), nor by the fact that the employer is failing to comply with the standards that apply to working conditions, labour relations and terms and conditions of employment.

Objective 2: The improvement of the allocation within the labour market

The employment of foreign nationals must not be allowed to lead to the displacement of other persons in search of employment. Thus it is important that a restrictive approach is adopted with regard to the issuing of employment permits. Having said this, the simple fact that there are other persons in search of employment does not automatically mean that all vacancies can be filled. When it comes to certain vacancies, it will be necessary to accept that there is no suitable labour amongst those currently seeking employment. In such a situation an employment permit will be granted.

The Aliens Employment Act also provides for the possibility of permits being issued for a limited period of time and subject to certain conditions. The issuing of such permits is intended to encourage employers to create the labour they need by means of (sectoral) training, for example. Thus the restrictive nature of the policy will continue to be upheld while at the same time the need for labour is not totally denied.

Objective 3: The countering of illegal employment

The employment of foreign nationals without an employment permit constitutes illegal employment. Illegal employment involves a number of undesirable aspects, such as the displacement of legal labour (in particular, those persons in search of employment who are entitled to some form of unemployment benefit). Because the employers in question generally omit to pay the relevant tax, employing workers on an illegal basis is cheaper. This also introduces a false competitive advantage. Furthermore, illegal employment makes it possible for illegal foreign nationals to stay in the Netherlands for extended periods and can also lead to an influx of foreign nationals who hope to establish a position for themselves in the Netherlands by engaging in illegal employment.

To make it easier for the authorities to counter illegal employment, both the Aliens Employment Act and the General Administrative Law Act bestow certain powers on the officials responsible for supervising the employment of foreign nationals. With a view to preventing exploitation, the act also makes it possible for a foreign national to bring an action to recover back wages. A court of law is also entitled to deprive the employer of the economic advantages gained by illegal employment.

Objective 4: Allowing foreign nationals who have been admitted to the Netherlands on a permanent basis the greatest possible choice of employment

Foreign nationals who have been admitted to the Netherlands on a permanent basis – amongst others, those in possession of a residence permit, refugees who have been allowed to enter the country and the partners of persons who have free access to the Dutch labour market – have free access to the Dutch labour market.

Furthermore, foreign nationals who are in possession of a residence permit during an uninterrupted period of three years for the purpose of employment and who have not established their main residence outside of the Netherlands by the end of this period, have free access to the Dutch labour market and, as such, they are entitled to greatest possible choice of employment. In this case an employment permit is no longer required for these foreign nationals.

Liability

The law holds the employer liable. In other words, the employer must be in possession of an employment permit and is liable to punishment under the terms of the Economic Offences Act if he – the employer - employs a foreign national without being in possession of an employment permit. The employment permit must be applied for by the employer and will be issued to the employer.

The foreign national in question is not actively involved in the application for an employment permit and is not liable to punishment under the terms of the Economic Offences Act in the event that he or she is illegally employed. However, the Ministry of Justice will check to ensure that the foreign national in question is entitled to reside in the Netherlands. If it turns out that the foreign national does not have a residence permit that is valid for the employment he or she is engaged in, the foreign national may be expelled.

There are certain groups of employees and certain activities that the Aliens Employment Act does not apply to. Examples of persons to whom the act does not apply include foreign correspondents and diplomatic and military personnel; examples of activities to which the act does not apply include the conducting of business meetings. In these cases it is evident that there is no displacement of priority labour.

The implementation of the Aliens Employment Act

The Dutch Minister of Social Affairs and Employment has delegated the authority to decide whether an application for an employment permit is to be granted or refused to the General Directorate of the Public Employment Service. This means that an employer wishing to apply for an employment permit must contact the Public Employment Service, not the Minister of Social Affairs and Employment.

The Public Employment Service

Until 1991 the Public Employment Service was part of the Ministry of Social Affairs and Employment. In 1991 the organisation was positioned outside of the Ministry. Thus the Public Employment Service is now an independent administrative body headed by a board of management made up of representatives of employers' organisations and trade unions and independent Crown-appointed members.

The Public Employment Service consists of a national organisation, 18 regional bureaux, some 220 local employment offices and about 65 training centres (Vocational Training Centres).

The choice of the Public Employment Service as the body to be charged with the task of implementing the Aliens Employment Act serves to emphasise the importance of the Aliens Employment Act as a labour market instrument. One of the stated objectives of the Aliens Employment Act is to enlist priority labour. To the extent that the people who fall in this category are unemployed, they are generally registered with the Public Employment Service. Thus every request for an employment permit is an opportunity for the Public Employment Service to help one of the unemployed persons on its register to find employment.

The application procedure for an employment permit

Five weeks before submitting an application for an employment permit, the employer in question must notify the local employment office of the vacancy in question. This gives the Public Employment Service the opportunity to suggest (unemployed) persons in search of employment for the vacancy. If the vacancy has not been filled within a period of five weeks, the employer is then entitled to apply to the Regional Manpower Services Bureau for an employment permit.

The Regional Manpower Services Bureau serves as the link between the employer and the national Public Employment Service, which will ultimately decide whether or not the application is to be granted.

Upon receiving an application the Regional Manpower Services Bureau will carry out an initial assessment. This assessment will cover both the procedural aspects (the personal details of the foreign national and the details regarding the pay and any training) and the intrinsic aspects (the availability of priority labour within the region, the employer's recruitment plans, the working conditions and the terms and conditions of employment).

On the basis of the above-mentioned assessment the Regional Director will make a recommendation to the Employment Permit Team of the national bureau. If the Regional Director is of the opinion that there is no priority labour available locally and that the employer has complied with all of the regulations pertaining to working conditions and terms and conditions of employment and has also made the necessary effort with regard to recruitment, he will recommend that the employment permit be granted. If the situation differs from the one outlined above, the Regional Director will issue a negative recommendation (Table 1). This recommendation made by the Regional Director is not binding for the manager of the national Employment Permit Team.

Upon receiving the application and the recommendation of the Regional Director, in the event that there is no supply of labour within the region, the national team will investigate whether the vacancy can be filled with national or European labour. The possibility of labour being available in the future via training and agreements with the two sides of industry – possibly in the form of a voluntary agreement – will also be taken into account when arriving at a decision. The outcome of this investigation may lead the national Employment Permit Team to disregard the recommendation made by the Regional Director.

The Employment Permit Team will make the ultimate decision regarding the application for an employment permit. If the decision is negative the employer can object to the legal team of the Public Employment Service. If the objection is declared to be unfounded, the employer can appeal to a court of law. If the matter is urgent, the president of the court can be asked to issue a temporary permit. This may mean that the president of the court will decree that the employer is considered to have been granted a temporary employment permit while awaiting the verdict regarding the objection or the appeal.

Table 1. **Work permits issued or refused, 1996-1998**

	Issued(total)	Refused(total)	Refused(after priority test)	Refused(without priority test)
1996	9 173	643	545	98
1997	11 062	570	530	40
1998	15 180	2 375	2 265	111

Source: Central Statistical Office.

Voluntary agreements

Large numbers of applications for employment permits may indicate that there is a problem regarding the supply of labour in a certain sector. The Public Employment Service has concluded various voluntary agreements with the two sides of industry – employers' organisations and the trade unions – in a number of sectors. These voluntary agreements aim to increase the influx of priority labour.

The action points covered by these agreements include, for example, improving working conditions and terms and conditions of employment, improving the image of a sector and increasing the opportunities for training. The Public Employment Service is also authorised to issue temporary employment permits, with a view to enabling employers to bridge the period within which the measures are supposed to have the desired effect.

The number of employment permit applications

Far from all of the applications for employment permits are subject to a full assessment in the light of all of the grounds for refusal specified by the Aliens Employment Act. An application for an employment permit to be extended will automatically be granted without any assessment being carried out if the employment permit in question concerns the same employment offered by the same employer. In a large number of cases, depending on the nature of the employment, only a limited assessment will be carried out if an employment permit is applied for. This applies, for example, to trainee placements, students doing lab work, key officials within an international concern and to artists and musicians who will be working in the Netherlands for less than four weeks. Above all, this limited assessment seeks to establish that the application in question actually applies to one of the above-mentioned categories. If this is the case, an investigation to find out whether there is priority labour available is redundant. Approximately 60% of the applications for employment permits are subject to a limited assessment, 25% are subject to a full assessment and 15% of the applications (applications that concern extensions of employment permits that have already been issued) are not assessed. From the point of view of labour market policy, the applications that are subject to a full assessment are the most relevant, because the granting of these applications may possibly lead to the displacement of priority labour within the labour market.

The upholding of the Aliens Employment Act

The Labour Inspectorate, which is part of the Dutch Ministry of Social Affairs and Employment, is charged with the task of supervising compliance with the Aliens Employment Act. The provisions for the enforcement of the Aliens Employment Act include a combination of (policy) instruments, actors and a tailpiece concerning criminal proceedings.

The Labour Inspectorate – the organisation and its adopted approach

The Labour Inspectorate is made up of six regional offices and a central office at the Ministry of Social Affairs and Employment. The regional inspectors are appointed by the Minister of Social Affairs and Employment and charged with the task of supervising compliance with the Aliens Employment Act within companies and organisations. The inspectors are also charged with the task of tracking down punishable offences in this context. Police officials authorised to track down punishable offences are also appointed to act as supervisors.

As from 1 January 1999, a total of 73 Labour Inspectorate officials were involved in upholding the Aliens Employment Act and combating fraud. The central office of the Labour Inspectorate carries out the various facilitative, coordinative and evaluative tasks and maintains contact with the policy directorates.

The mission of the Labour Inspectorate is worded as follows: "We instigate legal action against cases of abuse and provide politically relevant information". Given this mission, sectors of industry are singled out with a view to monitoring compliance with the Aliens Employment Act. Within these sectors the Labour Inspectorate will focus in particular on those companies that it suspects or knows to be deliberately evading the law.

In 1997 and 1998 the Labour Inspectorate developed a cyclical procedure with a view to coming up with a sensible selection of the companies to be visited. A study of the market was carried out to identify cases of illegal employment, in order to gain an insight into the nature, the manifestation and the consequences of illegal employment within the Dutch labour market.

The Labour Inspectorate has also developed a model for risk analysis. Armed with this model it is possible to estimate the risk of illegal employment within a certain sector. The model focuses on the objective characteristics of the sector in question (such as training requirements and labour-intensiveness), information regarding compliance with the Aliens Employment Act in the past and assessments of the sector carried out by experienced experts.

Analysis of the results and measurements of the effect after a period of twelve months of the various enforcement projects designed to uphold the Aliens Employment Act serve as input when it comes to planning future enforcement projects.

If the Labour Inspectorate detects an infringement of the Foreign Nationals Employment Act, the regional Labour Inspector in question will draw up a report. The report will then be sent in to the Public Prosecutions Department. The standard penalty for violation of the Aliens Employment Act is NLG 2 000 for each foreign national illegally employed. Repetition of the offence, poor working conditions and exploitation of the foreign national may lead to the penalty being increased.

Enforcement activities

Information

A sector is provided with information regarding the statutory regulations at various levels (sector, business group, and individual company) and any obstacles that stand in the way of compliance with the regulations can also be discussed at these same levels. The provision of information serves to promote greater awareness of the statutory regulations and can lead to greater compliance with the law.

Criminal investigation in response to tips

Specific detective investigation is carried out in response to tips, reports and signals from within the organisation itself regarding suspected violations of the law. These tips may also be incorporated in the projects designed to uphold the Aliens Employment Act.

Regional enforcement projects

Specific regional detective investigations are carried out in regions known to accommodate problem sectors, such as the regions in which workers are employed to harvest asparagus and pick fruit. Generally speaking, only one of the regions of the Labour Inspectorate will be involved in this kind of investigation and most of these investigations are also carried out in collaboration with the Aliens Department.

National enforcement projects

On the basis of the risk analysis referred to above, sectors of industry in which there is known to be a relatively high occurrence of illegal employment are singled out. The various regions of the Labour Inspectorate then take part in the systematic project-based investigation carried out in these sectors of industry. The staff of the Labour Inspectorate generally work in collaboration with the Aliens Department when working on these enforcement projects, though they may also collaborate with other investigative departments such as the National Transport Inspectorate and the Waterways Police. Examples of the sectors of industry singled out for investigation in 1999 include the inland navigation sector, the hotel and catering industry, the international road haulage industry, the fish and meat processing industries and the horticultural sector.

Multidisciplinary investigation

Since 1998 the Labour Inspectorate has been focusing increasingly on tackling organised illegal employment. Many different kinds of legal constructions are devised with a view to evading the regulations that apply to the employment of foreign nationals in the Netherlands. The Labour Inspectorate carries out multidisciplinary investigations to expose the organiser(s) of these *mala fide* constructions. One such construction is the setting up of a company, which may have anything from a few to a few hundred registered partners. The company then claims that all of these partners are self-employed which therefore means that they are not subject to the provisions of the Aliens Employment Act.

Co-operation

Many employers resort to illegal employment on account of the financial advantage that they stand to gain. Thus illegal employment also goes hand in hand with the evasion of tax and social security legislation. In order to be able to bring legal action against these fraudulent employers as efficiently and effectively as possible, in carrying out the investigations referred to above, the Labour Inspectorate often works in association with the Inland Revenue Department, the social security administration agency and the Aliens Department. Other investigative departments may also collaborate on these investigations. The Public Prosecutions Department is directly involved in the multidisciplinary investigations.

The illegal financial advantage enjoyed by the employer is confiscated by means of the imposition of a fine and the subsequent levying of non-paid premiums and tax.

The increase in the numbers of reports is accounted for by expanded capacity in terms of the number of Aliens Employment Act/fraud inspectors from 1996 onwards (Table 2).

3. ALIENS CONTROL WITHIN THE COUNTRY

Following the abolition of checks at the internal borders as a result of the introduction of the Schengen Agreement, the government decided in 1994 to take three additional measures:
- Introducing the concept of mobile supervision of aliens behind the national borders.
- Intensifying internal supervision of aliens, i.e. more specific and intensified checks carried out by the police.
- Stipulating that applications for asylum are henceforth to be lodged at two locations in the Netherlands only in order to be better capable of overseeing the entire process.

Table 2. **Numbers of reports of cases of illegal employment by sector, 1995-1997**

	1995	1996	1997
Agricultural sector	147	116	172
Industry			
Off-the-peg clothing	75	19	24
Bakeries	1	30	37
Food industry	6	2	3
Meat processing industry	15	16	3
Other industry	6	4	11
Construction	3	7	6
Trade			
Wholesale trade	22	25	46
Retail trade	11	58	56
Hotel and catering industry	201	564	735
Services			
Cleaning	2	5	3
Employment agencies	–	1	10
Financial institutions	–	5	2
Other sectors	37	64	72
Total	**526**	**916**	**1 180**

Source: Labour Inspectorate, Dutch Ministry of Social Affairs and Employment.

Efficient supervision of aliens strongly depends on an adequate insight into the stay and the situation of aliens in the Netherlands. This requires reliable data on the number of aliens, the places of residence, their means of support and their living conditions.

Administrative steps have been taken to adequately satisfy this requirement. These measures also cover the method of registration of aliens by the Offices of Civil Status in the municipalities.

Because intensifying internal supervision of aliens particularly requires extra efforts to be made by the police, the government decided in 1994 to provide the police constabularies with structural means to that end up to a sum of 650 million guilders on an annual basis.

Intensification of the internal supervision of aliens focuses on five categories. These are (in order of priority):

- Criminal aliens.
- Aliens disturbing the peace or causing any other form of nuisance.
- Deportation and supervised departure of aliens not entitled to residence in the Netherlands.
- Combating individuals and groups taking economic advantage of the illegality of aliens.
- Aliens coming into contact with the police following investigations or checks made under other laws.

The Ministry of Justice and in particular the Immigration and Naturalisation Service (IND) is the organisation primarily responsible for ensuring that the above policy goals are achieved.

For this purpose policy agreements (administrative covenants) have been concluded between the State Secretary of Justice (responsible for aliens policy matters), the Minister of the Interior and Kingdom Relations (responsible for the police organisation) and the 25 Chief Police Authorities (colleges of mayors of the cities situated in the territories falling under their police authority).

The police organisation in the Netherlands consists of 25 operational units plus an extra central unit. The mutually adopted general policies on this specific task have been laid down in these policy agreements.

In addition, implementation agreements are concluded annually between the regional IND directorates and individual Chief Police Authorities in which the policy agreements included in the administrative covenants are worked out.

These implementation covenants should provide insight into the agreements reached, into the mutual reporting obligations, the consultations, the implementation and the supply of information.

The experiences with the covenants gained so far have learned that an adequate understanding of each other's operations and the progress thereof is of key importance to being able to make feasible agreements. This essential insight sets particular requirements to the consultations and the supply of information.

It is now intended to work out the covenants to such an extent that the performance targets to be met will be defined more unambiguously than in the past. Moreover, the performance in relation to the admission and return of aliens will henceforth be covered by the agreements in addition to the performance in the field of supervision.

4.   POLICY ON ALIENS ILLEGALLY STAYING IN THE NETHERLANDS FOR EXTENDED PERIODS

This section deals with aliens who have already been staying in Holland for longer periods of time and who may or may not be engaged in paid work to pay for their living expenses.

In 1989 a regulation was introduced stipulating that aliens with a long-term history of illegal residence in the Netherlands could be granted a residence permit for urgent humanitarian reasons.

These urgent humanitarian reasons may arise from the duration of the illegal stay, their employment history in this country (without entitlement to a residence permit) or the existence of special ties with the Netherlands.

The basis for this regulation was the apparent status of legality the government had created in respect of some aliens because during the period of their illegal stay they had complied with all kinds of (statutory) public obligations such as paying taxes and social security premiums.

In the period between 1989 and the end of 1994 each case was individually assessed on its own merits. Court decisions in a number of these cases has resulted in a regulation of a more general character: at the recommendation of the Council of State (*Raad van State*) the unwritten policy was converted into several objective verification criteria.

Laying down this policy by means of recognisable verification criteria has led to a certain tightening of the rules and regulations.

To become eligible for a residence permit the alien now had to satisfy a number of clearly defined qualifying conditions:
- Showing that at the time of the application he had stayed in Holland for a period of at least six years without interruptions.

- Being able to prove that during that period he had received earnings from work or benefits.
- Income or unemployment insurance for at least 200 days, subject to payment of social security premiums, wage tax and national insurance contributions (*loonheffing*) and/or income tax.

This policy remained in force until 31 December 1997 because after that date it was no longer possible for aliens without a valid residence permit to enter the social security system, as a result of which documentary evidence of payments of social security premiums, tax/national insurance contributions or income tax could no longer be submitted. This took away the main source of the apparent legality of the aliens status thus eliminating the basis for the regularisation scheme.

As regards applications lodged by long-term illegal aliens after 31 December 1997, it is only verified whether any extraordinary circumstances apply on account of which admission could be allowed for urgent humanitarian reasons.

In the evaluation of urgent humanitarian reasons, attention should focus on a combination of factors as a result of which admission to the Netherlands is still to be considered justified. Examples of factors that could be taken into account in this respect are:

- The duration of the stay in the Netherlands.
- The special ties of the applicant and any family members with the Netherlands and/or the country of origin.
- The medical condition of the applicant and/or any members of his family.

This concerns individual factors which, in individual cases, may lead to a judgement that not granting a residence permit is likely to result in such a dire situation that it is still possible to issue a residence permit.

It also means that an exhaustive enumeration of relevant factors cannot be given beforehand because each time it concerns an assessment to be made in a individual case.

Also courts of law verify whether urgent humanitarian reasons are involved which could justify admission. Obviously, the scope for possibly using this inherent competence to decide otherwise is limited by any previous court rulings, in particular if these concern very recent cases.

The scope for using the above competence is also limited by what are called counter-indications, such as previous deportations from the Netherlands, the commission of criminal offences and the use of forged documents. In case of a previous deportation from the Netherlands, the ratio behind the regulation in force until 1 January 1998, namely the apparent status of legality created by the government, no longer exists.

Finally it should be noted in this respect that, for the time being, the Dutch government has no intention to set up a new regularisation scheme. The current verification based on urgent humanitarian reasons provides sufficient safeguards in individual cases for granting admission in manifestly poignant cases.

Status Report on Measures to Prevent and Combat the Employment of Foreigners in an Irregular Situation in Switzerland

by
Kurt Rohner
(Federal Office of Foreigners, Federal Department of Justice and Police, Bern)

1.   ATYPICAL SITUATION

The situation in Switzerland differs from that in neighbouring EU countries for a number of reasons listed below. For years now the total population of Switzerland has included a significantly higher than average percentage of foreigners[1] which is steadily increasing. Foreigners also hold one in every four jobs in Switzerland.[2] Furthermore, Switzerland is not a signatory to either the Schengen Agreement or the Dublin Convention. This may have certain implications for asylum.[3]

The Swiss Government and Parliament have voiced their unequivocal support for measures to prevent the illegal employment of foreigners, in the interests of the country's social and economic policy. The number of illegal migrants employed is increasing from year to year, through periods of economic growth and recession alike. The government is keen to improve the instruments it has at its disposal to combat this problem.

---

1. Currently, the number of foreigners permanently residing in Switzerland as a percentage of the total population is over 19%. Some groups of people - short stays, international civil servants, and applicants for asylum - are not counted. Furthermore, Swiss naturalisation legislation is, on close inspection, no more stringent than that of other countries, particularly EU/EEA countries.

2. Of whom some 75% are EU nationals.

3. For some years, Switzerland has been taking a higher than average number of applicants for asylum, as a proportion of total population. In 1998, 583 applications for asylum were registered per 100 000 residents, more than double the number registered by the EU member state most concerned.

2. MEASURES TO PREVENT AND COMBAT THE EMPLOYMENT OF FOREIGNERS IN AN IRREGULAR SITUATION

The current approach is founded principally on long-standing legal bases. First, it provides for *sanctions* (enforcement and deterrent measures) and *controls* (measures aimed at combating and halting illegal employment). Switzerland as yet lacks any wide-ranging *incentive measures*, although it is now clear that such measures are an essential component of any effective policy. Sanctions have recently been made more severe, chiefly against traffickers, those who knowingly work illegally and the employers of illegal foreign workers.

In contrast with other countries, Switzerland has not declared an amnesty for *"undocumented" foreigners* to date. In 1998 the government turned down a majority motion for an amnesty by the National Council. The main reason for its decision was that an amnesty would not be an effective or lasting answer to the problem of illegal foreign workers.

Administrative provisions

Foreigners must have identity papers showing their place of residence and, for those who are employed, their employer and place of work. The main identification data required are thus directly available to the relevant authorities, at customs or roadside checkpoints for example. The core of the system is the on-line Central Register of Foreigners (RCE).

As in some other countries, responsibility for verifying the conditions that apply to residence and gainful employment are shared by a number of Swiss authorities. Once a work permit is issued, the main statutory provisions relating to employment contracts become subject to considerations of public policy. Consequently, it is relatively easy for the employee to rely on the legislation for employment contracts, particularly in the courts. In addition, regional labour inspectorates check up on firms to ensure that they are complying with labour and with accident-insurance and unemployment-insurance legislation. In the event of non-compliance, employers may face a prison sentence or a fine, and employees, detention or a fine.[4]

Administrative sanctions

Sanctions against employers. For serious or repeat offences against the law on foreigners, the cantonal employment office can turn down all or some of the employer's applications, independently of any criminal proceedings.

Sanctions against service providers. For serious and repeat offences against mandatory requirements under the legislation on the protection of employees or its implementing regulations, particularly those relating to the entry of foreigners, service providers face having their licences revoked.[5]

Expulsion of foreign workers. Foreigners can be expelled from Switzerland (and may also be prohibited from re-entering the country) if convicted of a crime or offence or if their behaviour or actions suggest that they are unwilling or unable to conform to the established order.

---

4. Federal law on work, RS 822.114.

5. Federal law on employment services and the provision of services, RS 823.11.

Prohibition on entry of undesirable aliens. The competent authority can prohibit the entry into Switzerland of undesirable aliens. It can also prohibit, for a period not exceeding three years, the entry into Switzerland of foreigners who have committed repeated or serious offences against the regulations applicable to foreigners or decisions by an authority that are based on those regulations. While the entry prohibition is in force, the foreigner may not cross Switzerland's borders without the express permission of the authority that imposed the ban.

Criminal provisions[6]

Sanctions against employers. A person who knowingly employs foreigners not authorised to work in Switzerland is liable to a fine of up to CHF 5 000 for each such illegal employee.[7] A person doing so unknowingly is liable to a fine of up to CHF 3 000.

Subsequent offences. In addition to a fine, a person for whom an enforceable judgement has been made for knowingly committing an offence and who within five years again employs a foreigner illegally is liable to imprisonment for up to six months or to detention.

Sanctions for assisting illegal stays. A person who facilitates or assists in making arrangements for an illegal entry into, departure from, or illegal stay in Switzerland (who not only illegally employs but also provides lodgings for a foreigner) is liable to imprisonment for up to six months or a maximum fine of CHF 10 000 or both.

Breaches by employers and employees of regulations applicable to foreigners. Other breaches of regulations applicable to foreigners or of decisions by the competent authorities are punishable by fines of up to CHF 2 000. Penalties may be waived for minor breaches.

Sanctions for procuring work or hiring out services. A person who knowingly procures work for foreigners or employs foreigners for the purposes of hiring out their services, without complying with the statutory requirements applicable to foreign labour, is liable to a fine of up to CHF 100 000. An additional fine may be imposed by virtue of the Federal Law on the residence and settlement of foreigners.

3.   EXPERIENCE AND ANALYSIS

The problems of illegal work and the illegal employment of foreigners were addressed in the 1980s, a time of high economic growth, when they were further aggravated by a shortage of labour. Research[8] conducted in the late 1980s yielded a number of *findings:*

- Illegal earnings from jobs in the cleaning and hotel/catering sectors amounted to over 12% of declared earnings, followed by the building and repair sectors.
- There was no direct correlation between illegal work by foreigners as a percentage of illegal work in each economic sector and the proportion of foreigners employed in those sectors in relation to the total workforce there.[9]

---

6. Federal law on entry and settlement of foreigners, RS 142.20 (undergoing total revision).
7. CHF 1 currently equals ECU 1.60 or USD 1.50.
8. Including Frey, Pommerehne and Weck-Hannemann; Die heimliche Wirtschaft, Bern, 1986.
9. While undeclared work was higher than average in agriculture and the hotel, cleaning, domestic staff and repairs sectors, this was not the case for the textile, clothing and machinery industries.

- The rate of illegal employment of foreigners in Switzerland, according to various studies, was relatively low compared to that in other European countries and remains so.
- Of all illegal work, only one-third involved foreign workers.

This latter conclusion is particularly interesting, given the particularly high, and rising, proportion of foreigners in gainful employment in Switzerland. Today, illegal employment among foreigners is thought to be increasing more or less exactly in line with other countries[10] – a disheartening conclusion. As circumstances changed in some major respects in the 1990s, new studies are currently in view to provide a sounder basis for decision making. There has been a marked increase in the scale of immigration via the asylum channel.[11] Overall migratory patterns have also changed with growing globalisation. Of course, the economic situation has also changed (economic boom, followed by recession and a high unemployment rate, the reduction of working hours, not always on a voluntary basis, part-time working, second jobs, availability of cross-border staff, and so forth).

As yet, there are no reliable data on the deterrent effects of sanctions or on the volume of convictions. One-time surveys tend to confirm that the legal bases for criminal sanctions are adequate. However, not enough use is being made of controls. Basically, the main problem is that the sanctions imposed by the *courts* are not severe enough and are therefore not very effective as a deterrent.

Entry prohibitions do not provide a reliable estimate. However, if entry prohibition data can be observed over several years, they can be used with a number of other indicators to gauge trends in the illegal employment of foreigners. Data analysis produced the following:

- The number of entry prohibitions issued has risen slightly over the last few years, for virtually the same level of enforcement operations. Around 40% of entry prohibitions issued were for illegal entry and illegal stays with or without gainful employment. Their geographic distribution is instructive:[12] at any rate, it is not directly proportionate to the size of groups of foreigners in Switzerland. Over 30% of entry prohibitions were issued in connection with the banking, insurance, property and other services sector and around 25% involved the hotel and catering sector. These figures confirm earlier studies which found that occupations requiring good qualifications and commanding above-average salaries were heavily implicated in the illegal employment of foreigners. The construction and agricultural sectors each accounted for barely 10%. This low percentage may also be linked to difficulties in controlling these sectors. No evidence was found to support the theory that the major business centres (Zurich, Basel, Geneva and Bern) were the most affected by the employment of illegal foreigners.

---

10. See in particular current data in Schneider Friedrich, Prof., University of Linz (Austria), "*Shadow economies: size, causes and consequences*", September 1999.

11. The number of asylum seekers has risen sharply; the "pull" of the host country is also a problem (for example, labour market and social assistance as "pull factors").

12. A majority of European nationals, with some 25% from the former Yugoslavia and 15% from EU member states; less than 10% each from Africa and Turkey.

- Very few such penalties were imposed on traffickers. Most traffickers are from countries with political and economic problems or where the emigration of asylum seekers is high.[13] Conclusions can be drawn from this for more effective prevention.

Recent research has shown that the communes and cantons most aware of the illegal employment problem are those where the authorities, media or Parliament have been able to apply some pressure. Other cantons still do not seem to be very aware of the problem. Local authorities have virtually no hard data on the extent of the problem. In contrast, cantons that are actively trying to prevent illegal employment, and committing the necessary resources have met with some success: it seems that the problem is bigger than people generally want to admit.

4. CONCLUSIONS

Sanctions

Owing to legal loopholes and the spread of unsatisfactory judicial practices, specific problems relating to the illegal employment of foreigners are not receiving adequate attention. To remedy this, relevant measures – some of which have already been considered or introduced in other countries – are now being reviewed as part of the comprehensive revision of the Federal Law on the residence and settlement of foreigners. These include:

- Heavier penalties.
- Minimum penalties for employment offences and for traffickers.
- Closer alignment of the essential components of the offence under the law on foreigners and the general sentencing guidelines in the Penal Code (for example, detention or fine for failure to comply with a ruling by an authority).
- Confiscation of property (or award of damages to the injured party, confiscation of dangerous items, debarment from a profession, trade or business, publication of sentence, and so forth).[14]
- Limited exclusion from public office.
- Payment of maintenance costs – including costs related to illness and accidents - and the costs of returning illegally employed immigrants to their home country.
- The criminal liability of the employer, as strictly defined under civil law, to be extended to *de facto* employers/service providers (for example, provision of personnel).
- Extension of liability to both professional and non-professional principles.
- Deterrent campaigns in the media, publicising the penalties for employers and employees.

Controls

Everyone concedes that enforcement operations by authorities are not given enough priority and that the resources available are inadequate. However, given real "political will", more frequent enforcement operations, which would have a deterrent effect, could be carried out. A small official

---

13. Including the former Yugoslavia, Turkey and Sri Lanka, with a small minority from the European Union.

14. Theoretically possible since 1 August 1994, following the revision of the Penal Code, but not applied to date.

unit could be set up. Co-operating closely with other offices, this unit could combat abuses by stepping up controls and could be self-financing through the fines it collects.

The possibility of agreements between employees and trade unions and possibly the competent authorities should be examined with the aim of delegating to them the responsibility of enforcement, particularly in sectors that have signed collective-bargaining agreements.

Incentives and disincentives

The possibility of (temporarily) suspending workers/employers on whom a sanction has been imposed from their union/professional association is also under discussion. No one is unaware of the long-standing need to reduce tax and social security contributions and simplify the administrative procedures for employers and employees. This is more than just a matter of policy. In fact, it is vital for addressing the cumbersome day-to-day administrative procedures (complicated procedures for minor matters) that have imperceptibly crept in. This may seem trivial but, taken as a whole, they can be major disincentives for employers and employees.

Information

Better designed public information campaigns that explain the disadvantages and additional costs of illegally employing foreigners are needed. The same applies to incentives. Publicity should be instrumental in effectively combating illegal employment and in tarnishing the image of the "gentleman criminal" for good.